RESEARCH TO RESULTS: EFFECTIVE COMMUNITY CORRECTIONS

PROCEEDINGS OF THE 1995 AND 1996
CONFERENCES OF THE INTERNATIONAL
COMMUNITY CORRECTIONS
ASSOCIATION (ICCA)

REVISED AND UPDATED FOR THIS VOLUME

PATRICIA M. HARRIS
EDITOR

American Correctional Association Staff

Richard L. Stalder, President
James A. Gondles, Jr., Executive Director
Gabriella M. Daley, Director, Communications and Publications
Harry Wilhelm, Marketing Manager
Alice Fins, Managing Editor
Michael Kelly, Associate Editor
Sherry Wulfekuhle, Editorial Assistant
Dana M. Murray, Graphics and Production Manager
Michael Selby, Graphics and Production Associate

ICCA Executive Director: Peter Kinziger

Cover design by Michael Selby.
Photo by Al Francekevich/The Stock Market.

Printed in the United States of America by Kirby Lithographic
    Company, Inc., Arlington, VA.

ISBN 1-56991-092-6

This publication may be ordered from the:
American Correctional Association
4380 Forbes Boulevard
Lanham, MD 20706-4322
1-800-222-5646

For information on publications and videos available from ACA, contact our World Wide Web home page at:

http://www.corrections.com/aca

For information on ICCA, contact their home page at:

http://www.ICCAWEB.org

Library of Congress Cataloging-in-Publication Data

Research to results: effective community corrections/Patricia M. Harris,
    editor.
        p.   cm.
    Includes bibliographical references (p.)
    ISBN 1-56991-109-6 (pbk.)
    1. Community-based corrections--Congresses. I. Harris, Patricia M.
HV9279.F76 1999
    364.6'8—dc21   99-19231
                                                              CIP

TABLE OF CONTENTS

Section 4: Emerging Issues and Trends

FOREWORD

We are pleased to be issuing this second book with the International Community Corrections Association so that we can bring "what works" information to the corrections community. These essays will be useful to an audience far beyond those interested in community corrections. The principles discussed should be useful for practitioners in different types of facilities, academics, and policy-makers. We are learning what works and what does not work, and more important, what works with what groups and under what conditions. When we can apply this information, we can create programs that lead to less recidivism, greater rehabilitation, and more effective management of our correctional resources.

We have long believed that there are keys to effective programs and practices that would unlock the doors to success—even for those who have long-term substance abuse problems, criminal mindsets, and other seemingly unalterable conditions. This book describes some of these keys. The analysis at times may be difficult to sort out. But the unmistakable progress is reassuring. We have to continue researching, testing our results, and retesting them again under different conditions until we have further evidence of the most effective strategies that not only will keep individuals out of our institutions but will enable us to teach offenders the skills and habits that will enable them to lead productive lives when they leave our care. This is a worthwhile pursuit not just for this generation but for its children, due to the high rate of offenders' children who later will be incarcerated.

Toward this end, the American Correctional Association (ACA) publishes materials on successful practices, so that we can all find positive approaches to the dilemmas facing our profession. For almost 130 years, ACA has stood for positive and rehabilitative practices in corrections. As we enter the new millennium, we continue this goal and hope to widen the audience for our message. Thus, we welcome manuscripts from practitioners and researchers. By working together with the researchers, practitioners and educators can provide new successes.

James A. Gondles, Jr.
Executive Director
American Correctional Association

PREFACE

The issues of crime and justice loom large in our public discourse. Most people would agree that we know far too little of the solutions to crime and that our justice systems are not designed to find effective responses to the problem. Nevertheless, our criminal justice systems must forge ahead with developing broad policy positions responsive to the public at large. Too often, the national debates on crime and justice are reflective of the crime of the day, the solution of the moment, or the criminological theory of the year. In this ambiguous environment, it is easy for insights, common sense, and sound research to be ignored due to the exchange of opposing ideologies and competing sound bites.

In recognition of the politics of crime and justice, the International Community Corrections Association (ICCA) made a decision to support its members through the exploration of "What Works" research as a way of providing direction toward effective correctional interventions. Seven years ago, ICCA formed a committee consisting of practitioners, academics, and researchers and convened a meeting in Boston. The outcome of that meeting was a consensus agreement that ICCA should plan a conference that would focus on research supporting the effectiveness of treatment interventions for offenders.

The committee members felt that the time was right to develop a forum in which researchers would be commissioned to research specific areas of criminal conduct. The researchers then would author scholarly papers worthy of being published, and would respond publicly in detail to the questions and observations put to them by a distinguished panel, as well as an audience of practitioners. The end result was ICCA's first in an ongoing series of "What Works Research" conferences that continue to this day.

In discussions leading up to the research conferences, our committee had to recognize that we in community corrections have not used research and behavioral and cognitive curricula to our best advantage. We have not used the many assessment and diagnostic instruments that have advanced our understanding of effective interventions for offenders. We have not been influencing the public policy direction of the criminal justice systems by using the best thinking and best minds of our intervention researchers. It became clear that these issues need to be addressed in order to influence correctional policy.

As a means of promoting informed and rational discourse in community corrections, ICCA is now in its seventh year of sponsoring "What Works" conferences using the knowledge of some of North America's most prominent academics. The chapters contained in this book are the edited papers from two of ICCA's annual research conferences. The papers were written to provide the readers with a practical application of the research. It is ICCA's intention that the "marriage" of research and its practical application will provide a special learning environment that will help guide policy makers and practitioners in developing rational and effective intervention strategies.

The body of information coming from the "What Works" papers continues to build upon itself and increasingly provides direction for those interested in effective interventions. I encourage you to collect the "What Works'" series of books and to attend ICCA's annual research conferences.

Peter Kinziger
Executive Director
International Community Corrections Association

From Research to Results: Pathways to Effective Community Corrections

1

Patricia M. Harris, Ph.D.
  The University of Texas at San Antonio
  San Antonio, Texas

Introduction

This book is concerned with helping policymakers and practitioners promote and sustain effective innovation in community corrections. Primarily, it addresses three pathways for advancing effective community corrections innovations. The first is by fostering *strategic management* of community corrections agencies, to enable policymakers to successfully introduce and implement desired programs in complex and hostile political environments. The second is by facilitating *diffusion of research*, to accelerate the transfer of treatment-effectiveness knowledge across a greater number of practitioners, agencies, and policymakers. The third is by enhancing *treatment responsivity*, to broaden the number of offenders positively affected by correctional interventions.

The chapters in this volume are revised versions of commissioned papers initially presented at one of two research conferences sponsored by the International Community Corrections Association (ICCA) in 1995 and 1996. The conferences represented the third and fourth of an ongoing series of ICCA-sponsored annual meetings dedicated to the advancement of effective correctional interventions. The 1995 conference, which took place in Ottawa, Ontario, addressed the theme "Research to Results: The Challenge" and included papers on the strategic management of community corrections and the diffusion of treatment-effectiveness research. The 1996 conference, held in Austin, Texas, addressed the theme "Expanding on What Works" and sponsored presentations that elaborated on the relevance of the principles of offenders' criminogenic needs and treatment-program responsivity to effective correctional innovations. The 1996 conference also included presentations regarding two important trends in corrections, the first, the "adultification" of juvenile corrections, and the second, developments in the restorative justice movement.

This volume is divided into four sections. The first section includes three chapters on the strategic management of community corrections. The second section presents two chapters on innovative programs for facilitating the transfer of treatment-effectiveness research. A third section includes three papers, which discuss the criminogenic needs and responsivity principles of effective treatment. The fourth section presents a chapter on trends in juvenile justice and a chapter on developments in the restorative justice movement. The current chapter reviews the significance and contributions of each of these works, and contemplates important practice- and research-related questions that they provoke.

The Strategic Management of Community Corrections

Few would disagree that community corrections agencies struggle for credibility in the view of the public and the policymaking community. Support for incarceration dominates legislative policymaking despite a quarter century of research that favors less-punitive crime control measures (Blumstein and Petersilia, 1994). For much of the last thirty years, supporters of correctional treatment have been locked in battle with the detractors over whether empirical evidence favoring rehabilitation is of sufficient methodological rigor to justify a shift to treatment-oriented correctional policies (Martinson, 1974; Palmer, 1975; Gendreau and Ross, 1979; Whitehead and Lab, 1989). At the same time, crime-control initiatives rooted in far more inferior evidence (*see* Eck, 1997) flourish without a single rebuke from either the scholarly or policymaking communities.

Consequently, the viability of probation as a criminal sanction increasingly has become linked to its ability to render supervision experiences so severe and negative that they can substitute for incarceration. Nearly all attention given to probation in the last decade has been focused on implementation and evaluation of intermediate sanctions—though no greater than 10 percent of all offenders sentenced to probation participate in such (Petersilia, 1998). Most ironically, these more punitive-sounding community-based innovations—which enjoy greater appeal among citizens and legislators alike—fall short for want of organizational capacity to enable compliance with court-ordered conditions (Petersilia, 1997).

In summary, community corrections is ensnared in a paradox: When it should be most credible, it enjoys the least trust; when it seems most worthy of enhanced financial support, it remains underfunded. What factors account for this paradox? And what can be done to resolve it?

Section 1 of this volume addresses these questions with three papers on the strategic management of community corrections from the 1995 ICCA conference on "Research to Results: The Challenge." The chapters affirm two key lessons for managers of community corrections. One is the importance of taking political and organizational environments into account in planning correctional innovations. The second is the importance of portraying initiatives in a manner that is consistent with public values.

A Framework for Strategic Management

In Chapter 2 ("The Strategic Management of Criminal Sanctions"), Mark Moore considers how managers may overcome the sluggish pace of innovation in community corrections. His prescription, strategic management, calls for fitting community corrections goals to environmental conditions. The strategic leader takes stock not just of the task environment, but more important, the political environment, too. Managers need to recognize environments as a source of opportunities as well as constraints.

Moore presents a framework to assist public-sector managers assess the worth of community corrections initiatives, compared to the costs of achieving them. The framework includes three criteria. First, does the initiative have public value? Second, will it be viewed as legitimate enough to gain the support of those who provide money and authority to carry out the initiative? Third, is the initiative operationally and administratively feasible? It is important for managers to consider all three. The result is what Moore refers to as the "strategic triangle," a proactive decision-making tool for managers, which integrates politics, values, and operational management. The components of the triangle are dynamic— managers can be affected by them, or they can change them.

Moore directly attributes the miscarriage of rehabilitation-focused initiatives to the failure of corrections managers to consider the public value of community corrections activities. Moore suggests that the lack of principled arguments on the side of redemptive strategies has damaged the credibility and viability of such interventions. He writes: "This silence cedes the principled arguments to those who favor harsher, more expensive, and more controlling sanctions."

Applications to Community Corrections

In Chapter 3 ("Managing the Risk of Innovation: Strategies for Leadership"), Ellen Schall and Ellen Neises elaborate on the causes for rejection of innovations in community corrections. First is the public's low tolerance for risk relative to other arenas, such as health care, where there is greater receptivity to risks. In contrast to the field of medicine, where risks are couched in such safe terminology as "experiments," and "trial and error," in criminal justice risk is equated with failure. However disproportionate to potential gains, the "failures" of even a few individuals can jeopardize entire programs. Second is the lack of agreement about goals, which makes getting approval for new programs tougher. Third is a lack of agreement over the terms of accountability, which prevents innovators from revealing to the public how their programs relate to the problem.

Schall and Neises offer a seven-stage framework for educating the public to achieve greater success in gaining public support for innovation. Innovators in criminal justice seem to observe only the first two stages: a sense of awareness and urgency about the issue. Public education efforts must be more prolonged and thorough, to allow both intellectual and emotional resolution of issues. Strategic leadership entails facilitating the public's evaluation of risks and benefits of alternative correctional policies.

The authors provide three examples from the community corrections arena as illustrations of "innovations that managed their environments." These include intermediate sanctions programs in Minnesota and Georgia, respectively, and a community sentencing program run by the New York City-based Center for Alternative Sentencing and Employment

Services. For each example, Schall and Neises demonstrate how the strategic display of the public value of the sought-after initiative ultimately enhanced its successful implementation and longevity.

The Strategic Uses of Penal Purpose

In Chapter 4 ("Clarity About Penal Purpose and Correctional Strategy Require Individualized Sentences"), Michael Smith explores how community corrections managers can customize noncustodial sentences in an environment that values accountability, proportionality, equality, and public safety. This chapter is a guide to creating client-specific initiatives that have public value in the courtroom and beyond.

To introduce initiatives successfully, community corrections managers must emphasize the relation of programs and conditions to accepted penal purposes and convince judges of the validity of those associations. Smith demonstrates how community corrections managers can shape conditions of supervision that are both responsive to specific needs (for example, financial stability and employment) of individual probationers while observing widely accepted penal purposes. Conversely, he shows us how failing to match conditions to purpose can backfire in these same cases.

According to Smith, strategic uses of penal purpose should accompany both needs and risk management, including shaping responses to violations of probation conditions. Drug courts are an exemplar of this kind of approach, yet such formality is not a prerequisite for the successful individualization of probation conditions and sanctions. Well-designed and implemented conditions can each serve particular sentencing purposes as long as there is congruency of the character of the conditions and the sentencing purpose.

The Diffusion of Research Innovation

A main impediment to the introduction of effective community corrections programs is that much of the knowledge regarding effective offender rehabilitation is neither disseminated widely nor recognized outside of academia and subsets of the treatment community. Too little of "what works" knowledge reaches practitioners and policymakers, and no meaningful conduits for its transfer are yet established. As Gendreau (1996) observes, degree concentrations leading to specializations in

offender treatment are nearly nonexistent. By default, infrequently scheduled training workshops provide the sole means of technology transfer
for the community corrections field.

A different problem is the increasing magnitude and complexity of
knowledge related to effective correctional interventions. There is also
the question of whether agency managers and judges—parties with the
greatest program policy impact—would avail themselves of opportunities for education, were institutionalized sources of training on offender
rehabilitation widely available.

Outside of academic publications, avenues for the routine dissemination of information on treatment effectiveness do not exist, at least in the
United States. Very little of the empirical research sponsored by the
National Institute of Justice, an agency which aggressively distributes
reports of its research to practitioner audiences, focuses on studies of
treatment or treatment implementation. In fact, a review of the research
sponsored by the National Institute of Justice for the last twelve years (a
period corresponding to the recent renaissance of rehabilitation) reveals
that evaluations of relatively punitive intermediate sanctions, not treatment programs, have dominated the probation and parole literature widely
disseminated by that agency (National Institute of Justice, 1996, 1997).

The two chapters in Section 2 address innovations for facilitating
transfer of treatment effectiveness to program managers and policymakers. Originally presented at the 1995 conference on "Research to Results:
The Challenge," the papers highlight different approaches to the diffusion
of "what works" information. The first, by Alan T. Harland, L.L.M., Ph.D.,
and Wayne N. Welsh, Ph.D., examines organizational conditions and
processes favorable to transfer and adoption of research. The second, by
Donald Andrews, Ph.D., introduces a decision-making tool for structuring
treatment-program planning and implementation.

Formation of a Multiagency "Information Culture"

In Chapter 5 ("Towards the Strategic Management of Correctional
Innovation: Putting 'What Works' Information to Work"), Drs. Harland and
Welsh describe a sophisticated effort to facilitate and routinize cross-
agency transfer and use of research. The authors report on the
development and activities of an interagency forum, the Delaware County
Criminal Justice Advisory Committee. They describe the rational decision-making processes practiced by this forum and the broad-based
"information culture" that resulted from this effort. As an update to their

original conference presentation, the authors report positive outcomes in the areas of information-systems development, prison-population management, and court administration, among others, brought about by the work of the forum since the Committee's inception in 1994. The chapter underscores the significance of implementation processes and organizational settings in the successful diffusion of research.

To assist other agencies in engaging in similar efforts, the authors furnish readers with two management tools. The first is a detailed outline of a systematic approach to program development, accompanied by extensive narration of the tasks attached to each phase. The second is an assessment instrument, which enables decision-makers to choose between correctional options, and which takes the multiplicity of system goals and desirable impact measures into account.

Assessment of Evidence-based Practice

In Chapter 6 ("Assessing Program Elements for Risk: The Correctional Program Assessment Inventory"), Donald Andrews, Ph.D., provides an overview of a recently developed assessment instrument that uses correctional programs as its units of analyses. The purpose of the Correctional Program Assessment Inventory is to help managers assess the extent to which planned or existing programs are consistent with "evidence-based" practice. Programs implemented in a manner consistent with research on treatment effectiveness can be said to have crime reduction potential.

Features of the Correctional Program Assessment Inventory include sections which measure the qualifications of program designers and staff, the nature and scope of offender-assessment practices, and integrity of service delivery. The Correctional Program Assessment Inventory also measures whether programs have incorporated relapse-prevention components into service delivery. Additionally, the instrument examines the depth of a program's commitment to process and outcome evaluations and its consistency with ethical-treatment program practices.

An important feature of the Correctional Program Assessment Inventory is its capacity to facilitate a two-way flow of information. In addition to structuring treatment implementation, it also can help managers to articulate to stakeholders what their programs represent (who is served, in what ways); assess the "evaluability" of their programs; and facilitate process evaluations of existing programs.

The Principles of Needs and Responsivity

For supporters of correctional treatment, the 1990s have been good years. The meta-analytic research of Andrews et al. (1990) established the supremacy of treatment efforts over punitive sanctions in bringing about reductions in recidivism. Particularly important has been the confirmation of the viability of treatment in community corrections contexts. In her review of the effectiveness and impact of the intermediate sanctions movement, Dr. Joan Petersilia concludes: "The empirical evidence regarding intermediate sanctions is decisive: Without a rehabilitation component, reductions in recidivism are elusive." The increasingly frequent integration of treatment components into community supervision sentences, she writes, indicates "a major paradigm shift for community corrections in the United States" (Petersilia, 1998, 89-90).

Yet, enthusiasm over empirical support for treatment must be tempered by two realities. First, though treatment programs potentially outperform criminal sanctions, they do not always achieve such a result, and those which outperform criminal sanctions may do so by only a modest margin. As Donald Andrews, Ph.D., points out in his essay for this volume, while some programs produce far more substantial results, in the aggregate, treatment programs can be expected to bring about a 10 percent reduction in the recidivism rate of treated offenders. Second, positive findings of meta-analytic research are culled mainly from controlled experiments or other demonstration programs, which may not represent the norm in program implementation. An important question facing community corrections remains: How can community corrections programs increase, broaden, and systematize the positive impact of treatment programs?

Meta-analytic research confirms that effective offender treatment conforms to three principles (Andrews, Bonta, and Hoge, 1990; Andrews et al. 1990; Andrews and Bonta, 1994). The *risk principle* reserves delivery of services to higher-risk individuals. The *criminogenic needs principle* restricts programs to the treatment of only those offender risk factors that are dynamic (in other words, changeable) and which, when changed, bring about reductions in criminal behavior. The *responsivity principle* confines the manner and mode of treatment to interventions that are suited to the offender's learning style.

The importance of taking risk, criminogenic needs, and responsivity into account in designing correctional treatments is now widely accepted among scholars and informed practitioners in the community corrections field. There can be little question, however, that the risk principle has attracted more attention by criminologists than either the principles of criminogenic needs or responsivity. Elaboration of the principle of criminogenic needs, which has occurred mainly in the context of empirical research on predictors of risk (*see*, for example, Gendreau, Little, and Goggin, 1996), limits appreciation of criminogenic needs to their role as dynamic risk factors. Elaboration of the responsivity principle, which has occurred mainly in the context of meta-analytic research on evaluations of offender treatment, focuses attention on the significance of cognitive and behavioral modalities in positively shaping offender behavior and underscores the need for therapeutic integrity in treatment programs (Andrews et al. 1990; Andrews, Bonta, and Hoge, 1990; Gendreau, 1998).

The 1996 ICCA conference on "Expanding on What Works," revisited the less-studied principles of criminogenic needs and responsivity. The chapters included in Section 3 of this volume (1) accent the utility of developing aggregate profiles of offender needs for more effective management of correctional populations, and (2) integrate the concept of client "readiness for change" into the responsivity principle of effective rehabilitation. Collectively, these papers suggest ways for broadening and strengthening the impact of treatment programs to a larger population of offenders.

Offender Needs and Treatment Planning

In Chapter 7 ("Assessment Methods in Corrections"), Larry Motiuk, Ph.D., reports on the utility of the Correctional Service of Canada's automated Community Risk/Needs Management Scale as a tool for profiling and tracking criminogenic needs in community and institutionalized-offender populations. Dr. Motiuk demonstrates how combining needs information with data on risk level can better differentiate offenders likely to recidivate. In this study, ten of twelve traditional needs areas were significantly correlated with outcome on conditional supervision. Offenders who were assessed as high risk/high needs were more likely to fail than other categories of offenders, throughout the follow-up period, though rates of failure were markedly higher for the first six months of supervision. Offenders whose ratings increased were more likely to fail than those whose ratings remained the same, who in turn were generally more likely to fail than those whose ratings decreased.

Dr. Motiuk's study highlights two important benefits of computer-assisted monitoring of offender populations for treatment planning. First, automated offender-tracking systems can and should be used throughout the course of offender supervision to identify and monitor demand for a system's treatment resources. Second, offender tracking can determine what problems offenders face prior to incarceration and whether and how those problems change upon release.

One interesting result of Motiuk's work with the Community Risk/Needs Management Scale is particularly salient for audiences in the United States, where the Wisconsin style, eleven-item needs assessment continues to be widely practiced. As a result of Canadian research with the predictive utility of various offender needs measures, the Needs Management Scale evolved into just seven domains. Dr. Motiuk's work, in combination with other comprehensive research on criminogenic needs and which similarly confines needs to fewer domains (Gendreau, Little, and Goggin 1996), suggests that a comparable reassessment of offender-needs instruments now in use in the United States may be in order.

Enhancing Treatment Responsivity

In Chapter 8 ("Stages of Change Approach to Treating Addictions with Special Focus on DWI Offenders"), James Prochaska, Ph.D., architect of the influential transtheoretical model of behavioral change, explores the application of the stages-of-change paradigm to a specific correctional treatment context, the treatment of driving while intoxicated (DWI) offenders. Dr. Prochaska explains how the stage paradigm relates to five important phases of correctional treatment: voluntary participation rates; retention during treatment; progress through the stages of change during treatment; selection of treatment modality (which change processes are best suited for what stages of change); and treatment outcome.

The significance of the stages-of-change model for broadening the impact of offender-rehabilitation efforts cannot be overstated. Failure to tailor treatment programs to the client's stage of readiness for change results in substantial attrition from rehabilitation programs. The implication is critical for the appreciation of the relative-rehabilitation potential of different treatment programs. As Dr. Prochaska demonstrates using the example of two programs, an apparently "less effective" program (as would be defined by the recidivism rate of program graduates) that sustains high client-retention rates can bring about a *1,000 times greater impact* than a "more effective" program that experiences a low-retention rate.

In Chapter 9 ("Treatment Responsivity: Contributing to Effective Correctional Programming"), Sharon Kennedy, Ph.D., and Ralph Serin, Ph.D., provide a closer inspection of the application of the stage paradigm to the treatment of criminal offenders. Specifically, they report on the results of a pilot study to explore the feasibility of various methods for assessing offenders' readiness for change. Drs. Kennedy and Serin use six inventories, including one developed by Dr. Prochaska and his colleagues, in their protocol to measure offender readiness to change.

Their findings indicate that inventories for the measurement of readiness to change are not all alike. Some tools are more sensitive to measuring an offender's stage of change than others. Drs. Kennedy and Serin's results suggest that instruments validated using nonoffender populations may display less sensitivity to differences in readiness to change in offenders than tools validated specifically on offender populations.

Emerging Issues and Trends

The 1996 conference also invited two accomplished individuals from the fields of juvenile justice and restorative justice, respectively, to evaluate important developments in those arenas and to assess the implications of these changes for the practice of community corrections. Their papers are included in Section 4 of this volume.

The Transformation of Juvenile Justice

In Chapter 10 ("Trends and Issues in the Adultification of Juvenile Justice"), David Altschuler, Ph.D., surveys sweeping changes that have affected the juvenile court. Primarily, the new laws increase the potential for channeling youths, including a large proportion of relatively low-risk property offenders, to criminal court. Other provisions, involving the retention of youths in the juvenile court, replace criminal-centered, rehabilitative objectives with crime-centered sentencing aims that are purely retributive in focus.

Though their immediate impact appears to rest with institutions, the new wave of sentencing modifications affects community corrections, as well. By increasing the frequency of terms of incarceration along with their length, the new laws cause institutional crowding and the breakdown of classification practices. The difficulty of providing successful treatment under such conditions, combined with the impact of antisocial institutional cultures, causes a higher rate of recidivism upon release among juveniles who are subjected to the new harsher provisions than among those who receive more traditional processing. Presently, the juvenile justice system is too fragmented and ill-prepared to reintegrate offenders back into the community effectively. Demands upon community corrections agencies in the criminal justice system are exacerbated as well, in light of current practices, which channel transferred youths to intensive supervision upon release from institutions.

Dr. Altschuler makes several recommendations for addressing the negative impacts of the "adultification" movement. These include reduction of institutional populations (because meaningful rehabilitation does not take place there); the practice of more accurate risk classification; and the placement of nonviolent juveniles in intermediate sanctions programs that integrate treatment with monitoring.

The Restorative Justice Movement

In Chapter 11 ("Restorative Justice: What Works"), Mark Umbreit, Ph.D., provides an overview of research to date on the theory, prevalence, and characteristics of restorative justice programs. Due to their obvious public value, consistency with established penal purposes, advocacy by a wide spectrum of the justice system decision-making community, and capacity to reduce crime risks while increasing the likelihood of successful completion of restitution, restorative justice programs provide a practical example of community corrections initiatives, which embody the principles of strategic management expressed earlier in this volume.

Dr. Umbreit cautions readers away from likely avenues for the mismanagement of restorative justice programs. Because community corrections programs historically emphasize reintegration and restorative services for offenders, managers may overlook the need for and significance of active victim involvement when planning such initiatives. Programs should emphasize the concerns of victims, who rate dialog with the offender more highly than receipt of restitution, over mechanical compliance with monetary conditions of supervision. Finally, care needs to be taken to ensure that restorative justice programs drive true reductions in incarceration, and do not serve merely as "window dressing" for programs that are essentially retributive in nature.

A Look to the Future

The chapters of this book equip managers and other practitioners with credible new tools for introducing and sustaining innovations in community corrections. They also raise questions which invite further deliberation and research. This section briefly reviews some of the questions provoked by the various contributors to this volume.

The Probation-Judiciary Connection

One question generated by the readings in Section 1 relates to the ease with which the principles of strategic management may be implemented in community corrections. Are there not, in fact, special constraints that limit the capacity of probation and parole managers, and particularly the former, to successfully apply the techniques of strategic management? In some states, the close affiliation of probation and parole agencies to the judiciary and departments of institutional corrections, respectively, is a profoundly subservient one that presents far fewer advantages for the former than it does for courts and institutions. It is likely no coincidence that the examples offered as illustrations of various strategic management techniques involved managers who happened mainly to be judges, as opposed to chiefs of probation agencies.

The probation-courts interface is one which has not received probing attention. This presents a stark contrast to the case of law enforcement, which has enjoyed sustained attention to overcoming the limitations of relationships between police and prosecutors. A future conference that takes an unfaltering look at the constraints (and opportunities) that accompany the tethering of probation departments to courts, especially in jurisdictions where judicial selection occurs by popular and partisan election, would make a good beginning.

The Academy and the Diffusion of Research

A second question, provoked by the chapters in section 2, concerns additional avenues for the diffusion of scholarly research to community corrections practitioners and managers. Several contributors to this book have made meaningful inroads in removing knowledge deficits that slow the pace of correctional innovations. In contemplating alternate measures for the facilitation of knowledge transfer in corrections (and criminal justice, generally), it is only natural to weigh the potential impact that academia can have in better preparing future justice system employees for effective correctional practice.

In light of the status of criminal justice as an "applied discipline," the fact that individuals who pursue criminal justice degrees receive so little preparation to enter direct practice in justice-related occupations is uncanny. Few would argue that agency training adequately makes up for the absence of preparation at the university level. Consider the most egregious cases—probation and parole—where orientations of new employees to direct practice are frequently of two weeks duration or less. Inasmuch as criminal justice is now the fastest growing major in the United States, with a captive audience of 350,000 majors (Butterfield, 1998), the question of what obligation academic institutions owe to the preparation of persons who will enter direct practice and later management of criminal justice agencies is more consequential now than it ever has been.

Should academic preparation in criminal justice become more like nursing, engineering, and computer sciences? In these disciplines, failure to prepare students for direct practice would be unthinkable. Yet the structure of criminal justice education in the United States has remained fundamentally unchanged since its inception in the 1970s. It is time for earnest discourse between academics and practitioners to begin on the roles and responsibilities institutions of higher education should adopt in directly influencing future justice system policies and practice.

The Integration of Treatment and Probation Supervision

A third question provoked by contributors throughout this volume concerns the manner by which treatment may be better incorporated into community supervision. Five authors (Drs. Andrews, Motiuk, Prochaska, and Kennedy, and Serin) call attention to various means for strengthening and routinizing the positive effects of treatment programs. In the face of so much optimism over the future of treatment, it can be easy to forget that for most probationers and parolees, conditions of supervision consist of requirements other than mandates to participate in formal treatment, or conditions that make it difficult for offenders to participate in formal treatment.

The integration of probation conditions and treatment, a benefit now commonly bestowed upon offenders channeled through drug courts, continues to be withheld from the overwhelming majority of offenders processed under more traditional circumstances. The chapter by Dr.

Michael Smith addresses this problem and suggests strategies for securing conditions of probation that can enhance the treatment potential of ordinary probation supervision.

A main obstacle to the more widespread coordination of probation conditions and treatment, at least in the United States, is that in most jurisdictions the most rigorous assessment of risk and criminogenic needs (involving empirically based, actuarial instruments, versus the more subjective presentence investigation) takes place *following* sentencing and the setting of probation conditions and not before.

A different yet related problem concerns the scope of the formal assessment that does occur. In most community corrections agencies, formal assessment of needs places greater emphasis on documenting various deficits and their impact on the offender's daily functioning than on the determination of which offender characteristics are associated with ongoing risks of new criminal activity. That is, most community corrections agencies continue to place greater emphasis on the assessment of general versus criminogenic needs. The result is a focus on symptoms (for example, unemployment) rather than underlying problems (such as impulsivity or inadequate problem-solving skills) that may be the cause of both the symptom and further involvement in crime. An emphasis on symptoms can misdirect the officer to recommend programs that target improvement of skills (for example, job training) versus programs that remedy the actual criminogenic need (for example, cognitive deficits). More thorough integration of treatment into community supervision likely entails a reexamination of the point at which formal risk and needs assessment occurs, as well as a makeover of the needs-assessment tools now used in most community corrections agencies throughout the United States.

Attrition and the Quality of Evaluation Research

A fourth question relates as much to research as it does to practice. In Chapter 8, James Prochaska, Ph.D., refers to attrition of clients from treatment as "one of the skeletons in the closet of psychotherapy and behavior change interventions." That skeleton is nowhere more prominent than in the field of evaluation of correctional interventions, where, in marked contrast to the larger fields of psychotherapy and drug-treatment research, virtually no substantive attention has been paid to the topic of attrition from treatment. The diminutive emphasis on the study of attrition in correctional programs is surprising, when viewed against the backdrop of a decades-long debate over the efficacy of offender rehabilitation that consistently has emphasized the need for methodological rigor in evaluations of treatment.

As Dr. Prochaska demonstrates, substantial attrition saps a treatment program of its rehabilitation potential. In addition, attrition also poses formidable methodological obstacles for evaluations of correctional treatments. The failure of researchers in the field of corrections to neither assess and report the extent to which attrition occurs nor to question the impact that differential treatment across treatment and control groups can have on the interpretation of evaluation findings (including the findings of meta-analytic research) should be disturbing to all who engage in evaluations of correctional treatment, and to consumers of such research. In the future, greater effort should be expended by program planners and evaluators to acknowledge and address attrition from treatment.

Conclusions

The essays in this book show that effective innovations in community corrections are possible and that numerous avenues exist for bringing about innovation. The diversity of strategies suggested by the various contributors to this volume proves that innovation in community corrections can be implemented by a wide assortment of decision-makers in the criminal justice process, with wide-ranging skills. Though the provocative contributions stir up some new questions for research and practice, perhaps such questions can be the fodder of future conferences on advancements in community corrections. In the meantime, managers and practitioners may draw upon the versatile, evidence-based strategies presented in Chapters 2 through 11 to initiate positive and substantial change in community-supervision policy and practice.

References

Andrews, D. A. and J. Bonta. 1994. *The Psychology of Criminal Conduct*. Cincinnati, Ohio: Anderson Press.

Andrews, D. A., J. Bonta, and R. D. Hoge. 1990. Classification for Effective Rehabilitation: Rediscovering Psychology. *Criminal Justice and Behavior*. 17:19-52.

Andrews, D. A., I. Zinger, R. D. Hoge, J. Bonta, P. Gendreau, and F. T. Cullen. 1990. Does Correctional Treatment Work? A Clinically Relevant and Psychologically Informed Meta-analysis. *Criminology*. 28:369-404.

Blumstein, A. and J. Petersilia. 1994. NIJ and its Research Program. *In 25 Years of Criminal Justice Research*, the National Institute of Justice, ed. Washington, D.C.: National Institute of Justice.

Butterfield, F. 1998. With a Little Help from the Movies and TV, a Subject that Once Got No Respect Attracts Students. *New York Times*. 5 December, 7.

Eck, J. 1997. Preventing Crime at Places. In L. W. Sherman, D. Gottfredson, D. MacKenzie, J. Eck, P. Reuter, and S. Bushway, eds. *Preventing Crime: What Works, What Doesn't, What's Promising*. Archived at http://www.preventingcrime.org.

Gendreau, P. 1996. Offender Rehabilitation: What We Know and What Needs To Be Done. *Criminal Justice and Behavior*. 23:144-162.

————. 1998. What Works in Community Corrections: Promising Approaches in Reducing Criminal Behavior. In B. J. Auerbach and T. C. Castellano, eds. *Successful Community Sanctions and Services for Special Offenders: Proceedings of the 1994 Conference of the International Community Corrections Association*. Lanham, Maryland: American Correctional Association.

Gendreau, P., T. Little, and C. Goggin. 1996. A Meta-analysis of the Predictors of Adult Offender Recidivism: What Works! *Criminology*. 34:575-607.

Gendreau, P. and R. R. Ross. 1979. Effectiveness of Correctional Treatment: Bibliotherapy for Cynics. *Crime & Delinquency*. 25:463-489.

Martinson, R. 1974. What Works? Questions and Answers about Prison Reform. *The Public Interest*. 35:22-54.

National Institute of Justice. 1996. *The NIJ Publications Catalog, Fifth Edition, 1985-1995*. Washington, D.C.: National Institute of Justice.

————. 1997. *The NIJ Publications Catalog 1996-1997*. Washington, D.C.: National Institute of Justice.

Palmer, T. 1975. Martinson Revisited. *Journal of Research in Crime and Delinquency*. 12:133-152.

Petersilia, J. 1997. Probation in the United States. In M. Tonry, ed. Vol. 22 of *Crime and Justice: A Review of Research*. Chicago: University of Chicago Press.

————. 1998. A Decade of Experimenting with Intermediate Sanctions: What Have We Learned? In *Perspectives on Crime and Justice: 1997-1998 Lecture Series*, the National Institute of Justice, ed. Washington, D.C.: National Institute of Justice.

Whitehead, J. T. and S. P. Lab. 1989. A Meta-analysis of Juvenile Correctional Treatment. *Journal of Research in Crime and Delinquency*. 26:276-295.

SECTION 1:

THE STRATEGIC MANAGEMENT OF COMMUNITY CORRECTIONS

The Strategic Management of Criminal Sanctions

2

Mark H. Moore, Ph.D.
Harvard University
Cambridge, Massachusetts

Introduction

For organizations that deliver criminal sanctions (and those who lead them), these are heady times (Tonry and Hatlestad, 1997). The demand for their product is up. Legislators want stiffer sentences for particular offenses, and sentence enhancements for repeat offenders. Criminal courts are churning out felony convictions, most with dispositions to be administered by corrections agencies. In these respects, business is booming. Yet, tightfisted legislators increasingly are reluctant to pay the operational costs for the sanctions so enthusiastically inscribed in legislation and meted out by judges. The net result is intense pressure on correctional agencies (and their contractors) to perform: to meet public demands to produce just, effective, and low-cost criminal sanctions.

In the private sector, conditions such as these would be expected to produce high rates of innovation (Clifford and Cavanagh, 1985). In the face of escalating demand, any company that developed a cost advantage in delivering the desired product could expect substantial growth and high returns. Thus, one would expect wide experimentation and rapid diffusion of successful innovations.

In corrections, this has not occurred. It is not that there has been no innovation. Indeed, many "alternative sanctions" have been designed and field-tested (Anderson, 1998). In principle, they could be deployed to meet some—perhaps a significant portion—of the escalating demand for criminal sanctions. The problem is simply that the industry as a whole has not much capitalized on these alternatives.

It is not hard to imagine why this is so. The politics of criminal sentencing are so passionate that it is hard for corrections officials to focus serious legislative attention on the relatively straightforward issue of how they plan to pay for the tougher sentences, to say nothing of the far more difficult issues of the potential injustice, or needless waste of human potential that such laws might entail. Similarly, the swirling passion limits the political room needed to innovate: there is little tolerance for the new and different; much enthusiasm for the tried and true. And, unlike the private sector, correctional administrators have few incentives to take the risk of personally championing innovations.

The purpose of this paper, and the others presented in this conference, is to help remedy the slow rate of innovation in the corrections industry by arming those individuals who wish to exercise leadership with the analytic frameworks and techniques of strategic management. More specifically, this paper will do the following: (1) set out the general idea of strategic leadership; (2) develop a conception of strategic management specifically for the public sector; (3) apply that conception to the current problems of corrections; and (4) by way of summary and conclusion, suggest specific steps that correctional managers should take to establish an overall strategic conception of corrections that makes room for some of the important innovations that we need in the field.

This should set the stage for subsequent papers that will do the following things: (1) describe how community corrections programs must be designed and engineered for effective performance; (2) explain how managers can make room for introducing innovative programs; and (3) describe what managers must do to sustain high-quality performance in innovative, individualized, community-based correctional programs.

Strategic Management

In contemporary management theory, "strategic" approaches are definitely in vogue (Porter, 1980; Bryson, 1988; Moore, 1995). Yet, it remains unclear what this means, particularly what it means to manage strategically in the public sector. This author will begin by clearing up these mysteries, or at least explaining how he intends to use the term.

Looking Ahead (But Not Too Far)

Perhaps the most common idea associated with strategic management is that it should be about the future, preferably the long-run future. In this respect, strategic thought seeks to overcome the enormous gravitational pull of the concrete present; to focus managers' attention on imagined futures, and what must be done now to prepare for those futures rather than expend all their energy reacting to current demands.

Forward thinking is certainly an important part of strategic thought; strategy should be focused on goals beyond the horizon. Yet, it is quite easy for managers, and particularly planners, to reach too far into the future—to establish planning horizons that are too distant to be practically useful.

The difficulty with looking too far into the future is that, as one does so, uncertainties multiply. The farther one looks ahead, the more varied environmental conditions can become. The more varied conditions can become, the harder it is to define the best organizational response. This is particularly true if the environment one faces is changing rapidly. In such circumstances, commitments to specific long-run objectives can lead one dangerously awry, for the future may turn out to be quite different from what one imagined.

In addition, even if one guesses right about the future, the further ahead one looks, the more attenuated the link becomes between the imagined future, and the particular, concrete actions that must be taken today to prepare for that future. The more tenuous the link, the looser the grip the future has on the imaginations of those whom managers must persuade to act in the present, and the harder it is for managers to focus the attention of their organization on the demands of the future. Long-run plans, based on imagination and calculation rather than concrete, current experience, fail to command the attention that the concrete demands of the present can. For both reasons, then, long-run plans may fail to guide organizations usefully because either they are mistaken, or widely ignored, or both.

If it is a mistake to stay focused too much on today's operations, but also to look too far in the future, there should be some optimal time horizon to use in strategizing. But it is not the same for all situations. The optimal planning horizon depends on how clearly one can see into the future, and one's ability to act now to prepare for that future. The more dynamic and changeable one's environment, the shorter the optimal planning horizon. The tighter the constraints on one's authorization to invest and innovate (and, thereby, to produce returns in the future), the shorter the horizon. What this means for most public-sector organizations is that two years is probably too short, and ten years much too long. Four or five years is probably about right.

Focusing on Key Investments and Innovations

The focus on preparing for the future means that, in strategic management, managerial attention is focused intensively on the investments being made today, which will ensure success tomorrow. Relatively less attention is focused on maintaining the larger number of routine activities that constitute the totality of the organization's current activities. In essence, managers must learn to look away from current operations.

This does not mean that the routine operations are not important. They are. Their continuation is necessary to the future of the organization. It just means that strategic managers have to relax their exclusive preoccupation with managing current operations, and become focused on the investments they are making that will improve performance in the future.

The investments that matter are, generally speaking, innovations (Altshuler and Behn, 1997). The investments that will improve performance are at least new to the organization; they also may be new globally. They can be of many different types. Some involve more efficient methods of achieving old goals, or delivering old services. Others involve introducing new products and services. And, some involve a whole new strategic idea about both the ends and means of an organization.

Because strategic management is focused relatively more intensively on investments and innovations, strategic managers tend to think of themselves as "change agents" rather than "status quo managers" (Moore, 1995). But the change cannot be change for change's sake; it must be designed to achieve a purpose. But what purpose?

Fitting Goals to Environmental Conditions

This leads to the third idea commonly associated with strategic management: organizational goals should be fitted to realistic assessments of the following: (1) what the environment demands, makes possible, or considers valuable, and (2) what the organization can do to meet the demands, exploit the opportunities, or produce what is valued (Porter, 1980). Environments do not allow organizations to become just anything (Wilson, 1989) (Indeed, they sometimes require an organization to be a particular something!) Moreover, organizations are not capable of becoming anything they want, even if the environment allows or requires it, and even if managers are skillful change agents. The discipline of strategic management requires that organizational goals accommodate this reality.

In the private sector, the important environmental conditions include such factors as the following: (1) the future demand for the company's (more or less varied) products; (2) the organization's current market share in each of its product markets; (3) the organization's "distinctive competence," and the rate at which that is being transformed by technological innovation; (4) the factors that give the organization an advantage or disadvantage vis-a-vis their competitors in each of their product markets; and so on (Porter, 1980). In the public sector, the relevant factors are less well established, but include at least the following: (1) projected increases in client populations; (2) the emergence of new programs, administrative systems, or technologies that widely are believed to or actually do improve the performance of the organization in traditional missions; (3) the rebalancing of political priorities to give greater emphasis to one kind of activity, or one dimension of value over another; (4) the emergence of new political demands or aspirations to which a public organization could choose to respond; and so on (Moore, 1995).

These diagnostic skills have a strategic quality not only because they are directed outward and toward the future, but also because the environments are assumed to be dynamic and heterogeneous: dynamic in the sense that demands and expectations for the organization will change (partly on their own accord, and partly in response to what managers do); and heterogeneous in the sense that different stakeholders will want different things from the organization. The world that most managers would prefer—one in which the demands on the organization remain stable, specific, and coherent—is treated as a special (and not particularly likely) case.

Positioning Organizations

Because organizational environments are dynamic and heterogeneous, organizational planning cannot be formulated as an "optimization" problem. Instead of "optimizing" the performance of the organization against a consistent, clear set of objectives, strategic managers "position" their organizations in complex, changing environments. This means several different things.

First, it means centering their organizations' efforts within (what seem to be) the strongest and most durable demands on the organization. They must find and exploit their core business opportunities.

Second, it means developing sophisticated methods for continuously scanning their environment. This includes initiating formal planning efforts. But it also includes paying close attention to the feedback that they are getting from various stakeholders about the value of current products and the efficiency of current operations.

Third, it means developing a diversified portfolio of activities distributed across many different products or activities that might turn out to be valuable or important. The diversified portfolio is important as a hedge against the uncertainty about how the environment will change, and as a way of accommodating the heterogeneity of the environmental demands.

Note that holding a diversified portfolio implies that an organization is less efficient in achieving any specific objective. If the organization could be sure of what will be demanded of it, it can focus all of its resources on achieving that goal. If, however, it must be uncertain about the particular things required of it, it must be ready to produce several different things. And that is generally less efficient than producing one thing.

Summary

In sum, strategic management is about judgment and poise. It has to do with looking far enough ahead into a complex, changing environment to make an accurate judgment about what is valuable and feasible for an organization to achieve. And, it has to do with positioning the organization in that environment in a way that allows it to pursue and exploit opportunities through sustained effort, but also to adapt and respond quickly when environmental conditions change in unexpected ways.

Strategic Management in the Public Sector

If the challenges of strategic management are as follows: (1) to focus managerial and organizational attention and effort on ensuring success in the (midrange) future rather than the present; (2) to focus on the few, large investments and innovations that allow an organization to fully exploit their best environmental opportunities; (3) to base planning on hard-nosed assessments of both the constraints and opportunities in an organization's dynamic and heterogeneous environment; and (4) to remain flexible and adaptive by monitoring continuously the organization's external environment and sustaining a diversified portfolio of activities; then, it is not hard to see why strategic management is particularly difficult in the public sector.

The Difficulty of Focusing on the Future

Take, for example, the injunction to focus on the (midrange) future. In principle, that should be possible in public-sector organizations. The missions of public-sector organizations are relatively stable. Their leaders are technical experts in their fields. It, therefore, ought to be possible for organizations to make steady progress in improving their performance. To many public sector managers, this is the ideal.

What stands in the way of achieving this ideal, however, are the insistent and fickle demands of politics. The hot currents that pulse through public-sector organizations are not the pressure of competition, or unpredictable shifts in consumer demand; they are the demands of their political overseers (Moore, 1995). These are particularly hot when managers and their organizations are exposed to intense public scrutiny: for example, when damaging news stories occur, or elected overseers in legislative and executive branches of government make an issue of an organization's performance, or (much less frequently) when a court steps in to declare an organization's operations unconstitutional.

Such moments often seem unpredictable; they seem to come from nowhere. Moreover, they often seem to focus on one particular incident, or on one particular attribute of an organization's performance, not on the organization's overall performance, or the full set of dimensions along which an organization's performance should be evaluated. For both reasons, they are distracting, and they throw a monkey wrench into the planned, orderly development of the organization's operations.

Even the more formal and systematic mechanisms of accountability (such as budget reviews, audits, performance evaluations, or contract renegotiations), which in principle could operate to keep organizations focused on a more orderly course of development, tend, instead, to be focused on the past or the immediate future. At best, public-sector budgeting processes ask managers to look one or two years out, not four or five.

Planning efforts may make a contribution by noting some important environmental changes that require increased spending (such as project- ed increases in workload or clients), or by proposing certain kinds of investments needed to improve current operations (such as new infor- mation systems). But these tend to be closely tied to current missions and operations, not to scenarios that require radical new thinking about products or productions processes. What is particularly missing in the usual budget-based planning systems is important investments in human resources, or important experiments that could lead to new products or production processes. These expenditures are viewed as administrative overhead in existing operational budgets rather than as the value- creating paths to the future. Thus, managers in the public sector have few occa- sions or incentives to look far ahead.

Hostility to Innovation

Consider, next, the idea that strategic management should focus on the investments and innovations that pave the way toward a value-creat- ing future. The private sector clearly has learned that investment and innovation—both in products and processes—are valuable, even essen- tial, for private sector organizations to succeed (Clifford and Cavanagh, 1985). In their dynamic world, organizations must reinvent themselves continuously if they are going to survive. The public sector has been far less enthusiastic about continuous innovation. The reason is simply that the public sector is much less comfortable with the risks of innovation than the private sector (Moore, 1993).

All innovations entail risks. By definition, one cannot be sure that the innovative program will work, or work well enough to justify its cost. Thus, to innovate is to expose both investors and customers to risks.

The public sector is exceedingly hostile to risky investments. The common thinking is that if public-sector executives cannot be sure that a new program will work, the effort should not be undertaken. They should not gamble with public money, or with their clients' lives and fortunes. They are paid to be expert, and to know how to solve public problems; they are not paid to experiment with untested ideas.

These prevailing views, reinforced on a daily basis through the vigor- ous pillorying of public officials who dare experiment and then fail, teach public managers to stay well within the boundaries of conventional practice. They create a climate in which errors of omission (in other words, failing to invent or adopt an innovation in a situation where they might have done some good) are complacently tolerated, while errors of commission (in other words, undertaking an innovative program that ultimately fails) are punished harshly. This makes it hard for individual managers to behave strategically, and slows both the overall rate of innovation in the public sector, and the rate at which valuable innovations can be diffused.

What is the Relevant Environment?

Take, next, the exhortation to make hard-nosed assessments of the environment. The question for public-sector managers is, what particular features of the environment should be monitored?

The most obvious answer is that they should focus on their task environment: for example, on the particular problems the organization is charged with handling, and how those are changing over time. Thus, in the context of corrections, it is important to know whether more prisoners are coming into the system, and what their particular needs will be. It also may be important to keep track of programmatic, administrative, or technological innovations in the field that can help the organizations deal successfully with the problems that are their unique responsibilities. This is the function of program planning, and a very important part of strategic planning in the public sector.

But it is equally, or perhaps even more important, for managers to monitor what is happening in their political environments (Moore, 1995). After all, it is citizens and their elected representatives who pay for the correctional programs and are authorized to dictate the particular purposes to be achieved and values to be expressed through them.

Of course, elected representatives are influenced by interest groups, the media, and expert professional opinion, as well as by citizens' views. Whatever the sources, however, it is ultimately the values of elected representatives that transform ideas about public goals and objectives into the collective aspirations that will be publicly funded and authorized. And it is these collective aspirations that will define the terms in which managers will be held accountable. In this sense, elected overseers are more like the customers of public sector organizations than the clients who are met at the business end of the organization. Their preferences and aspirations are a surer guide to what is valuable and important to produce.

What is Valued and Valuable in the Environment?

Not only is it difficult to determine what part of our environment should be monitored, it is difficult to figure out what particular attributes of organizational performance are wanted or needed, and how managers and their overseers could determine whether those aspirations are being met. In the private sector, the overall goals of the organization are relatively clear: the aim is to maximize long-term shareholder wealth by conceiving, producing, and selling products and services at prices that can more than cover the costs of producing them. If these broad goals can be achieved, there is a presumption that the organization has produced something of value, and will be rewarded with continuing support from investors, employees, and customers.

In the public sector, however, it is often less clear what the overall goals are. There is dispute, for example, about whether the goals of a correctional system primarily should be the principled goal of ensuring justice and accountability, or the practical goal of reducing crime. There is also dispute about what the principled goals require, and how the practical goals best could be achieved. To some, for example, the goal of ensuring justice requires a detailed examination of the context of an offense and the background of an offender, and a suitably individualized disposition.

To others, justice requires the opposite: a relentlessly rigorous focus on acts rather than contexts or individual backgrounds, and a disposition that is consistent with respect to the acts across all individuals. Similarly, some think crime may be reduced most effectively over the long run through rehabilitation efforts of various kinds. Others think the best ways to reduce crime are through the devices of deterrence and incapacitation.

How Is Organizational Performance Assessed?

Note that even if the public could reach a consensus on the goals of a public sector enterprise, the problem of how to value the attainment of the goals relative to the cost of achieving them remains difficult. In the private sector, one can see whether an enterprise was profitable or not; all one has to do is subtract the costs of producing the goods or services from the revenues earned by selling them.

In the public sector, one might be able to see whether goals were achieved, but it is not obvious how one compares the value of achieving the goals with the costs incurred. This is particularly difficult in the public sector because not all the costs used to achieve public sector objectives are financial. Public-sector enterprises often use public authority as well as money to achieve their results (Moore, 1995). Since there is a real cost (in liberty foregone) when public authority is used, it is important that public enterprises economize on the use of authority and money, and that the ends achieved be valued enough to justify these costs. Yet, it is difficult to account for these particular costs.

Of course, one could treat the willingness of the elected representatives to spend public money and authority to achieve the goals as indicative of the net value of a public enterprise just as we treat the customer's willingness to pay for products and services in the private sector as indicative of value. But this often feels unsatisfactory because elected representatives are spending other peoples' money, and we all easily can imagine the ways in which political judgments about the value of a public enterprise might be faulty or corrupted.

This has led many public administrators to want to place their trust in analytic techniques such as program evaluations, or cost-effectiveness analysis, or cost-benefit analysis to gauge the value of their enterprises more reliably (Wholey, 1986). While potentially useful, these techniques have proven more expensive to deploy, and less definitive in their conclusions than they first appeared. Thus, they have been less valuable for purposes of routine oversight and evaluation, than for the investigation of the value of experimental and innovative programs.

In short, the question of what constitutes a valuable performance by a public-sector organization remains both conceptually and operationally cloudy. For all practical purposes, public administrators have remained accountable for achieving operational goals, keeping total and average costs low, and minimizing any fraud, waste, and abuse that might occur in their organizations. It is these attributes of performance that are used by overseers to gauge the effectiveness and value of public enterprises.

A Conceptual Framework: The Strategic Triangle

One way that managers in the public sector can begin to cope successfully with these obstacles to strategic management is to fix them in their sights as problems to be managed rather than conditions to be deplored. One way to accomplish this objective is to develop an analytic framework that brings the problems and opportunities of managing in the public sector clearly in view.

Integrating Politics, Values, and Operational Management

Over the last decade or so, faculty at the Kennedy School at Harvard have developed just such a framework to help public-sector managers assess the potential and actively pursue imagined public sector initiatives (Moore, 1995). The framework is symbolized by a triangle (*see* Figure 2.1). The three points of the triangle define particular calculations that managers must make in deciding whether an enterprise is worth pursuing. They also point to particular activities they must undertake to ensure the success of their venture.

FIGURE 2.1. Strategy in the Public Sector

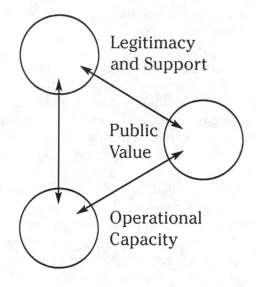

Legitimacy
and Support

Public
Value

Operational
Capacity

The first point of the triangle—the one labeled "public value"—reminds managers of the obvious point that they are responsible for producing things that are valuable, and publicly valued. There must be something that is produced or delivered—some way in which the world is changed by their efforts—that would justify their expenditure of public resources. There must be a vision of important values to be achieved through their efforts—some kind of story that connects their efforts to important public values.

The second point of the triangle—the one labeled "legitimacy and support"—focuses managerial attention on the idea that their particular conception of value must be able to capture and sustain enthusiasm from those who oversee their operations. As a practical matter, this is important, for without the support of elected representatives in legislative and executive branches, the organization will lack the resources (both money and authority) it needs to continue operations. But support from overseers is also normatively and ethically important, for it is only the support of elected representatives that can reassure public-sector executives that their particular visions of public value—the ones they now are using to guide their organizations' efforts—are sufficiently widely shared to ensure they are producing genuine public value rather than idiosyncratically or self-interestedly conceived conceptions of value.

The third point of the triangle—the one that is labeled "operational capacity"—is designed to focus managerial attention on the question of whether a particular initiative is operationally and administrative feasible. The most obvious way to think about this problem is to ask whether a given organization is capable of implementing a particular new program—whether it has the financial resources, the human resources, the particular kinds of procedures, equipment, and facilities the program requires, and the ability to monitor performance of the program on the appropriate dimensions.

By labeling this corner of the triangle "operational" rather than "organizational" capacities, however, managers are reminded that, often, much of the operational capacity they need to achieve their objectives lies outside the boundaries of the organizations they lead. For example, if one is responsible for educating children, one needs parents to help ensure the children do their homework; if one is trying to keep the streets clean, one needs shopkeepers to sweep the streets and homeowners to put their garbage in trashbags; if one is trying to eliminate street-level drug markets, one may need citizens to resist drug trafficking in their neighborhoods. If the total operational capacity one needs includes resources and efforts outside the boundaries of one's organization, it may be important for managers to operate their organizations in ways designed to mobilize and use that external productive capacity, as well as to maximize the direct contribution of their organization to the task at hand.

At one level, the idea meant to be conveyed by this simple diagram is utterly trivial: it says that for a public sector to be usefully undertaken, it must be valuable, authorizable, and feasible. What could be more obvious? Yet, at another level, this idea is quite challenging, for it reminds us of how many times we have launched an initiative or committed ourselves to an organizational purpose, with only one or two of these bases touched.

We have known that something was valuable and doable, but we may not have been sure from where the political support would come. Or, we have had support for a valuable enterprise, but not looked closely enough at the magnitude and character of the investment required to achieve the purpose. The reason these three things are joined together in an inter-locking triangle is to remind us that all three bases must be touched if the enterprise is to succeed. And, that is difficult to accomplish.

Using the Triangle to Chart Paths to the Future

What makes this framework useful for strategic management is that it reminds public sector managers that *politics* must be integrated with *substance* and *administration*. Less emphasized in the diagram but implicit in the notion of strategic management is that the prevailing social, political, and organizational conditions could support several different goals. There may not be a unique solution to the question of what would be valuable for an organization or a manager to do. Thus, public managers may have the discretion to decide which of several plausible visions is most valuable to undertake.

Also important is the fact that changes can occur in the conditions illuminated by the strategic triangle. Ideas about what would be valuable to achieve could change over time (at least in the relative emphasis to be given to different attributes of performance if not the overall set of value dimensions). The political forces that emphasize some dimensions of value over others might change. And the available administrative, programmatic, and technological capacities might change. As a result, goals that seemed impossible at one moment might become possible at another, and things that seemed possible and valuable suddenly can be foreclosed.

Moreover, these changes can occur independently of managerial effort, or be a consequence of managerial action. Managers, paying attention to how their organization is performing and what results it is achieving, are often in a good position to see important dimensions of value currently being neglected by the political environment. For example, a community corrections official might be in a position to notice the impact of work release programs on the level of support that a convicted offender could give to his dependent children, and use that information to remind the political environment that when offenders are locked up, families are weakened even as communities are made safer. Similarly, managers can take actions that change the balance of forces in their authorized political environment. By talking about neglected values, they may be able to mobilize a latent political constituency to demand that the priority of those neglected values be increased in the operations of an agency. Finally, and most obviously, managers can reengineer the administration and operations of their agency, and put new capacities within the organization's reach.

Leadership and Strategic Management

In sum, this particular conception of strategic management in the public sector assumes that public-sector managers face the challenge of integrating conceptions of public value, with political demands, and with operational capabilities. It assumes that managers have some discretion in setting goals for their organizations, for many different goals, which are consistent with environmental demands, and because circumstances change, both on their own and in response to what managers do. Among the conceivable goals, some are riskier and more difficult than others; some require more work and more skill from the managers than others; and some are more valuable over the long run than others. In principle, the quality of leadership that managers give to an enterprise can be measured by the value of the path they choose, the diagnostic skill they revealed in conceiving of the path, and the operational skill they showed in exploiting the opportunities they discerned (Heifetz, 1994).

Strategic Management in Corrections

Let us now apply this general conception of strategic management in the public sector to the specific context of corrections, or the production of criminal sanctions. Before we begin this general analysis, however, we must keep one important point in mind. Strategic management begins with an accurate diagnosis of the particular situation one confronts, now, and as best one can see, into the future. Generally speaking, the best diagnoses will be quite specific to particular times and places. Consequently, there are distinct limits to what can be usefully said in general about the conditions that correctional managers face. Nonetheless, as long as we remember that managers must look closely at their local circumstances, there may be some utility in relying on the categories of the strategic triangle to diagnose the potential for deploying community-based innovations in corrections.

Values at Stake

Strategic management begins with identifying the important values at stake in the operations of a correctional system. This step is particularly interesting in the management of criminal sanctions, because both principled and instrumental values are supposed to govern, and be expressed through, the operations of the correctional system.

Principled Values: Just Deserts

The principled values focus on what, as a matter of justice, individual offenders *deserve*. In one such conception, offenders should be held accountable for their crimes. It is just that they be tried and punished. Indeed, the principle of accountability is so strong that even if punishment had no practical effect on levels of crime, offenders nonetheless should be punished as a matter of principle. The particular punishment to be administered is also governed by principles. One is that "cruel and unusual punishment" should be avoided. A second is punishment should be proportional to the seriousness of the crime. (The seriousness of the crime, in turn, should be judged largely by the harm produced by the criminal act.) A third principle is that like offenses should be punished equally.

A slightly different (but equally principled) conception would give greater weight to the moral culpability of the offender in determining the appropriate punishment. In this alternative view, it is the "blameworthiness" of the offender as well as harmfulness of the act that justifies criminal punishment (Moore et al., 1984). Blameworthiness, in turn, cannot be judged solely by the act itself; one must look to the offender's intent, and the context in which the offense was committed. A cold-blooded murder committed for money is a different crime than an accidental homicide occurring in the midst of a drunken argument among friends. It deserves, as a matter of justice and morality, a different punishment.

An additional idea, formulated as a principled rather than practical concern, is that even convicted offenders have certain rights that correctional administrators are bound to protect. They are entitled to be safe within correctional institutions, to have access to medical care, and to be held in conditions that are sufficiently benign as to avoid "cruel and unusual punishment." The society makes these promises because it is part of our idea of what constitutes just treatment of criminal offenders.

While these ideas about what constitutes just punishment differ from one another, they operate within the same moral framework. Punishment is to be guided by principled concerns about what offenders deserve, not by any practical considerations about the practical impact of punishment on levels of crime.

Practical Values: Crime Control Cost-Effectiveness

In this respect, these principled ideas may be contrasted with more practical or utilitarian conceptions of the value produced by criminal sanctions. Utilitarian conceptions of criminal sentencing begin with a practical concern for reducing crimes. In this view, the value of any given punishment depends on its effectiveness in reducing crime. Indeed, it is principally that value in reducing crime that justifies punishment. If no practical effect were produced by punishment, there would be no reason to impose it.

Punishment is thought to be causally related to future criminal offending through four different causal mechanisms. One mechanism, general deterrence, reduces crimes by threatening potential offenders with the prospect of arrest and punishment if they should offend. A second mechanism, specific deterrence, reduces crime by giving convicted offenders a taste of punishment. That experience, in turn, is expected to dissuade the offender (though not necessarily others) from committing future crimes. A third mechanism, incapacitation, reduces crimes by making it physically impossible for offenders to commit crimes by imprisoning them, isolating them, or so closely supervising them that they are never free to commit offenses against other citizens.

A fourth mechanism, rehabilitation, reduces crimes by altering offenders' inclinations to commit offenses. This effect, in turn, is achieved by several different methods including: (1) providing offenders with general education or specific vocational skills so that they can earn a living through legitimate means; (2) treating their mental illness or drug addiction to eliminate some of the factors that predispose them to criminal offending; or (3) training them in rational, nonviolent means of resolving disputes so that they are less inclined to resort to violence.

There are other values at stake in utilitarian conceptions of punishment beyond crime control. In practical conceptions, one must be concerned about keeping the financial costs of producing the sanctions and treatments low as well as keeping the crime control effectiveness up. Indeed, the ultimate value of the punishments depends on the size of the gap between the public costs incurred in meting out punishments and the crime-reduction impact that the punishments produce. In looking at the cost of punishments, citizens and their representatives may be particularly sensitive to comparisons between the average costs of supervising offenders and the average costs of supporting people in other kinds of "total institutions" such as universities, mental hospitals, or nursing homes (Goffman, 1970). They also may focus their attention on the total costs of correctional budgets, their share in overall state spending, or even the rate of change in either of these dimensions.

In addition, most utilitarian conceptions of punishment also acknowledge the claims that principled conceptions of justice can make on the operations of a correctional system. They would accept the idea that cruel and unusual punishments should be barred (even if they were cost-effective in controlling crime); that punishments should be roughly proportional to the seriousness of the crime; and that punishments should fall equally across offenders. They also would accept the idea that even prisoners have rights that are to be protected, and would judge the value of a correctional operation in terms of the reliability with which it could keep prisoners safe from one another, from abuse at the hands of correctional officers, and ensure that inmates would have the medical care, legal assistance, and visitation rights to which they are entitled. Still, these values, so prominent in principled conceptions of the goals of criminal punishment, would be less prominent in utilitarian conceptions. In the utilitarian world, any discretion left to judges and correctional administrators should be guided by concerns for achieving the maximum crime-reduction effect at the minimum financial cost.

The Political Resonance of These Values

The author reviews this familiar terrain not because these points are new, but because he wants to make a point about the stance of those who favor community corrections in the current political environment. In his experience, those who make the argument for community corrections are relying principally on utilitarian arguments to advance their cause. They point to the high total and average costs of criminal dispositions and the limited effectiveness of prisons in reducing crime. They then argue that a different set of dispositions would be cheaper and no worse in controlling crime than the current reliance on prisons (Rubin, 1997).

They have been surprised to discover that this argument has relatively little political resonance. Part of the reason for this is that the empirical claims made by this common argument are not well developed: we still do not know whether increasing aggregate levels of imprisonment increase, reduce, or leave crime unaffected over the long run. Those who favor imprisonment can and do make utilitarian calculations that suggest that prisons are "cost-beneficial" (Zedlewski, 1987).

But, a larger part of the explanation for the lack of political resonance is that citizens and their representatives do not want to have the practical, utilitarian discussion about crime control. They want to have the principled discussion that focuses on what is just, and what is deserved (Bessette, 1997).

Currently, that discussion focuses crudely on the culpability of offenders, and adopts a relatively harsh, unforgiving stance. Yet, it is important to keep in mind that there might be principled, desert arguments for both less and different forms of criminal punishment as well as for longer and more secure imprisonment. After all, some of the most powerful arguments for rehabilitative sentencing were arguments about justice and practicality. It seemed *just* (as well as *prudent*) to give offenders a chance to redeem themselves, particularly if they had previously been badly neglected by society, if their crimes were not serious, and if they showed some desire to improve themselves.

The current political conversation about the values to be served through criminal punishment has been impoverished by the lack of principled, moral arguments on the side of redemption and atonement as well as prosecution and condemnation. This silence cedes the principled arguments to those who favor harsher, more expensive, and more controlling sanctions.

Multiple Objectives and the "Production Possibility Frontier"

In any case, it is possible to identify the values at stake in the operations of a correctional system. Table 2.1 (on the next page) presents an initial conception of what those values might be.

One important feature of the discussion about the management of criminal sanctions is that we often act as though society had to choose which of these different values was to be the *only* or *primary* goal of a correctional agency. We have to decide whether principled or utilitarian goals should guide operations. Or, we have to decide whether our primary utilitarian goal is deterrence, incapacitation, or rehabilitation.

It is true, of course, that as an analytic and logical matter, the system only can be designed to maximize one goal. It also may be true that it would be easier to administer the system if we decided explicitly once and for all what our principal objectives in criminal sentencing were. And

TABLE 2.1. Dimensions of Value in the Production of Criminal Sanctions

1. Principled Values: "Just Deserts"
   —Absence of cruel and unusual punishments

   —Proportionality

   —Consistency

   —Protection of inmates' rights

2. Utlitarian Values: Crime Control Cost-Effectiveness
   —Reduced crime through:
     • General deterrence

     • Specific deterrence

     • Incapacitation

     • Rehabilitation

   —Cost to public of producing supervision and services

   —Level of order and amenities within programs

   —Ability to mobilize informal social control

arguing with one another about the proper goals of sentencing and corrections is certainly a morally compelling enterprise.

Yet, reflection reminds us that it is also true that any correctional system produces effects that can be measured and observed along each of these dimensions of performance. If we designed a system to maximize deterrence, for example, that system would produce effects on dimensions such as: (1) the presence or absence of "cruel and unusual punishments;" (2) the proportionality of the sanctions imposed; or (3) crime reductions achieved through incapacitation as well as through deterrence whether intended or not. It is even possible that a system designed to deter would reduce crime through the mechanisms of rehabilitation as well by achieving the cognitive-restructuring objective of

reminding offenders that it is both morally wrong and practically consequential for them to commit crimes. In short, regardless of our particular
objectives, a correctional program or system produces results in all the
relevant dimensions. And a system can be evaluated on any particular
dimension of interest.

This observation raises several interesting possibilities. One is that
instead of continuing to argue about what our goals should be, we should
get on with the task of measuring the results of our efforts; further, that the
results should be measured in each dimension that the political world
judges to be important. This tack would have the enormous utility of
releasing those who oversee correctional agencies from the task of agreeing on the single important objective to be achieved. They, instead, could
be free to examine performance of the organization along any dimension
that interested them. The organization, for its part, would be responsible
for trying to improve its performance on each of the particular dimensions.

Of course, some immediately will insist that the organization cannot
achieve all its objectives simultaneously; that in order to improve its performance on one objective (say reducing overall costs), it has to take a
loss on some other objectives (such as the protection of inmates' rights).
That may be true. But, it is important to keep in mind that this is only true
if the organization is now operating at what economists call *the production possibility frontier*; that is, at a place where all the resources of the
organization are being used most efficiently to achieve the organization's
various objectives. That need not be true.

There may be many organizations that are operating well inside their
"production possibility frontier." To the extent that is true, there will be
ways of operating to achieve more of both things that are valued. The private sector has found that this is true far more often than they first
thought. When they looked closely at their operations to see if they could
produce more quality and reduce costs, they found many such opportunities. Perhaps the same is true for correctional agencies. Perhaps they
can produce more justice, more crime control effectiveness, and less cost
than they now do. It is hard to know whether this is possible until we begin
measuring the performance of programs and systems in these terms.

Emergent Values

It also is worth noting that new values are emerging in politics, and
in discussions of criminal sanctions. In the wider political debate, there is
a great deal of enthusiasm for reminding citizens of their responsibilities
to the wider society: to refrain from committing crimes, to meet their

obligations to their children, and to remain drug free and employed. There is also greater interest in the impact that governmental operations have on primary social institutions such as families and communities. There is more respect for the power of these informal institutions, and more interest in trying to ensure that they be protected, and allowed to do their work.

Within discussions of criminal sanctions, there is increased interest in allowing victims to participate in the adjudication and punishment of offenders through programs such as victim restitution. Implicit in this interest is the rediscovery that crimes are not just offenses against the state to be punished by and through state agencies, but also events that happen between offender and victim, in which the victim has an important stake.

Values like these are not necessarily hostile to innovations in corrections programs, and particularly not to the development of community corrections. In fact, they suggest some importantly different ways of thinking and talking about community corrections.

In the past, we have conceived of community corrections as devices that could be used to help manage the transition from prisons back to the community, that would help maintain connections to the community, or that could reduce the stigma associated with imprisonment. These were all purposes closely linked to rehabilitation objectives.

But many of these same features of community corrections can be seen in a different light: as a way for informal, private institutions to participate in the control and reformation of offenders, and as a way of reinforcing the obligations that offenders have to their families and communities. In short, community participation in correctional programs is not just support for offenders; they are ways of making more concrete, vivid, and exacting the obligations that offenders have to their communities and families. Insofar as the connection can be made between the enthusiasm for rebuilding families and communities and the development of informal systems of control on one hand, and community corrections programs (including, in particular, notions of restorative justice) on the other, a new political constituency for community corrections may be created.

Political Support and Legitimacy

For correctional programs and systems to succeed, they must be able to command support and legitimacy from their external political environment. The values that justify their existence and guide their operations must be shared by those who grant them the authority and money they need to operate. Not everybody has to agree with everything the correctional system is trying to do; but there must be enough people, in powerful enough positions of authority and influence, who *do* agree to ensure the success of any given correctional strategy, and to reassure those who are leading the initiative that they are pursuing something that is publicly (as well as merely personally) valued.

This discussion concerns gaining political support *and* legitimacy from the external environment. This author also separates the concepts of support and legitimacy from the public value that is to be produced. This may seem wrong-headed. One could argue that these are all the same thing: that the only appropriate way for a public enterprise to gain legitimacy in a democracy is through the political support of the citizens; and that one cannot be sure that something is publicly valued until citizens and their representatives declare the value of an enterprise through legislation or executive proclamation.

Certainly, it is important to the success of a public sector enterprise that it pursues goals and operational objectives that can combine these qualities: in other words, that are popular, legitimate, and objectively valuable. Yet, there is some utility in separating these different concepts, and reminding public leaders that part of their task is to work to align them. This is useful partly because the concepts are different: a popular cause (capital punishment, for example) is not necessarily either a legitimate or valuable one; a valuable purpose (individual rehabilitation of offenders, for example) cannot always capture political support, nor be carried out legitimately.

Separating these ideas is also important because different groups and agencies attend to these different sources of legitimacy. When one is looking for political or popular support for an idea, one looks to public opinion, the platforms of those who run for elected office, and the views that elected officials hold while in office. Staying aligned with the values explicitly or implicitly expressed through politics ensures political support.

When one is looking for legitimacy, one looks to somewhat different overseers, and different kinds of ideas. Courts, and generalized concepts associated with the rule of law such as restraints on governmental power, the protection of individual rights, and procedural fairness in establishing and applying the law, all are linked closely to the idea of legitimacy. Staying aligned with these values can ensure that a correctional enterprise can operate with the support of courts as well as legislatures. And, insofar as the public as a whole tends to support legal institutions and legal concepts, being aligned with these legal institutions and values increases the political support a correctional system enjoys.

When one is looking to be sure that one is delivering something that is intrinsically valuable in the most efficient and effective way, one relies on those institutions that embody different kinds of instrumental expertise: for example, substantive experts in penology who are supposed to know "what works" in corrections, and how correctional systems might best be operated; or auditors, budgeters, and program evaluators whose measurements can reassure overseers that something valuable is being accomplished with the resources that are committed to the enterprise.

Note that, to a degree, these different bases of support and legitimacy for a public enterprise correspond to the different kinds of values that are evoked in debates about what is valuable in criminal sentencing and the administration of criminal sanctions. Concerns about what is just, about what offenders deserve, and what prisoners are entitled to, tend to be associated with concepts of legitimacy and to tap into these particular sources of support. Concerns about what works, about how crime can be reduced most effectively, and whether the benefits of imprisonment outweigh the costs tend to be associated with concepts of effectiveness in delivering public value, and they tap into the public's concerns for instrumental effectiveness. Since both of these frames evoke important values that the public has (intermittently) on its mind, both are potentially available for building the overall support and legitimacy for a correctional strategy.

Weaknesses in one or the other frame are, conversely, sources of vulnerability for any given strategy. Indeed, the support for rehabilitation tended to collapse in the first instance when doubts arose about the effectiveness of the programs, but then accelerated as doubts about the fairness and justice of rehabilitative sentencing came to the fore.

Given the different sources of support and legitimacy, what do we now know about what sorts of values, realized through particular kinds of programs, will be supported by the public, by elected legislators, and by the courts? What will the authorizing environment for correctional agencies demand, expect, or tolerate?

Public Opinion About Criminal Sanctions
In examining public opinion about criminal sanctions, one first must consider what kinds of public opinion should count as normatively compelling in guiding administrative action. One answer is that public opinion

is captured by a certain kind of public opinion poll in which a random sample of the population is subjected to a telephone interview posing questions about what kinds of sanctions they support. A different answer is that public opinion only can be captured through a quite different process in which people first are asked about their raw opinion, and then given information, a chance to try to apply their views to particular situations, and an occasion for talking to one another. This sort of public opinion tends to be more informed and more stable, and in some sense, more normatively compelling than the off-the-cuff response one gets from more superficial opinion polling.

This issue is important because the two different methods for tapping into public opinion produce different answers to the question of what kinds of correctional program the public will support. When one conducts the first kind of poll, one learns that the public supports harsh sentencing, and is deeply suspicious of community corrections. When one conducts the second kind of opinion survey, one discovers that the public will support a variety of community corrections programs for many different kinds of offenders.

They want offenders to be held accountable for their offenses, and for some punishment to be delivered, but they are open on the question of what form the punishment should take. They are willing to use community sanctions because they think such sanctions are fairer, and because they can save money. (The argument that they are consistent with supporting rehabilitation, however, has less general and less powerful resonance.)

The fact that the two different kinds of polling activities produce somewhat different answers raises the interesting question of which poll results ought to be heeded by correctional managers. The practical question for them might be which of these different kinds of opinions will govern their world: will elected representatives align themselves with the first or second type of poll? The ethical question is which of these kinds of opinions does democratic theory sanction as the normatively compelling kind of public opinion: does democratic theory say that untutored, raw opinion should guide public action, or that opinion based on information, reflection, and discussion should guide public action?

In the view of this author, it is the better founded public views that are the proper guide to public action. Raw public opinion has relatively little normative status as a guide to public action. For it to become a powerful normative and practical guide, the raw public opinion has to be transformed into settled and shared views through a process of reflection and deliberation. Only then can it be viewed as a legitimate public aspiration. Of course, this view offers little comfort to public officials who, as a practical matter, often are buffeted by the waves of raw public opinion that sweep over them in times of crisis, and by the demands of elected representatives who are prepared to pander to and manipulate raw public opinion. Yet, it does remind them that one of the important challenges of strategic management in the public sector is to bring as much of the public along as possible in developing a correctional strategy, and to do this through hearings and media coverage of the full range of activities and values being expressed through those values, rather than wait for the occasional crisis. In short, to build legitimacy and support, correctional officials have to find ways to encourage a public deliberation about correctional policy, not just a public reaction.

Legislative Attitudes

From a quick review of recent legislation, it would be easy to conclude that legislative attitudes were quite hostile to community corrections programs. They have voted for longer sentences for particular offenses (principally drug offenses); and for sentence enhancements for repeat offenders. They also have attacked parole and probation programs, and reduced the amount of "good time" awarded to offenders.

And yet, despite this, little of the authorizing legislation that grants corrections officials the power to classify prisoners, to operate intermediate sanctions, and to distribute prisoners across the different levels of security and kinds of programs has been repealed or changed. In fact, one can detect a certain amount of legislative enthusiasm for some new kinds of criminal sanctions such as community service, victim restitution, and electronic surveillance. There may be some emerging political enthusiasm for "restorative justice."

In these respects, legislative attitudes seem (not surprisingly) to reflect the attitudes of the broader public. They want offenders to be held accountable for their offenses—not allowed excuses, or "treated" for mental illness. They are open to the idea that punishment could take the form of work and/or close surveillance in the community, but they want to be sure that if offenders commit any additional crimes while under correctional supervision, they will be held accountable. This means that offenders who violate conditions of probation or parole or community service should be imprisoned, and that some scarce prison capacity should be reserved for that purpose.

They are interested in saving money, but find it hard to believe that correctional institutions cost as much as they do. They cannot believe that the high costs are necessary to control and protect prisoners. They suspect the high costs are associated with luxuries of various kinds that the prisoners could and should do without.

Note that these views are animated much more by concerns about justice than by concerns about effectiveness. They are interested in keeping costs low, and find it hard to believe that punishing offenders through confinement and close supervision does not reduce crime through deterrence and incapacitation. But their primary motivation seems to be to uphold the principle of accountability for criminal offending.

The concerns also leave a great deal of room for different kinds of intermediate sanctions, but the sanctions have to be understood in terms of specific values. Boot camps are good because they are tough and demanding, and because they demand accountability and teach discipline. (This is a kind of rehabilitation that the public and legislators will support!) Mandated abstinence from drug use, supported through mandatory urinalysis, and swift punishment for infractions, is good because it compels drug users to be sober, and depends on their self-control. (In this respect, it differs from drug treatment which is thought to be less demanding, and less reliant on an individual's self-control.) Community service is good because it holds offenders accountable and requires them to work rather than lie around at taxpayers' expense. So, there is a great deal of room for experimenting with certain (but not all) kinds of intermediate sanctions.

One final point about the political support for community corrections is worth considering. Spending on corrections is now so large, and is growing so fast, that decisions about the production of criminal sanctions have taken on aspects of public works and economic development as well as crime control and justice aspects. This means that important decisions that affect the future supply of criminal sanctions (such as the number of prison beds or other kinds of facilities) sometimes are made by different legislative committees, or are guided by a different set of values than we have so far discussed. Sometimes, decisions about capital construction are made in public works committees rather than justice committees. Sometimes, the most important value on the table is not justice or crime control effectiveness, but jobs and public spending in particular communities.

For the most part, this fact has worked against investments in community corrections. The constituency that benefits from the construction and operations of prisons and other kinds of secure facilities is well developed, and usually well connected. The constituency that could benefit from increased spending on community-based alternatives is less well developed and less well connected. In time, such a constituency might emerge.

Indeed, the development of this constituency might be an important reason to support community corrections programs even when their principal short-run effect will be to "widen the net" rather than substitute for prison placements. The strategic calculation would be that community corrections and intermediate sanctions never can compete successfully with prisons until they have an infrastructure of sufficient scale, and that now would be a good time to build that infrastructure so that when the current enthusiasm for longer punishment ends, the community-based alternatives successfully can maintain their position as overall spending on criminal punishment declines.

Judicial and Legal

Ordinarily, in looking for sources of legitimacy and support, one could focus most of one's attention on public and legislative attitudes. The views of the courts, while potentially important, could be given lower priority simply because the courts would not be much involved in the oversight of public enterprises. This is not true in corrections, however. In corrections, courts are crucially important for two reasons.

First, the prisoners' rights movement, and the litigation associated with it, has brought correctional agencies under the direct authority of the courts. The courts have used this authority primarily to improve conditions within prisons: specifically, housing conditions, access to medical care, visitation rights, and so on. They also have focused attention on due process rights prisoners might have in probation and parole hearings, and other administrative decisions affecting their length of stay in prison.

The courts have had much less direct influence over the development of intermediate and community-based sanctions, however. Of course, by requiring governments to maintain constitutionally permissible prisons (and thereby effectively increasing their cost), prisoners' rights litigation has created incentives for legislators and correctional administrators to search for lower-cost alternatives. But, this is an indirect and uncertain effect. Courts, by themselves, cannot sustain the development of a large, differentiated system of intermediate punishments.

Moreover, it is not clear how long this pressure from the courts will last. Public sympathy for offenders seems to be declining. The Supreme Court has expressed reluctance to continue to regulate the details of prison conditions and operations. Thus, whatever energy was linked to prisoners' rights litigation now may be ebbing.

Second, in addition to overseeing court operations, courts decide whether and how to use correctional services. They are the ones that decide for the society what particular kind of correctional program to use in responding to individual criminal offenders. Although the discretion of judges in making sentencing decisions generally is being reduced through the passage of determinate-sentencing laws, some still remains, particularly with respect to the use of intermediate sanctions. Consequently, judges are important coproducers of dispositions, and important customers for intermediate sanctions. If criminal court judges do not know about or want to use intermediate sanctions, they never can emerge as an important part of a correctional enterprise.

Based on this author's limited experience, judges have been reluctant users of intermediate sanctions. No doubt, they fear the prospect that an offender, sentenced to a community-based disposition, will commit a serious crime, and that they will become the focus of public indignation. Their reluctance also may be linked to their own attitudes of what is just and appropriate. But reluctance to use intermediate, community-based sanctions could be based on nothing more than lack of familiarity with the programs. They may not have gotten comfortable with the idea of community corrections, or with specific providers. To the extent this is true, their reluctance may be overcome by more intensive marketing of the programs.

Judges, like legislators, may be more willing to support community-based intermediate sanctions if they are used as devices for increasing control over offenders who otherwise would be headed for probation than when they are used to divert prison-bound offenders. While that can be seen as a problem in the short run, it need not be that in the long run. As noted above, it could be a wise strategic move to widen the net now to allow judges to accumulate experience with intermediate programs, and to build the operational infrastructure and political support these programs need, so that when the current enthusiasm for harsher sentencing abates, one has a firm base for alternatives. In any case, in the short run, the important task is to market the programs to sentencing judges. That is as important as any other part of building support and legitimacy.

Operational Capacity

In our survey of the factors shaping the strategic potential of correctional systems, we come, finally, to the traditional focus of management:

the deployment of assets in operational programs to achieve objectives. The natural focus of operational management is on the design of innovative programs to deal with a particular class of offender in a way that is equally consistent with the demands of justice, lower cost, and equally or more effective in controlling crime (in the short and long run). Innovative programs are clearly an important part of strategic management; they are to the management of correctional systems what the creation of new product lines to meet the tastes of particular segments of a market are to the management of private enterprises.

Yet, strategic management also should be concerned with the performance of the entire *system* of corrections as well as with the development of individual programs. The entire system of corrections consists of the following things.

First, a correctional system has a portfolio of supervisory programs. The programs include different levels of security in prisons and different kinds and levels of support programs in prisons (such as drug treatment, general education, or vocational education). In addition, the portfolio of programs includes a variety of intermediate, community-based sanctions such as intensive probation, electronic surveillance, community service, boot camps, and so forth. Some of these programs are used as substitutes for prison; others as prerelease programs. Ideally, the portfolio of programs would include some programs that are innovative, and therefore risky, since it is from these programs that we might learn new ways to deal more effectively with offenders. But, one ordinarily would expect most of the portfolio to be programs whose operational characteristics were reasonably well known.

Second, in addition to these different kinds of supervised programs, a correctional system must include some kind of classification or risk-assessment system that is used to sort the correctional population into separate groups that are eligible for different kinds of dispositions. Often, a piece of this system supports the judge at the point of initial sentencing; another supports correctional administrators as they transfer prisoners among different parts of the system; and another supports probation and parole decision-making.

Third, a correctional system includes an information system that keeps track of the status of the clients of the system, at least for as long as they remain clients. It also would be desirable for the system to have some way of monitoring the behavior of offenders even after they have ceased being clients to measure the long-run impact of the system on recidivism rates and other indicators of effectiveness. In short, what is needed is an accounting system that captures and records the performance of the system on relevant dimensions of value such as cost, levels of crime while under supervision, and rates of recidivism once released from supervision.

Generally speaking, when one surveys correctional systems, one tends to find the following: (1) inadequate total resources; (2) representation of many different kinds of programs in the correctional system, but most of the resources committed to (and most of the inmates supervised within) a small number of traditional programs—largely prisons; (3) fragmented classification systems; and (4) weak systems for measuring the status and performance of offenders. This means that generally there is much managerial work to do to build a correctional systems that can be accountable, accommodate the large and heterogeneous client demand, and innovate in search of more just and cost-effective dispositions. The question thus becomes which problem to tackle first?

One of the important ideas in strategic management is that the first step nearly always is to take steps that make the system more accountable. The reason is that becoming more accountable is the route to more legitimacy and support, which is necessary to get additional resources, and the political room needed to innovate. In short, increased accountability establishes the base on which all the other things can be built. As a practical matter, this means finding out the particular attributes of performance which are important to overseers, and developing measurement systems to record the system's performance on these particular valued dimensions.

The second step is not to hide the capacity problems of the system, but to make them visible and explicit. Instead of looking at the number of clients being admitted to correctional institutions, one ought to be measuring the number and characteristics of offenders convicted of felonies in criminal courts. That is the population to which the correctional system as a whole has to respond. What is important to keep in front of citizens and their representatives is the total number of people who "deserve" or "need" some kind of correctional response, and the proportion of the offenders who get different kinds of responses, ranging from probation to maximum-security incarceration. That will keep the pressure on not only to increase overall capacity, but also to diversify.

The third step is to build capacity in the particular kinds of intermediate, community-based sanctions that can capture support from the population, and to monitor their operations very closely. Everyone has to get more comfortable with the operations of these programs, and the only way to do that is to actually invest in them. This also helps to build an infrastructure that can help build a political constituency for these programs.

The very last step is to conduct explicit experiments with very risky but potentially high pay-off sanctions. It is only after a correctional system has built credibility with its overseers, that it will be given the room to experiment widely. Yet, it is important that we get to these experiments, and that we use them effectively to learn what works, or corrections as a whole will never make any progress towards more just, and more cost-effective corrections.

An important question in all this is where contracting fits in, and in particular, where nonprofit or profit-making firms can make a contribution. One important contribution that contracting out might be able to make to the development of more just and more cost-effective correctional systems is to create more room for innovation by reducing the risk to government officials. If private groups (whether nonprofit or for profit) are willing to operate a program, they may take some of the risk from public-sector officials. The private sector may enjoy enough legitimacy to be able to get away with more innovative activities than the government can undertake.

Private firms also may have some important cost advantages over public bureaucracies. Nonprofit firms may be able to recruit volunteers, or complement government payments with voluntary financial contributions, and thereby increase quality without raising costs. Due to more flexible personnel policies, they also may do better in attracting and deploying high-quality people to the demanding work associated with intermediate sanctions. But none of this is certain. It could turn out that the quality of private contractors is lower, or their costs higher than public-sector providers. We will not know much about this until we try.

Perhaps, the hardest thing over the long run, however, will be to create correctional systems that can be accountable to their overseers, capable of producing relatively individualized responses to their heterogeneous client populations, and capable of experimenting with and learning about new kinds of programs. It is hard to build that much flexibility into operational systems that are subjected to the demands for accountability that are common in the public sector. The only way to accomplish this goal is to work the political problem of building legitimacy and support as hard as one works the operational problems of building the complex operational capabilities that a first-rate correctional system requires.

Summary: Managing the Transition to a More Diversified, Higher Performing Correctional System

In all likelihood, correctional systems can produce more public value if they grow, become more diversified, improve their capacities to tailor dispositions to individual offenders, and engage in much more systematic experiments in search of more just and cost-effective criminal sanctions. Ordinarily, this means that they will have to increase their investments in intermediate, community-based alternatives. To do that, however, they will have to regain legitimacy and support for their overall traditional programs, and for the particular pieces of work that constitute their investment and risk portfolio that carries them into the future. Exactly what path should be taken to achieve these objectives only can be revealed by taking the following steps.

Performing a Market Analysis

First, they must look closely at the market in which they are operating. This means not only paying attention to the number and characteristics of clients committed to their safekeeping, and clients who were eligible but have been diverted elsewhere, but also to the values that citizens, legislators, elected executives, and courts want to see expressed through the operations of the correctional system. It is impossible to know what is worth producing until one finds out what those who give the resources for the production desire.

Embracing Accountability

Second, they must embrace their accountability to citizens and their representatives by developing ways to measure their performance on dimensions of performance that matter to their overseers. If their overseers are focused on reducing costs, they must get good at measuring costs. If they are preoccupied with crimes committed by people who are under state supervision, they must get good at measuring this quantity, and finding ways to reduce it. If they are preoccupied with conditions inside the prisons, they must find ways of revealing what conditions really are inside the prison. By making it possible for overseers to look at the organization's operations in ways that respond to their interests, managers increase their accountability, and their legitimacy and support.

They also may be able to get their organizations to focus more effectively on the key dimensions of performance, and through that device, actually improve performance.

Stimulating Innovation

Third, with the confidence built by embracing accountability, they have to be willing to risk that through experiments and innovations. They also must be organized to take maximum advantage of experiments for continued learning. Correctional organizations must perform this way if society as a whole is to find more just and more cost-effective responses for convicted offenders.

References

Altshuler, A. A. and R. D. Behn, eds. 1997. *Innovation in American Government*. Washington, D.C.: Brookings Institution Press.

Anderson, D. C. 1998. *Sensible Justice: Alternatives to Prison*. New York: New Press.

Bessette, J. M. 1997. In Pursuit of Criminal Justice. *The Public Interest*. 129 (Fall):61-72.

Bryson, J. M. 1988. *Strategic Planning for Public and Nonprofit Organizations*. San Francisco: Jossey-Bass.

Clifford, D. K., Jr. and R. Cavanagh. 1985. *The Winning Performance: How America's Midsized Companies Succeed*. New York: Bantam Books.

Goffman, I. 1970. *Asylums: Essays on the Social Situation of Mental Patients and Other Inmates*. Chicago: Aldine Publishing Company.

Heifetz, R. A. 1994. *Leadership Without Easy Answers*. Cambridge, Massachusetts: Harvard University Press.

Moore, M. H. 1993. *Accounting for Change: Reconciling the Demands for Accountability and Innovation in the Public Sector*. Washington, D.C.: Council for Excellence in Government.

―――. 1995. *Creating Public Value: Strategic Management in Government*. Cambridge: Harvard University Press.

Moore, M. H., S. R. Estrich, D. McGillis, and W. Spelman. 1984. *Dangerous Offenders: Elusive Targets of Justice*. Cambridge, Massachusetts: Harvard University Press.

Porter, M. E. 1980. *Competitive Strategy: Techniques for Analyzing Industries and Competitors.* New York: Free Press.

Rubin, E. L., Ed. 1997. *Minimizing Harm as a Goal for Crime Policy in California.* Berkeley: California Policy Seminar.

Tonry, M. and K. Hatlestad. 1997. *Sentencing Reform in Overcrowded Times: A Comparative Perspective.* New York: Oxford University Press.

Wholey, J. S., M. A. Abrahamson, and C. Bellavita. 1986. *Performance and Credibility: Developing Excellence in Public and Nonprofit Organizations.* Lexington, Massachusetts: D.C. Heath and Company.

Wilson, J. Q. 1989. Bureaucracy: *What Government Agencies Do and Why They Do It.* New York: Basic Books.

Zedlewski, E. F. 1987. *Making Confinement Decisions.* Washington, D.C.: National Institute of Justice.

MANAGING THE RISK OF INNOVATION: STRATEGIES FOR LEADERSHIP

3

Ellen Schall, J.D.
The Robert F. Wagner Graduate School of Public Service
New York University
New York, New York

Ellen Neises
Associate Director
Working Today
New York, New York

Introduction

Academics and practitioners alike are intrigued with understanding what promotes innovation—why some fields, some states, some countries, some eras have more of it than others—and what barriers inhibit its growth. Compared to other policy fields, the level of innovation in the criminal justice system in the United States has been relatively low, which suggests that the barriers to innovation in this field merit examination.

The need for innovation in criminal justice policy and practice is certainly great. The "pulls" that typically drive the demand for innovation in the public sector include: (1) serious problems that government activities do not adequately address, (2) substandard performance of routine functions, (3) ineffectual current solutions, (4) limited understanding of what has been tried before, (5) preference for the new over the old, and (6) crises (Schall, 1991). With the possible exception of the fifth, all of these factors apply to the justice system and help to create a demand for change which, in most jurisdictions, has not been met.

Mark Moore distinguishes between four kinds of innovations: *programmatic innovations* reflect changes in particular programs to better accomplish specific purposes; *administrative innovations* shift the ways in which organizations are staffed; *technological innovations* depend on new capital equipment or new uses of existing technology; and *strategic innovations* make fundamental changes in purposes, central means, or key financial relations (Moore, Sparrow, and Spelman, 1997).

The kinds of innovation that are most prevalent in criminal justice tend to be technical (and, in many cases, technological) in nature rather than strategic. Bicycle patrols, mobile computers in patrol cars, video documentation of arrests, automated fingerprint matching, remote video arraignment, electronic monitoring, and acupuncture treatment for addiction are among the recent technical advances in the field. Programmatic and strategic innovations are concentrated in a relatively small number of areas. Community policing, victim-offender reconciliation programs, community-based defender services, community courts, case management and aftercare in juvenile detention, and intermediate sanctions demonstrate the field's capacity for this more complex type of change.

This paper examines several barriers to innovation and suggests strategies for overcoming those barriers. We take a particular interest in one area of the criminal justice system—sentencing programs and policy. Sentencing should be particularly ripe for innovation because the demand factors are both strong and abundant, but two decades after the first wave of intermediate sanctions was created, the vast majority of convicted offenders in this country continue to be imprisoned or placed on a rudimentary form of probation. Innovators and the intermediate sanctions they have created have not yet had a significant impact on safety, sentencing patterns, the allocation of resources among sentencing options, the total cost of the justice system, or people's perception of the integrity and effectiveness of corrections policy (Morris and Tonry, 1991; Lemov, 1991).

Barriers to Innovation

The explanation for the relatively low level of innovation in sentencing programs and policy is complex. This is a field where feelings run so high that "error" is not tolerated, even at the conceptual level. Communities and individuals may not like the status quo, but they also fear change. The reluctance to take risks is magnified by the confusion about the purposes of sentencing. And finally, there is no public agreement on the terms to which programs and their staff should be held accountable. It should come as no surprise, then, that lacking consensus on what would constitute success, what kinds and levels of nonsuccess would be tolerable, and what might happen if something went wrong, there is so little innovation in the field.

Low Tolerance for Risk

Criminal justice is a particularly difficult policy field because it seems that every citizen has potent, though not necessarily fully developed, views about how the system should be run. Few are untouched by fear of, or fascination with, crime. And, as unhappy as people may be with the current system, they seem unprepared and unwilling to accept the possibility that it might get worse.

Risk-management scholars have found that, across a variety of disciplines, lay people tend to give greater weight to catastrophic potential than experts (Slovic et al., 1984). The sentencing end of the justice system is, of course, full of catastrophic potential, replete, for example, with the fear that a judge will take the "risk" of sentencing an offender to a noncustodial sentence and that person will reoffend and commit a serious crime or the risk that someone will escape from custody and reoffend. Framed this way, risk is about the chance that something bad will happen. "Risk" also could refer to the concept that we cannot foretell an outcome, that the result of an intervention is uncertain. Innovation would be stymied, of course, if neither any uncertainty nor any bad outcome could be tolerated.

Risk decisions, of course, are not about risks alone. People are willing to accept large risks if they are expected to bring large benefits; they may reject even small risks if they seem likely to bring little good (Fischoff, 1995). Unfortunately, at this point in the public policy debate, the benefits of intermediate sanctions and innovative-sentencing strategies are perceived to fall almost entirely to offenders. The community is seen as having little to gain and much to lose.

In some policy arenas, both program and individual risks are tolerated. In health care, for example, we seem to accept the fact that finding cures inevitably will entail experiments that do not work, including experiments where the entire line of inquiry behind an intervention may be flawed, or where individuals may die because the intervention is inappropriate. Both the risks and benefits of health-care innovations are seen as being connected to the same group—people who are at risk of contracting, or who have contracted, a particular illness. The terms commonly used in the field are revealing. Innovation in health care is premised on "experiments" and the idea of "trial and error." In criminal justice, no one talks of experiments—the only allowable direction is forward.

The calculus of criminal justice policy differs from that of health care and many other policy areas. Individual failures of offenders supervised by intermediate sanctions put whole programs and sentencing strategies at risk. When a patient dies in a hospital—even from a clear mistake such as an overdose of chemotherapy—cancer treatments are not suspended; the mission of hospitals is not questioned. Individual clinicians responsible for the mistake are punished. After a series of mistakes, a particular hospital's accreditation might be in jeopardy or the institution might be fined, but the enterprise as a whole would not be called into question.

But, when a client walks away from a community sanction and commits a serious crime, everything is at risk—not because the program architects were wrong about how the innovation related to the problem or they were unable to build a mandate for it, but because they were unable to sustain the mandate as a result of an individual failure. While the public sector will tolerate routinely poor performance of the justice system, people are reluctant to accept innovations that possibly might result in a calamity.

Lack of Agreement About Goals

In addition to the lack of tolerance for risk in this field, innovation is blocked by confusion about the goals of sentencing policy and programs. There is no consensus about the abstract goals of sentencing or the definition of the problem to which probation, intermediate sanctions, corrections, and parole authorities are supposed to be responding. People hold wildly divergent views about the "textbook" purposes of sentencing: incapacitation, just deserts, retribution, deterrence, and rehabilitation. Their confusion is amplified by the weakness of evaluative research on sentencing options. We are clear that prison incapacitates and punishes, but beyond that, professionals are not in agreement about what sanctions actually provide—for example, what level of deterrence for whom, or under what conditions offenders can be rehabilitated.

Determining what tradeoffs should be made among these goals, and how vigorously each should be pursued, depends in part on technical judgments about feasibility, methods, risk, and cost (Larivee and O'Leary, 1990). This determination must be made at least twice (Smith, this volume). The authorizing environment, whether it be the legislature or some other body, has to consider the tradeoffs in creating a systemwide sentencing schema, and the sentencing judge needs to reconcile the tradeoffs given the person being sentenced and the offense committed. Tradeoffs depend as well on political and moral judgments about what the system should achieve through sentencing.

The absence of an adequate consensus about goals makes it tougher to gather up front the political support and authorization to launch an innovation. In many fields of public management, innovators introduce new methods or programs without prior approval or public agreement about goals, as long as they can find the money and other resources to back them. With the program's early results in hand, they can push for acceptance of the pilot and the goals it represents. But to develop a sentencing innovation, advocates of change usually need to get approval from quite a few constituencies to get an idea off the ground.

Many of the interesting system-level innovations in this field have required prior legal authorization in the form of amendments to sentencing guidelines and laws, or transfers of administrative responsibility. And the operational success of community sanctions almost always depends on the participation of prosecutors and judges, and often on a wider group of stakeholders, including residents who must accept sighting plans, business owners who will be called upon to employ offenders in the program, and social service agencies needed to provide treatment, sponsor community-service projects, or lend other resources. Given this need for authorization and cooperation, some consensus about goals is required for most innovations to proceed. But even if prior approval is not required, agreement about goals is needed to keep the program going because, without it, innovators find it difficult to set reasonable terms of accountability and insulate the program against the risk of a high-profile individual failure.

Lack of Agreement about Terms of Accountability

Because the public is so intrigued with crime and punishment issues, practitioners in criminal justice are accountable to virtually the entire public as in no other area. The more people one is accountable to, of course, the greater the potential for conflict between and among their many views, interests, and demands. The conflict is compounded when each constituency's demands are not even internally consistent.

Sometimes innovators can get over the authorization hurdle by keeping a low profile and privately offering each important constituency vague reassurances about how the program relates to its views and interests. But if an agreement about goals has not been established prior to the development of an innovation, accountability issues are treacherous. The measures chosen say what the program is trying to achieve, which in turn makes it clear what the values behind it are, and the program then must fend off all the constituencies that disagree with those values (Moore, 1993). This is the source of much of the risk that innovators face.

Of course, this is not a complete account of the barriers to innovation. There are numerous other inhibiting factors. For example, new mandatory sentencing laws, "truth in sentencing" statutes, and other restrictions on the release and administrative reassignment of offenders limit the discretion of innovators and the space within which programmatic change can occur. But we would argue that these formal barriers (and many other informal ones) are largely the result of suspicion that innovators represent values that much of the public does not share, and awareness that the consensus they are operating under is very brittle. To launch and ensure survival of a greater number of innovations—and specifically more intermediate sanctions—leaders in the field need to increase the public's willingness to take risks and to see that the potential benefits of taking those risks may accrue to them, not just to offenders; to help the public reach some consensus on realistic goals for the criminal justice system, and to develop terms of accountability that call for measurement of outcomes linked to the public's expectations. These expectations, in all but a very limited number of jurisdictions, must first be shaped.

Strategies for Overcoming Barriers to Innovation

Developing a political agreement about a problem, and the goals of government enterprises intended to resolve it, is what Mark Moore (1993) sees as the basis for effective public management. Philip Heymann suggests that most decisions about what public organizations do hinge on the public manager's vision of the agency mission and his or her choice of plans to present for consideration. Constituents, he says, make decisions on the following basis (Heymann, 1987, 14):

> Those outside the organization whose support or opposition is crucial to the agency will decide whether to provide that support or opposition by looking first at three things: what the organization *does* that affects their interests; what its activities and language *say* about what is important in government and whose concerns or views of the national interest are to be given great weight; and what *alliances* with powerful organizations and individuals its words and actions seem intended to cement.

If innovators say little to the public about how their programs relate to the problem, the interests of stakeholder groups, and the views that are given credence, people must form their judgments unguided, on the basis of what they think they already know and what they see. If the public is unprepared to do this work, the program and its promoters are in danger.

Program developers often feel they must weigh the interests of their own operation against the interests of the "cause"—promoting wider (and wiser) use of intermediate sanctions. Laying low sometimes seems like the best way to protect one's own innovation. Professionals who are responsible for managing programs that involve risk tend to focus on the difficult tasks of trying to master the design and execution of their technology or program to reduce that risk and enhance benefits to the greatest extent possible. Baruch Fischoff, a professor at Carnegie Mellon University who has studied risk, notes that, "Quietly doing diligent technical work will often suffice. The risks of many enterprises attract no attention at all. Unfortunately, if a risk does become an issue, the preceding silence may raise suspicions" (Fischoff, 1995, 138).

In the justice field, choosing to be silent is very risky. Intermediate sanctions tend to attract attention (sooner or later), and so effective communication and public education are critical strategies for leaders. Professionals must learn to manage the political environment if they want to innovate successfully. Simply trying to stay out of the press generally is not a reasonable course of action because this endangers the program in the long-term and provides little cover for those behind it in the short term.

Having tried in the past to communicate with the press, the public, and elected officials, many innovators in the justice field may find this argument frustrating. The work of Daniel Yankelovich and the Public Agenda Foundation offers a useful perspective on why the task of shaping public opinion seems so Sisyphean and why, even so, there is reason to invest in long-term public education activities (Yankelovich, 1991). Yankelovich's work suggests that advocates in this field have not had much success in moving the public because they tend to collapse the steps of public education. They try to communicate (in some cases strenuously, but not always strategically) and then move on to other issues, assuming that they have reached people and getting discouraged when they find they have not.

The Public Agenda Foundation (n.d.) suggests there is a logic to how the public confronts and make decisions on complex issues. It offers the seven-stage framework outlined in Table 3.1.

TABLE 3.1. Public Agenda Foundation's Stages of Public Opinion

1. Awareness

2. Urgency

3. Discovery of choices

4. Resistance to making tradeoffs and wishful thinking

5. Evaluation of the pros and cons of choices

6. Intellectual acceptance of a particular stand

7. Full acceptance based on emotional, moral, and intellectual judgments

Stage one and two constitute consciousness-raising. In the first stage, the public is just becoming aware of a problem or issue, even if not of all the specifics. At stage two, people start to feel a sense of urgency about an issue—they recognize that a problem is worthy of attention. Yankelovich explains that on issues that are in the early stages of development, "Many people express strong feelings, but vehemence does not mean settled views. Opinions at this stage are unstable, flip-flopping at the slightest provocation" (Yankelovich, 1992).

Stages three, four, and five are where the public works through an issue. Shortly after developing a sense of urgency, people enter stage three and begin focusing on the possible courses of action. Depending on the number and complexity of proposals that are presented by professionals, stage three may be relatively short or quite prolonged. In stage four, people "raise a barricade of wishful thinking" and are resistant to facing the costs and tradeoffs involved in choosing a course of action.

It is worth noting that sometimes this resistance is the result of feeling excluded from the decision-making process—people do not feel obliged to act responsibly because they are not personally engaged. People start to seriously consider the alternatives and weigh the pros and cons of each as they move on to the fifth stage, where they weigh choices. While in the earlier stages, the media, professionals, and politicians do most of the work, here the public must make an effort to resolve conflicting values and think through the consequences of their choices.

Stages six and seven are the two stages of resolution. At stage six, the public takes the first step: they accept a particular solution intellectually. After grasping and weighing the facts, they believe that a particular choice is logical. At the seventh stage, people confront their feelings of ambivalence and desire to procrastinate (which sometimes stem from the realization that what seems to be right is unappealing to them personally). At this point, they make an emotional and ethical commitment to a particular policy option. Polls are informative in the resolution stages because opinion is stable.

Sentencing policy issues seem to have moved through stages one and two already. People are aware and concerned about how the justice system manages convicted offenders. But there are some significant barriers that make passage through stages three, four, and five difficult. At the "discovery of choices" stage, poor formulation of the problem, slogans about program and policy options, and uncertainty about the risks of community sanctions and the consequences of wider policies impede progress. The expert advice of many innovators ignores some of the public's concerns and fears; anger is often rejected as an invalid concern. Advocates fail to acknowledge the primitive feelings that crime stirs up (Gilmore, 1987).

The barriers at the fourth or "resistance" stage include compartmentalized thinking about crime, poverty, unemployment, race, and the value of preventive services; wishful thinking about the efficacy of cracking down; the many conflicting values at stake; and fear for personal safety and what people think of as "the fabric of society." The cost-containment issue, which advocates often highlight, is not resonant with the concerns of people at this stage.

A relatively small segment of the population seems to have made it to the fifth or "evaluation" stage. The impediments to progress here are that people have no incentive to choose, the range of choices is too narrow (the options appear to be polar opposites), and the pros and cons of the choices are unclear. Development of opinion on this issue has not begun to move into the resolution stages in most jurisdictions.

The Public Agenda Foundation's work suggests that leaders in this field have their work cut out for them. Public education efforts cannot stop short. The public must be given opportunities to work through the issues and reach resolution both intellectually and emotionally. Program innovators have much to offer when it comes to helping the public overcome the barriers to discovery of the options. Policy innovators—interested citizen groups, politicians, high-level appointees, foundations, and others—can have an impact on the barriers that block progress in the resistance and evaluation stages. By doing so, innovators at both levels will help to increase people's capacity for reasoned risk, full understanding of the goals sought, and the terms of accountability with which they must contend.

Baruch Fischoff (1995, 138) points to another reason why professionals might want to engage the public—to learn something. "Those who work within a discipline accustom themselves to its limitations. They learn to live with the reality of critical unsolved problems." Shielding the public from the work of evaluating risks and benefits is what he refers to as "dispensing niceness" (Fischoff, 1995, 142-43):

> Doing so respects the public's ability to prevent solutions, but not to create them . . . Often, though, members of the public want, and can fill a more active and constructive role . . . Partnerships are essential to creating the human relationships needed to damp the social amplification of minor risks—as well as to generate concern where it is warranted. Often controversies over risk are surrogates for concern over process.

"Dispensing niceness" is the opposite of what Ronald Heifetz (1994) defines as adaptive leadership—helping people work through tough challenges. Although some public problems are technical, most interesting and longstanding problems, he says, are difficult to diagnose and solve by technical means alone. When neither the issues nor the solutions are clear, the burden of responsibility for tackling and working through those problems is primarily on the public. Under these circumstances, the role of the expert or leader is to facilitate learning and adaptation.

Heifetz' (1994) definition of leadership is helpful if probation and corrections professionals conceive of the sentencing problem as changing the way the justice system responds to crime. Before people can recognize and evaluate the choices, professionals have to help them adjust their values, attitudes, habits, and conception of the problem.

While the task of managing the political environment in these terms may seem daunting on top of all the other work involved in designing and running good community sanctions, it is critically important. Michael Reich (1993), from the Harvard School of Public Health, draws a similar conclusion based on his studies of efforts to implement changes in health policy in developing countries. He argues for a deliberate process of political mapping that assesses the political dimensions of the contemplated innovation and then organizes an approach designed to maximize success. For those overwhelmed by the size of the task, Tom Gilmore, a well-known consultant and author, offers a place to start, recommending that innovators simply, "Look for focused, small actions that are valuable in their own right, yet also have a power to educate and lead because of their resonance with wider themes" (Gilmore, 1987, 2-3).

Innovations That Managed Their Environments

Below are some examples of innovators and innovations that paid attention to risk, to goals, to the terms of accountability by which they would be evaluated, and to the need for ongoing education work aimed at shaping and stabilizing public opinion. Each jurisdiction faced a particular set of problems and possibilities. Some had to manage the relationships with private-service contractors; some had to orchestrate program development in a fragmented county-based system; some had to work around (or against) mandatory sentencing laws. Legal and administrative structures, popular sentiment, the political environment, and availability of funds varied widely and had an impact on the range of sanctions feasible in each area.

Paying Attention to Risk and Goals

Minnesota was one of the first states in the country to invest substantial public money in community sanctions. It is also one of the few states that reached an adequate consensus about the tolerance for risk and the general objectives of sentencing and sanctions before making that investment. This consensus laid the groundwork for innovation nearly twenty-five years ago, and it has helped sustain support for community sanctions ever since.

The mission of corrections in Minnesota was defined on the basis of open debate among legislators, with substantial input from the judicial and executive branches. The working documents that define the goals of sentencing to this day—the Community Corrections Act of 1973 and the Sentencing Guidelines of 1980—reflect a consensus that expenditures on prisons and jails are not intended to prevent crime. While the particulars of the guidelines have been adjusted over the years, the philosophy of the Minnesota Department of Corrections, which oversees all community sanctions contracts, has remained the same.

Minnesota's intermediate sanctions—more than 200 local programs—were developed on the basis of a well-defined view of the value of money spent on corrections relative to alternative uses of public funds. This included: investing in education, economic development, health, and preventive services as the best way to reduce crime. And so managing the state's offender population at a reasonable cost became a key goal of the Department of Corrections. Offenders were programmed at the local level because doing so was consistent with public safety and fiscal objectives and more humane and fair than incarceration. The department of corrections sought to provide opportunities for treatment to offenders who were motivated to take advantage of them, but the mandate to which the department was held accountable, and to which it held programs managed or contracted for by counties, was not rehabilitation.

The department's responsibilities were clear and the expectations of politicians and the public were consistent with what corrections and local contractors were trying to achieve. As a result, practitioners did not spend all of their time in the early days trying to determine if community corrections programs worked in the sense of producing low-rearrest rates or eliminating all chance of a high profile reoffense. In other words, they had some space in which to grow and perfect their methods.

In the last four years, the state and all eighty counties have introduced restorative justice programs—the most recent wave of community sanctions in Minnesota. With these programs, some new goals for sanctions have been added, and the department of corrections has made itself accountable for helping to heal victims and the communities where crime occurs. In the last few years, the Minnesota legislature has put some pressure on the department to measure outcomes. But here, unlike many other jurisdictions, most legislators seem to understand that elimination of the risk of reoffense is not the primary measure of effectiveness, nor is recidivism. As a result, the consensus that first supported innovation in the state is expected to remain stable.

Paying Attention to Terms of Accountability

In earlier sections of the paper, we have talked about accountability in terms of making the goals of an innovation concrete, and demonstrating that the goods promised have been delivered. Almost all innovative sanctions that prosper over the long term seem to do this. We have selected the example of the Center for Alternative Sentencing and Employment Services (CASES), a nonprofit contractor in New York City, whose oldest community sentencing option was launched in 1968.

Over the last five years, CASES has built an unusually strong reputation for performance with its funders in city and state government, and with policymakers in the judicial, legislative, and executive branches. The state legislature and city council have augmented budgets for the organization on several occasions, demonstrating their faith in its programs despite a conservative shift in city and state politics around both crime and spending.

Unlike most community sanctions, CASES can give you a precise (and highly favorable) comparison of the rearrest rates for its clients to those for statistically similar groups sentenced to prison, jail, probation, or split sentences over a period of three years. Strict sentencing criteria, tailored to the idiosyncrasies of local sentencing policy and practice, decide which offenders the programs will accept from the courts, and these criteria are at the center of the organization's high credibility ratings.

The selection criteria for CASES' programs were designed to communicate on an ongoing basis what each program does and for whom. The criteria helped judges choose among community sanctions, and between community sanctions and jail or prison terms. They reminded judges and attorneys that the courts are a blunt instrument when it comes to addressing the social needs of troubled people who are also offenders.

And they helped CASES' court liaisons turn down judges when they wanted to put an otherwise probation-bound offender in the program.

CASES developed its sentencing criteria on the basis of not only careful analysis of the offender population in New York City to determine which groups behind bars could be managed effectively in some other way, but also used an elaborate outreach effort to relay the information gathered to judges, prosecutors, and defenders. Over time, as CASES demonstrated good performance on the measures of interest to stakeholders, city officials increasingly became comfortable with the idea that tough cases (including a large number of robberies) could be handled effectively in the community, and the selection criteria were narrowed to focus on more serious offenders.

Most importantly from the standpoint of CASES' mandate, the selection criteria helped to balance the competing interests of those who paid for intermediate sanctions—the city and state of New York—and those who applied them in the courts. Without tight restrictions on which kinds of offenders could be sentenced to the program, CASES never could have diverted enough offenders facing significant time behind bars to save the city and state substantial money. If the program could not prove it was saving money, the mandate for the program would dry up, regardless of its performance on service delivery, supervision, and rehabilitation measures.

Unfortunately, this point is now being proven as a result of a decision by the Mayor's Office to centralize all initiatives to match offenders with community sanctions beginning July 1997. While it seems to have helped the poor performers somewhat, the bureaucratization of the selection process has had disastrous effects on the confidence of judges and the performance of programs like CASES that depended on reaching serious offenders and demonstrating accountability.

Treating Communication as a Program Maintenance Activity

Most well-meaning public officials view sentencing issues as tough and time-consuming, and they tend to gravitate to issues with higher payoffs in terms of visibility and perceived need. We have argued that communications is a way for innovators to support their current allies and increase their number over time. The strategy of adopting a proactive approach to community relations, educating the press before a crisis hits, and making headlines intentionally worked particularly well for innovators in Georgia. And while this story dates back a number of years, it is still a textbook case and worth considering.

A number of jurisdictions have used grassroots public education campaigns to educate citizens, judges, and local leaders, but the Georgia Department of Corrections placed greater emphasis on a centralized communications strategy when it launched a statewide continuum of five public intermediate sanctions to control crowding in the 1980s. In Georgia, communication was not seen as a gratuitous effort designed to make the public and members of state government feel better about what the corrections system already was doing or planning to do. It was actually an important aspect of Georgia's innovation. (The programs, in and of themselves, were not that unusual, but the marketing effort was.)

The promotional efforts of the department of corrections were designed to show that intermediate sanctions constituted "no break with Georgia's history of public interest in punishment." Advertised as "law and order," the new programs were intended to quell anticrime hysteria to some extent, and in so doing, make the public more receptive to counterintuitive information.

Interestingly, the Georgia Department of Corrections sought national recognition to secure acceptance for alternatives at home. Stories about Georgia's programs were placed by the Office of Information and Legislative Services and carried by most of the nationally circulated dailies and news programs on all the major television networks. Criminal justice and corrections journals published numerous articles on the Georgia intermediate sanctions, and at least two books described the Intensive Probation Supervision program in detail. In 1989, the department applied for and won a prestigious award for its intermediate-sentencing options from Innovations in State and Local Government, a joint project of Harvard University and the Ford Foundation.

"We wanted to make people feel that, whether or not they agreed with the programs, they were Georgia's and they should be proud of them," explained the director of department's communications campaign at the time. The strategy seems to have been effective with many elected officials. Some key conservative judges, for example, said they first learned Georgia was considered a model for intermediate sanctions at a national judicial conference, and came away with a positive feeling about the direction of corrections policy in their state.

Over time, as the programs matured, many of the department's communication functions were integrated at the local level and the Office of Information and Legislative Affairs gradually withdrew from coordination of all public education projects, tours, and media relations. Recognition of communication as an on-going program maintenance activity, rather than a sporadic effort to be made each time a program was up for reauthorization, forestalled disenchantment with the concept of alternatives and led to expansion of Georgia's sentencing options for quite a number of years (prior to the current commissioner's prison-centered agenda).

Georgia's experience in the eighties and early nineties shows that the press can be used to build goodwill and illustrate the connection between intermediate sanctions and widely held beliefs and values, as well as it can spread word about the latest probationer gone awry. While working with the media often seems like a treacherous tool to use to communicate with the public, it can have enormous benefits if done strategically. As Joan Petersilia of the RAND Corporation has commented with respect to the state's flagship intermediate sanction program, "Georgia's development and implementation efforts were 'textbook' examples of successful adoption of innovative programs" (Petersilia, 1987, 23).

Some Conclusions about Innovations that Manage their Environments

Many barriers to innovation in the sentencing field seem to be the product of public awareness that the consensus professionals are operating under is brittle. The insights of the Public Agenda Foundation help probation and corrections professionals identify specific barriers to the resolution of the debate about the merits of increasing reliance on intermediate sanctions. Those impediments of greatest concern to participants in this conference—innovators at the program level—seem to be poor formulation of the problem, dependency on slogans as references to program and policy options, uncertainty about the risks of community sanctions and wider policies, and the failure of experts to take into account some of the public's concerns.

We have argued that to help the public overcome these barriers, innovators cannot "dispense niceness" or shield the public from the work of evaluating risks and benefits. Instead, they should work toward a political agreement about the problem, and the goals of the sentencing programs and policies intended to resolve it. This public agreement makes it possible to set terms of accountability that allow innovative programs to demonstrate performance, to insulate themselves against the risk of high-profile individual failures, and to ease introduction of future innovations. To shape an adequate consensus, professionals have to extend their focus beyond the technical issues of program design and management, to include public education and negotiation. As Peter Drucker (1974, 79) argues, "What the business thinks it produces is not of first importance . . . What the customer thinks he is buying, what he considers value, is decisive . . . ."

Management of the political environment is not simply advertising or sales, but a problem-solving tool that facilitates development of intermediate sanctions that fit their local contexts and assists the public in tackling tough problems. By looking at risk, goals, accountability, and ongoing communication separately, we mean to suggest that while all are worthy of attention, an innovator need not come up with a sophisticated strategy that encompasses all of the ideas presented here in order to launch and protect innovations from the risk of failure. Professionals can begin by doing something in any one of these areas and moving toward a more holistic strategy over time. Understanding the barriers to innovation, we suggest, helps us appraise the environment and recognize the possibilities for change.

References

Drucker, P. 1974. *Management.* New York: Harper & Row.

Fischoff, B. 1995. Risk Perception and Communication Unplugged: Twenty Years of Process. *Risk Analysis.* 15:137-145.

Gilmore, T. 1987. Being Effective as an Advocate with Newly Elected Officials: Being Against Is Not Enough. Unpublished briefing note.

Heifetz, R. 1994. *Leadership Without Easy Answers.* Cambridge: Harvard University Press.

Heymann, P. 1987. *The Politics of Public Management.* New Haven: Yale University Press.

Larivee, J. and W. O' Leary. 1990. *Managing the Development of Community Corrections.* Washington, D.C.: National Institute of Corrections.

Lemov, P. 1991. The Next Best Thing to Prison. *Governing.* (December):34-36.

Moore, M., ed. 1993. *Accounting for Change: Reconciling the Demands for Accountability and Innovation in the Public Sector.* Washington D.C.: Council for Excellence in Government.

Moore, M. H., M. Sparrow, and W. Spelman. 1997. Innovation in Policing: From Production Lines to Job Shops. In A. A. Altschuler and R. D. Behn, eds. *Innovation in American Government: Challenges, Opportunities, and Dilemmas*. Washington D.C.: Brookings Institution Press.

Morris, N. and M. Tonry. 1991. *Between Prison and Probation: Intermediate Punishments in a Rational Sentencing System*. New York: Oxford University Press.

Petersilia, J. 1987. Georgia's Intensive Probation: Will the Model Work Elsewhere? In B. McCarthy, ed. *Intermediate Sanctions*. New York: Criminal Justice Press.

Public Agenda Foundation. n.d. *The Seven Stages of Public Opinion: from Public Opinion to Public Judgement*. Copyrighted monograph.

Reich, M. R. 1993. *Political Mapping of Health Policy: A Guide for Managing the Political Dimensions of Health Policy*. Boston: Harvard School of Public Health.

Schall, E.1991. Unpublished manuscript.

Slovic, P., S. Lichtenstein, and B. Fischoff. 1984. Modeling the Societal Impact of Fatal Accidents. *Management Science*. 30: 464-474.

Yankelovich, D. 1991. *Coming to Public Judgement: Making Democracy Work in a Complex World*. Syracuse, New York: Syracuse University Press.

————. 1992. How Public Opinion Really Works. *Fortune*. October:102-108.

CLARITY ABOUT PENAL PURPOSE AND CORRECTIONAL STRATEGY REQUIRE INDIVIDUALIZED SENTENCES[1]

4

Michael E. Smith, J.D.
  University of Wisconsin School of Law
  Madison, Wisconsin

Introduction: Why Can't This Be Simple?

The question to be addressed is whether noncustodial sentences of the kinds community corrections agencies mount should be individualized and, if so, how might this be done in the current environment? The current environment simultaneously values accountability (obligations imposed by sentencing courts are to be enforced), proportionality (a sentence's punitive weight should be proportionate to the gravity of the offense), equality (cases alike in facts relevant to sentencing should get like sentences), and public safety. Each of these values should inform, but will complicate, efforts to customize community-based sanctions to accommodate offenders' individual characteristics and circumstances.

That task is made still more difficult by sloppy thinking about purposes of sentencing—the objectives sought by use of penal power in the particular case (Smith, 1984, 172-175; 1987). This sloppiness is distributed widely among sentencing courts, legislators, and, unfortunately, community corrections enthusiasts as well.

In this author's view, imprisoning and noncustodial sentencing are alike in requiring clarity about the court's penal purposes, in each case. But, the need is much more obvious in noncustodial sentencing, because different conditions of supervision in the community serve different purposes. And, every additional condition imposed as part of a sentence increases the risk of nonperformance by the offender. Further, nonperformance of a sentence condition threatens our interest in public safety (or it probably should not have been imposed). It also damages the offender (if he or she is punished additionally for the violation imposed without a purpose) and may damage our interest in accountability (if any violation is not punished). Clarity about the court's purpose at sentencing makes possible a parsimony of conditions. This, in turn, makes possible enforcement of the conditions actually imposed. Without parsimony of purpose (and of conditions imposed to achieve it), courts and the managers of community corrections programs cannot avoid putting at risk, for no purpose, the court's integrity, the offender's liberty, and our own public safety. (*See* Smith, 1995, for a discussion of public safety as a condition of place—where we are free from the threat of harm to our persons and property—not simply for a lower crime rate.)

Custodial sentencing in the 1990s is—or is thought to be—much simpler. In custodial sentencing, the accountability of offenders is achieved by stripping them of any responsibility for implementation of their sentences.[2] Proportionality and equality are not assured so easily. In recent years, they have been pursued vigorously through promulgation of presumptive grid-guidelines to control the discretion of trial courts. By artificially limiting relevant facts to two—current crime and prior criminal record—durations of confinement can be arrayed according to the severity (and perhaps the riskiness) of commonly occurring combinations of those offense and offender characteristics. In this two-dimensional environment, individualizing sentences is a trivial task.

A long tradition of judicial concern with individual characteristics and circumstances, found relevant in choosing a proper sentence for a particular offender, largely has been displaced in the United States by legislative concerns about sentencing disparity and (for some) leniency. Justice is offended when judicial consideration of certain characteristics (for example, race or sex) or circumstances (for example, employment, reputation, and family) lead one individual to be confined for a longer period than another convicted of the same crime and who carry the same prior record—unless there remains some relevant difference between them not accounted for by the offense and the prior record.

So, as the guidelines movement unfolded, the lack of clear answers to the question "relevant to what?" made it difficult at sentencing to defend taking into account facts about offenders' characteristics and circumstances. During a period when the field of community-based corrections was more primitive than it would be twenty years later, a period when durations of confinement were the only sanctions taken seriously—and the only ones for which guidelines were thought to be required—little seemed lost by embracing the grids.

This paper argues that, to get accountability, proportionality, and equality from sentences using community-based corrections, sentencing courts must be required to customize sentences. These values are put at risk when sentencing courts fail to relate individual characteristics and circumstances (the stuff of individualized sentencing) to the dominant penal purpose in particular cases. Drawing these connections properly requires fact-finding and reasoning—functions for which trial courts are well-suited but which themselves require specificity, clarity, and parsimony of penal purpose. Without clear specification of the essential penal purposes to be served, customizing noncustodial sentences is likely to produce unwarranted disparity, and poor performance—by offenders and by the community corrections agents charged with supervising them.

The argument leads the author first to explore the general territory of penal purposes; second, to sketch the ways in which the penal significance of particular characteristics and circumstances is shaped by the purpose or purposes a particular sentence is intended to serve; and, finally, to discuss some of the argument's implications for sentencing judges and for the community-based correctional personnel who implement their sentences.

Why Specificity, Clarity, and Parsimony of Penal Purpose Are Important in Noncustodial Sentencing

If our only purpose in imposing sentences were to assure rough proportionality between the seriousness of cases and the penal burden we impose, it would be a virtue to have only one penal measure about which we care. It would be fortunate that the burden of that sanction can be quantified so easily (in months or years), and it would suffice, to achieve our purpose at sentencing, for judges to use a two-dimensional grid guideline arraying presumptive or mandatory durations of confinement against the seriousness of the offense and the severity of the prior record. Although we also would need a mechanism (for example, judge-made common law or commission-made policy) to rank-order the gravity of offenses and to characterize the severity of various patterns of prior criminal record, the work of a score or more of sentencing-guideline commissions over the past ten years makes these difficulties appear quite manageable.

Although we would need a starting point from which to array the numbers of months or years in the grid, choosing numbers to place in such a grid is another disturbingly simple task.[3] It is simple so long as proportionality is preserved, and so long as the upper reaches of the grid do not offend consensus views about the limits of just desert. It remains simple for so long as the only means of accomplishing penal purposes is incarceration and the cost of building and staffing prisons is not considered prohibitive.

Grid guidelines are unquestionably powerful (but by no means perfect) instruments for reducing the kind of disparity in custodial sentences that arises from idiosyncratic interpretations of the significance of the individual characteristics and circumstances of offenders. But, they are inhospitable to subtlety about the purpose for which a court might exercise its sentencing power in particular cases. Offenders are herded into cells defined by crime and prior record to discourage (or forbid) judges from imposing one sentence on an offender whose specific deterrence is called for, and another on an offender who is unlikely to be deterred but is a good prospect for rehabilitation. Any cell in a guidelines grid is likely to capture cases in which quite different purposes (or penal strategies) ought to be paramount, given these normative and public-safety values. Once a jurisdiction has reduced its core penal policy to a two-dimensional grid, it is hard to work backwards to find the penal purpose that might lie behind any particular number in it—hard for a sentencing judge and hard for anyone trying to create or manage a noncustodial penal sanction.

When, as today, the policy debate is about how long the term of imprisonment should be, this paper's concern about sentencing purpose may seem a bit exotic: incarceration is nearly perfectly incapacitating. It is hard to find rehabilitative value in it,[4] and—since it is widely viewed as "tough"—it appears a plausible means for achieving specific and general deterrence. From this perspective, if durations of imprisonment are ordered correctly, according to a just desert philosophy, a guideline sentence covers any purpose a sentencing judge might have when an individual stands convicted before the court.[5]

Noncustodial penal measures, on the other hand, are of many types. They can be combined in almost infinite variation, and cannot be reduced usefully to duration or any other single measure of the penal burden they place on individuals with different characteristics and circumstances. Grid-based guideline systems are hostile to all penal measures except incarceration.Their allure to sentencing reformers is making life difficult for those who are trying to devise, impose, and implement noncustodial sentences; but this author concedes that our thinking about the purpose of individual sentences was not very good before grid guidelines either.

In any event, fascination with two-dimensional grid-guidelines and the long-standing primacy of imprisonment in our thinking about how to accomplish penal purposes have eroded our capacity for serious analysis of the purposes we are (or ought to be) trying to achieve through the application of state power at the time of sentencing.[6]

Why is Specificity of Penal Purpose Important?

For example, though most would agree that deterrence of thievery is a *permissible* purpose of sentencing a thief, it is much harder to get agreement (or good empirical information) about the mechanism through which tomorrow's would-be thief might be dissuaded from thievery by the sentence imposed on a thief today (Cook, 1980; Zimring and Hawkins, 1973, 1996). Without such agreement (or without the sentencing court weighing evidence relevant to the plausibility of a deterrent penal strategy to address this part of the theft problem), it is impossible to say whether deterrence would be a good purpose, or which penal measures, and in what quantity would be plausible instruments for accomplishing it. We have not had such agreement, nor have we required such fact-finding to date, so it is likely that a sentence of, say, twelve-months confinement will be imposed in one case by a judge who believes the example will dissuade other thieves, in a second case by a judge concerned only with desert (because theft is bad but he is not persuaded that prospective thieves expect to be caught and sentenced when they decide to steal), and in a third case by a judge who is content to put a dent in thievery by incapacitating for six months someone known to have been a thief in the past.

The ordinary methods for setting penal policy, or for creating guidelines, would settle on twelve months as the normal or presumptively correct sentence for this level of theft, and would ignore the very different purposes for which judges are imposing that sentence. This author doubts that a year in prison would serve all those purposes, but doubt about that is not as important in the current context as our knowledge that no noncustodial sentence is powerful enough to serve in this way, given all the combinations of characteristics and circumstances thieves bring with them to sentencing.

If such a sentence were constructed, to achieve all those purposes in each case noncustodially, it would be unjustly burdensome and excessively expensive in every case in which it was imposed and it would undermine proportionality. Assuring the rehabilitation of a homeless, addicted, and persistent petty thief, for example, would strain the purse and patience of anyone attempting it, as would assuring his incapacitation until the risk of his thievery dissipated. In either case, if deserved punishment is a constraint, the penal intervention would have to end long before reaching its strategic objectives.

If we wished to incapacitate him *and* rehabilitate him, we might pursue the strategies sequentially. In this case, we are likely to constrain his liberty even farther beyond what he deserves for his theft. If we incapacitate and rehabilitate him concurrently, we are likely to compromise the efficacy of the rehabilitative or the incapacitative penal measures we use, or both. Incapacitating conditions are valuable in noncustodial sentencing of offenders whose propensity for harm to public safety calls for some degree of incapacitation. But even if we were to ignore the expense and injustice of such an undeservedly burdensome sentence for theft, enforcing the conditions of such a sentence would interfere substantially with whatever we might have in mind for rehabilitation of the thief.

Partly for these reasons, a noncustodial sentence designed to serve all penal purposes would be very hard to finance and to enforce adequately (undermining accountability and public safety). Sentences imposed under any scheme will advance their purposes only if they are reliably enforced; and noncustodial sentences that cannot be enforced reliably (whether because it is too expensive to do so, or because doing so would be too harsh) are not used much by judges who care about achieving penal purposes. Conversely, when achieving penal purposes does not matter, courts cannot be expected to play their essential part in responding to violations by enforcing obligations of the sentence, which further undermines accountability.

Those who have labored to design and execute noncustodial penal measures know this slippery slope. If the public and courts do not view cases in which a noncustodial sanction is used as serious cases, sufficient resources cannot be assembled to enforce burdens that do any of the following things: punish, deliver services that may rehabilitate, or maintain conditions that partially incapacitate.

Without the resources necessary to realize the penal objectives, and without evidence that the penal measure produces the effects that would justify its imposition, the court will not impose the defective noncustodial penal measure in cases in which the court thinks the sentence matters. When the court does not view cases in which a particular penal measure is used as serious, violators are not likely to be held accountable when brought back to that court on an enforcement action. Lack of potency, inability to demonstrate efficacy, and inability to enforce the obligations of a noncustodial penal measure assure such sanctions will continue to lack both resources and judicial confidence, and consequent association with dispositions that move the court's calendar. Such sentences are not associated with strategies that advance penal purposes. For all these reasons, case-by-case specificity of penal purposes is critical to the successful introduction and use of noncustodial penal measures (Smith, 1984, 172-175).

Why is Clarity about Penal Purpose Important?

Being clear about penal purpose is not likely to have much effect on the implementation of sentences when it is widely believed that a prison cell is the preferred (perhaps the only) penal measure that can accomplish serious penal purposes. But the resulting lack of accumulated wisdom on the subject is a major obstacle to our creating and maintaining quality in community-based corrections. In all but the most trivial cases, clarity about purpose matters very much when a court chooses from an array of penal sanctions.

These sanctions include everything from the community-service order, through compulsory drug treatment, to electronically monitored house arrest. Yet, the community service order is a form of involuntary servitude, which can serve retributive and deterrent purposes, but is not well-designed to incapacitate or rehabilitate. Similarly, compulsive drug treatment has punitive weight and rehabilitative value to varying degrees, depending on the offender and the regimen, and which, depending on regimen, may or may not have incapacitative value. Likewise, electronically monitored house arrest may have deterrent and retributive value but the most valuable practical effects of it are some degree of accountability and partial incapacitation. As discussed more fully in the final section of this paper, clarity about the penal purpose of a sentence also matters very much to community corrections personnel—because the effectiveness of their supervision and enforcement activity depends on it.

Why is Parsimony of Penal Purposes Important?

A major pitfall for managers of community corrections programs, in general, and for "client-specific planners," in particular, is that, by promising to accomplish more than would be required if the penal purposes of the court were properly specified, they risk accomplishing nothing at all. This is most evident in the proposals of defense attorneys or professional sentence planners who, in order to increase the odds of avoiding a prison or jail sentence for their clients, recommend imposition of a dozen or more conditions, justified by reference to every permissible purpose of sentencing, without much regard to sensible penal policy or to the offender's ability to perform the resulting sentence.

It would help the field enormously if judges, when sentencing such badly represented offenders, at least would say in open court why some of those purposes are not particularly important in the case, or why some of the proposed conditions are not plausible ways of advancing the purpose. And, it would help if courts issued sentencing orders that properly related a limited set of conditions imposed to the purposes actually present in the case. If judges cannot on their own become parsimonious as to penal purpose, this kind of parsimony could be required by statute or by sentencing-commission guideline.

Without such discipline, however, the noncustodial sentences the courts impose undermine orderly development of essential operational capacity in the community corrections field. This occurs because an offender's violations of nonessential sentence conditions either goes unpunished or is punished without good reason (because none was specified at sentencing). Further, the individuals charged with supervising an offender burdened with such a sentence either must waste resources on interventions and enforcement actions that are without penal purpose, or make independent judgments about which (if any) elements of noncustodial sentences they should treat seriously.

In the view of this author, many intensive supervision probation programs fall into a similar trap. Probation, as it is implemented in much of the United States, widely is viewed as little more than an exhortation to offenders to be good. The reporting burdens it conventionally imposes cannot be thought of as particularly punitive. The conditions it conventionally enforces (if any are specified) cannot be expected to incapacitate very much.

Finally, the limited resources it, on average, can bring to a probationer's treatment and other needs leave rehabilitation beyond its reach. More of the same—making conventional probation several times more intensive—is not likely to serve any serious deterrent or incapacitative purpose a court might have. Worse, imposing a standard set of heavier conditions on top of conventional probation orders and applying them across an undifferentiated set of serious cases undermines the potential efficacy of each one of them.

In many jurisdictions today, an intensive supervison probation officer is likely to have in his or her caseload a variety of individuals. They include those whose liberty ought to be substantially curtailed for reasons of community safety, individuals whose behavior while under sentence is of little concern, but whose punishment is necessary for deterrence or just desert, and individuals about whom the court's penal purposes are almost entirely rehabilitative.

In any of these cases, a failure to accomplish the purpose for which sentencing power was invoked leads to a failure to protect public safety from an inadequately supervised offender, a failure to extract deserved punishment, or a failure to socialize those who, unsocialized, are likely to find new ways to get the attention of the criminal justice system. Parsimony of purpose is essential if we are to avoid the waste of authority and resources that results from such intensive supervision probation programs.

The same kind of point can be made about stand-alone community service, drug and alcohol treatment, home detention, and other noncustodial penal measures. Each of them, if well-designed, adequately resourced, well-implemented, and seriously enforced, can serve a particular sentencing purpose and penal strategy. But, this will be true only if they are imposed in cases where the purpose of the sentence is congruent with the character of the sanction. When individuals whose future misbehavior is what concerns the court are sentenced to community service, the community-service sentence before long will come into disrepute for its failure to incapacitate.

When home confinement, curfews, and other surveillance techniques are imposed too widely, and caseloads include offenders whose unsupervised behavior really is not viewed as risky, the conditions are not likely to be rigorously enforced. Once again, the result is likely to be that the community-based sanction falls into disrepute for its apparent inability to accomplish a penal purpose that would justify its imposition.

If Purposes Are So Important, Where and How Will We Find Them?

This difficulty, if it is one, is in part the product of a perceived paucity of effective penal measures with which to accomplish anything of importance. That is, purposes do not spring to mind if there is little expectation that if a purpose were specified it could be successfully pursued.

Although some jurisdictions, over the past decade, have developed community corrections programs with substantial capacities to punish and to incapacitate without resorting to prison and jail cells, this is an emerging field in which a great deal of program-development work needs to be done. Poorly designed programs, poorly implemented programs, and most importantly poorly targeted, and poorly focused programs are still all too common.

What is required is the careful construction of program capacities, within probation services and alongside them. These capacities should specify and enforce very specific conditions of noncustodial sentences, and demonstrate the power of those conditions, properly enforced to accomplish their purpose: sentencing to them the category of offenders for whom they are designed.

For this to happen, either sentencing judges somehow must begin to articulate and be quite specific about what purpose they have in mind when imposing penal measures for various offenses committed by various types of offenders, or community corrections program managers must develop new capacities for imagining what those purposes might be and new techniques for getting sentencing judges to see it their way.

This author would not count on a sea change in judicial behavior, so the rest of us will have to become more imaginative and sympathetic observers of their behavior. This means we will have to become more assertive, vis-à-vis the courts, in limiting the use of the various noncustodial penal measures to cases in which the court will treat violations seriously and limit the conditions imposed on various categories of offenders to those that suit the penal purposes actually at stake.

Undesirable as many effects of the movement toward presumptive grid guidelines have been, we would not be much better off if judges remained forever free to construct and impose "packages" of noncustodial penal measures, unconstrained by purpose and without legal obligation to reason openly, from purpose to sentence, by articulated inferences from relevant facts. Because noncustodial penal measures are so much more purpose-specific than prison cells, and because they are not self-enforcing sanctions, both the courts and community corrections program managers need guidance in their use. Norval Morris and Michael Tonry have made this point perfectly:

> Once the principle of rough equivalence between incarcerative and nonincarcerative punishments is accepted, it follows that the choice of punishment should be guided by the purposes sought to be achieved in the individual case. Sentencing choices from among interchangeable punishments (or packages of punishments) should be shaped by governing purposes at sentencing, not by the general crime preventive or retributive purposes of sentencing (or punishment). . . . Once the principle of interchangeability is accepted in a system of structured sentencing discretion, the importance of purposes at sentencing becomes unarguable (Morris and Tonry, 1990, 90-91).

How Purpose Shapes the Significance of Individual Characteristics and Circumstances in Noncustodial Sentencing

Notions of fairness that run deep in our culture support the demand that like cases be treated alike, for penal consequences. But, we also value the uniqueness of individuals, and, when we consider individual characteristics and circumstances, we have trouble agreeing about which cases are "like." One solution—the guidelines solution to unwarranted disparity in custodial sentencing—is to limit or prohibit consideration of them. In the community corrections field, however, the efficacy of many penal measures depends on a proper fit between the penal obligation and the offender's characteristics and circumstances. And differences among offenders' characteristics and circumstances will make use of certain conditions of noncustodial sentences possible in one case and impossible in another—even though the penal purpose is the same.

Without any attempt at comprehensiveness, this author will survey some ways a handful of individual characteristics or circumstances is likely to be important in the community corrections context. It quickly should become apparent why one cannot prohibit consideration of these matters in the noncustodial sentencing field and expect the sentences to accomplish their purposes.

Homelessness

Despite the tugs of charitable feeling, it is relatively easy to see why residential stability ought not generally be considered when courts gauge an offender's culpability. Gut feelings about homelessness are awkward to express, but all of us (including judges) have powerful emotional reactions to it, ranging from fear (there but for the grace of God go I), through sympathy (What stress! What discomfort! What humiliation! And all because real estate developers converted all the Single Room Occupancy hotels to condominiums), to contempt (get a job . . .). So, it is probably a good thing that sentencing-guideline schemes, such as the one now operating in federal courts, which are focused on fair distribution of custodial sanctions and are constructed with culpability and just desert as dominant rationales, ban or severely limit judicial consideration of the individual circumstance when a judge is choosing the term.

But anyone who has managed a noncustodial community corrections program knows that it is harder to secure compliance with most sentence conditions from a homeless person than from a person of fixed abode.

Community Service?

If you are homeless and caught up in New York City's shelter system, you may not know, from one day to the next, in which of the City's five boroughs you will awake tomorrow—so you may be late or simply unable to get to the site of your involuntary servitude. You may have to wash at a hydrant (or show up embarrassingly ripe at a senior citizens' center or a school for disabled children). If you do not get there, or are too embarrassed by your smell to show up, you will be hard for a community corrections agent to find—until you next appear in arraignment court. Thus, to punish a homeless person through community service sometimes requires a community corrections program to provide transportation, hygiene, food, and even shelter—all so that offenders in that unhappy circumstance will be enabled to perform involuntary servitude. There are reasons this is worth doing—and we did it at the Vera Institute when we developed community service sentencing for New York City (Smith, 1984; MacDonald, 1989).

But if sufficient ancillary services are not or cannot be mounted, should we imprison the nonhomeless who otherwise could be effectively punished through enforcement of community service orders? If not, we better find an alternative community-based sanction for equally culpable homeless offenders who are unable to perform community service.

Curfew? Home Confinement? House Arrest?

These are essential incapacitating noncustodial measures, but, by definition, they are hard to impose on homeless people, or on those who have a home today but may not have one tomorrow. Absent comparably burdensome incapacitating community-based measures suitable to the homeless and the residentially unstable, unwarranted disparities will plague the use of house arrest and the like—unless the less fortunate offenders are provided supported housing of some kind during their partial incapacitation, or the more fortunate are incapacitated in a rougher and more expensive way outside their own homes.

Using halfway houses and hostels to achieve a modicum of incapacitation when homeless offenders pose moderate risk while serving community-based sentences is the more appropriate solution to the dilemma presented by homeless offenders. But, is the disparity warranted or unwarranted when the fortunate are incapacitated at home and the unfortunate are incapacitated in a public hostel?[7]

Poverty

Is theft more culpable when there is no need? Maybe, but there are villains in every class and condition—there are plenty with hungry children just as there are plenty with law degrees. The risk to core values is great if sentencers are permitted to consider relative wealth and income when fixing culpability or blameworthiness. Custodial sentencing schemes grounded in just desert properly prohibit it. But some noncustodial penal measures cannot be imposed fairly without allowing for differences in offenders' means.

Fines?

Most monetary penalties are defined by formal or informal tariff systems: $100 for this, $750 for that. Day fines were devised to transform the sanction—first into some nonmonetary measure (100 "units" for this, 750 "units" for that), and then into a fine—by multiplying that tariff for an offense by the average daily disposable income of any individual convicted of it (Morris and Tonry, 1990, 111-49; Hillsman and Greene, 1988). By taking account of our different circumstances, Donald Trump's fine for indecent exposure might properly be $200,000, when this author's fine is $1,000, and a disabled veteran dependent on Social Security is fined $100. We would feel roughly the same pain from these apparently disparate sentences. We would not, if we all were fined $100.

Treatment

Here, the conceptual and practical problems get much more difficult. The rich and competent can get good treatment—treatment that may or may not "work," but treatment looks good to a court interested in imposing conditions that, by rehabilitating the offender, reduce the risk of further offending. Those offenders get good treatment because they can pay for it, but also because they can afford to live in places where good (adequately resourced and well staffed) treatment programs are likely to locate. These sources of disparity are compounded for the working poor, because so many day programs and outpatient treatments, even if located nearby, are open only during working hours. The solution for these disparities is obvious, but expensive.

Skills

This author cannot disguise his disappointment when judges sentence skilled offenders to perform a community service in which they get to exercise the skills whose mastery is the source of their deepest pleasure: when a billionaire businessman is sentenced to teach business techniques to adoring students; when a famous and socially assertive actress is required to host and speak at fundraisers for local charities; when three yachtsmen who stepped way over the line in business dealings are sentenced to take slum kids out on their boat to teach them sailing. This sort of customizing gives involuntary servitude a bad name (*see* El Nassar, 1995, reporting reactions to the community service elements of sentences imposed on Michael Milken, Zsa Zsa Gabor, and other celebrity offenders).

Community service is enormously useful in the community corrections repertoire because, as involuntary servitude (which in the United States is permissible under the Thirteenth Amendment *only* as punishment for a crime), most would consider it a burden, a price to pay, a punishment—not an occasion for additional celebrity, professional accolades, or recreation.

The problem under this heading is that most judges do not agree with this author, and many community corrections managers oblige the courts without thinking through the implications of these sentences for the future use of the sanction. Perhaps they hope that the dismal business of punishing folks can be made happier, if they use their sentencing power to create special value (charitable funds, profitable skills, ocean breezes). To avoid unwarranted disparity, and to preserve the integrity of community service as a *punishment* (serving retributive and deterrent purposes), it would be far better for judges to restrict themselves to requiring service that calls for unskilled labor, and for community corrections managers not to help implement the more exotic varieties.

Responsibilities to Support Family and Access to Family Support

There ought to be considerable discomfort in the idea that a sentencing judge would consider an offender's family circumstances in an assessment of his or her culpability. That is why desert-driven custodial-sentencing schemes tend to prohibit it. But, surely, it is relevant when rehabilitation or an element of incapacitation is called for in a noncustodial sentence. After all, a properly functioning family is a far more powerful socializing instrument than any formal penal measure we have yet devised, and is in the right place at the right time to help enforce incapacitating curfews and attendance at programs or jobs that have incapacitating *and* rehabilitative effects.

Curfews and Other Constraints on Time and Movements

Offenders lacking such families—whether or not that circumstance turned them to crime, whether or not it tugs at our sympathies, and whether or not it makes us worry that they will develop into more serious offenders—cannot be incapacitated noncustodially as easily as those with such families. Because development of a robust community corrections system requires penal measures that incapacitate as well as those that punish or reform, concern for unwarranted disparity ought not to cede the incapacitative purpose to custodial sentences. It should inspire our best creative thought about mobilizing other informal institutions in offenders' communities to assist (as a good family might) in enforcing and supporting compliance with incapacitating conditions of sentence.

Employment

Noncustodial sentences often require offenders to get jobs and to stay employed. Whether employment is required for its rehabilitative force or for its power to incapacitate during working hours, offenders who are already (or easily) employed obviously are positioned better to receive noncustodial sentences than the chronically unemployed. Everyone is offended by the disparity that results from incapacitating the employed at their jobs and the unemployed at prisons, or from using an individual's job to help rehabilitate him while using maximum-security group counseling to help others go straight.

Nevertheless, the remedy is not to send all to prison who require the degree of incapacitation a steady job provides. Rather, it is for community corrections managers to build programs that effectively move hard-to-employ, unemployed offenders from mandatory training and counseling into mandatory full-time labor market participation. community corrections programs with this capacity are rare, but they exist. They are difficult to create and to sustain, but building more of them and tending to the ones we have may be the most important tasks facing the field.

Customizing Risk Management—Penal Purpose Matters Here, Too

When a noncustodial penal measure is used, offenders' conditioned liberty may or may not put victims, families, or communities at risk of some harm during the term of their sentence. It is more than just useful for sentencers (or community corrections personnel who are responsible to the court for implementing sentences) to consider whether the offenders pose risks that the sentence itself to some extent should contain and, if so, how serious is the potential harm, how likely are the offenders to cause it, and how perfectly must the sentence contain it? These are questions for the sentencing judge, as well as for the community corrections manager or agent. Once again, the answers are shaped by the individual characteristics and circumstances of offenders,[8] and getting answers requires specificity, clarity, and parsimony of purpose in the sentence itself.

The following three subsections illustrate some of the interplay between penal purpose and offender characteristics in risk-management issues.

How the Same Condition of Sentence, Imposed for Different Reasons, May Require Different Responses to its Violation: Drug Treatment

Take a "simple" case of drug possession by an addict. A sentencing court may intend to punish the addict for his addiction, though hopefully not. It may want to "send a message" to those about to become addicts so that they change course, though it is past time for courts to stop wasting their sentencing power that way. The court may want to cure the offender of his addiction, though such a court should take the long view and be willing to bend its enforcement powers to case management and risk management purposes.

Residential Drug Treatment

Let us consider a case in which the court is lucky enough to have access to a quality residential-treatment program and the offender is unlucky enough to have committed a crime serious enough to deserve the burdens and deprivation of liberty that a sentence to such a facility entails. What risks need a court guard against when imposing the residential treatment condition?

If the offender walks away from the residence, he *could* murder the governor, or the shopkeeper, or his own child. But, absent good reason to think such grievous harms likely, rather than just conceivable, courts ought not to impose sentence conditions to contain those risks—or any other no-more-than-conceivable risk. Parsimony and specificity of purpose again should be the guiding principles. Piling on conditions to guard against every conceivable risk adds to the cost of noncustodial sentences, squanders scarce personnel resources in community corrections agencies, and increases the likelihood of sentence conditions being violated and courts being presented with most unwelcome enforcement problems and violation hearings.

But there are realistic concerns: If such an offender were to "walk" from the program to which he had been sentenced, he *might* steal to finance a binge—a risk very much worth trying to contain if there is evidence in his past record or current circumstances suggesting a likelihood of his robbing or burglarizing. And, whatever his past record, the court and the community corrections manager should assume he will get drugs and get high.

It turns out to matter why the court sentenced the offender to a residential treatment facility in the first place. If the addict's past record and current circumstances led the court to believe him likely to rob or burglarize to finance drug purchases unless he were incapacitated for a period of time, the court is likely to have counted on the residential element of the treatment program to help contain those risks. Under those circumstances, violation of the residency condition is necessarily a more serious matter than in a case where an addict appears to pose risks principally to himself—where the risk of concern at sentencing is that the offender will get drugs and get high if he violates the condition. In the first case, violation of the residential condition, particularly if coupled with relapse, would call either for a more incapacitating treatment condition or for other, more effective means of incapacitation (even if the prospects for effective treatment were reduced by that condition).

In the second case, violation of the residential condition might call for no more than a return to treatment. After all, if the penal purpose at the time of sentencing was to cure the addiction, and if the addicted offender posed no special risk of harm to others, there is no reason to send him to prison because the treatment did not "take" perfectly the first time—or the second.

Enforcement Issues in Drug Treatment Generally

For judges to make good use of substance abuse treatment in sentencing—and for treatment programs to get the improved prospects of success that legal coercion can provide—a court needs to be clear about the effects it expects from treatment, and it needs some sophistication about relapse. The way the sentencing court's power is applied over time, by the judge or by the community corrections agents to whom it is delegated, directly can affect an offender's retention in treatment, thereby enabling the offender to achieve success in treatment or to lead to certain failure.

Both sentencing judges and treatment providers seek sufficient leverage over an addicted offender's behavior to limit the number and to reduce the frequency of inevitable relapses, and to prevent relapses from escalating into other offenses. Efficient and assertive application of the court's power toward those objectives is supported by the following practices at the time of the sentence :

- Specifying conditions to minimize the risk of ancillary crime when a relapse occurs (for example, curfew, prohibition of activity or companions that put the particular offender at risk of return to crime)

- Specifying the means of enforcing the treatment and other conditions of the sentence

- Communicating to the offender that the court itself will be informed of any violations and will be involved in deciding how to respond to them, including revocation of the noncustodial sentence itself

- Specifying at key points along an addicted offender's passage through treatment, a comprehensive case-management plan— something that a sentencing judge is unlikely to produce, but that a good treatment program will conceive, refine, and modify over the course of treatment

A good case-management plan has provisions for measuring an offender's compliance with treatment conditions and for matching specified consequences to progress and backsliding. It anticipates the need for loosening and tightening the restrictions placed on the offender, and for swift but modest punishment of violations of the sentence (or of the treatment regimen) that fall short of crime and do not constitute complete failure of the treatment. The postsentence behavior of an addict-in-treatment almost always will raise issues for a sentencing court—whether or not they are brought to the judge's attention, and whether the judge deals with them directly or delegates all or part of that task to a community corrections program. If a court imposes a sentence mandating treatment, but treats violation of any treatment condition or any relapse as grounds for revoking probation, the court either will have to be shielded from knowledge of the violations and relapses or will have to revoke most of the sentences.

The nature of addiction, and the state of our knowledge about effective treatment cry out for judicial involvement in the specification of the conditions of sentences when treatment is a condition, and in postsentence case management, as well. In part, it is a growing awareness of this need (and of a corresponding capability of sentencing courts) that fuels enthusiasm for specialized drug courts—courts that try to maximize judicial presence in case management and try to take advantage of judges' ability to mete out rewards and punishments tailored to individual offenders' progress in treatment. But thoughtful judges do not need a special "drug court" to be clear about purposes and to customize treatment conditions and enforcement mechanisms to match offenders' individual characteristics and circumstances.

Circumstances Presenting Low-to-Moderate Risk of Grave Harm

Next, let us consider a first-time robber. He is probably young and marginally socialized. A sentencing court might believe he needs education and exposure to the labor market (and the legitimate income and maturation that goes with holding a job), as well as housing, drug or alcohol treatment, or any number of things that would make his transition to crime-free adulthood more likely. And the court might be inclined to use its sentencing power to see to it that he gets them, or at least gets led to that water.

But whatever a sentencing court thinks might help turn this offender away from crime, it cannot (and should not) avoid worrying about the harm that could follow from failure of the conditions of the sentence to rehabilitate—or from insufficiently incapacitating this offender while waiting for the conditions of the sentence to have their desired impact. Adolescents are risk-takers. Those who come before the court having risked others' lives (and their own) by taking or trying to take money or property from a stranger by force or threat of force ought to worry courts and community corrections managers a lot. The probability of a convicted robber repeating or escalating the behavior that poses such serious threats to the safety of others may be only moderate (it is not low), but the potential harm is very grave indeed. If we are to have the many advantages a noncustodial sentence offers in cases of young offenders—even serious ones—the sentences and our administration of them will have to be well-designed to contain the risk of another robbery.

Perhaps the court imposes a sentence requiring curfew, steady employment, regular attendance at church, and so forth. The curfew might be intended to reduce the risk of robbery—or it might be intended as a punishment, for robbers deserve to be punished. Steady employment might be required, because of its incapacitating effects—a job occupies time and draws away a lot of nasty adolescent energy—but it might merely be intended to hasten the maturation of this adolescent offender.

Again, if the offender ends up back before the court for having violated the condition of his sentence, it turns out to matter why the employment condition was imposed in the first place. If requiring his participation in the labor market was to aid in his "rehabilitation," the court (or community corrections program) should look for some other condition having rehabilitative effect if he has not complied with that one. But if the court relied on this condition as a means of reducing the risk of robbery that attends this offender's idle liberty on the streets, violation of the condition ought to be met by a condition that is likely to look harsher (and less rehabilitative)—because the need for incapacitating conditions in his sentence is not diminished by this offender's inability to connect with a job and the legitimate income a job produces.

Perhaps the sentence required the young robber to participate in a "day-treatment" program, which has its own rules of behavior and attendance requirements, and aims to help troubled youth get their lives together and so forth. Assume that the program was not constructed as a community corrections sentencing program—that is, assume the program is interested in the kids, not in the court's various sentencing purposes, and that its services are available to the court under contract with the community corrections agency. Again, if the condition of attending the program was imposed because the court wanted the offender at the program and not idle on the streets, his violation of an internal rule of the program is likely to concern the court, if at all, because it puts the offender at risk of expulsion, and expulsion puts the community at risk of robbery. The court is likely in such a case to respond vigorously to the offender's nonattendance or expulsion, but not to his violation of conditions imposed by the day-treatment regimen to protect the internal integrity of its program.[9]

Sentencing judges (and community-based correctional managers) ought to keep in mind that, when noncustodial sentences need to contain risk of a serious harm, they need conditions that:

- cannot easily be violated without detection

- can be violated without substantially increasing the risk that the sentence was intended to contain

- can be tightened (made harder to violate) if the offender violates or exhibits behavior indicating that violation of the condition is imminent

Although there may appear to be good reasons for imposing them, courts ought not rely for risk management on conditions that:

- depend for their enforcement on the offender's prudence, good will, or self-interest

- offer only a last line of defense against the harm (for example, no contact with the victim)

- depend for their efficacy on the success of a treatment or on an offender's rehabilitation

High Probability/Low-to-Moderate Harm

There is, for example, little risk of physical harm to a member of the community from a petty thief with a long record of swiping things from retail displays but no record (or no recent record) of robbery, weapon possession, assault, and the like. On the other hand, the risk of another petty theft is very high. A noncustodial sentence for such an offender ought to punish the theft, and might aim to expose the offender to a treatment, a service, or an experience with rehabilitative potential, but it probably should not aim to cure his thievery or to incapacitate him sufficiently to prevent theft.

Unless he is incarcerated, the probability of another theft during the period of his sentence (say, a probationary period of a year) is so high that the degree of incapacitation required to contain it both would place unreasonable demands on scarce noncustodial resources for incapacitation (in other words, various forms of intensive supervision or residential programming), and would entail conditions so tight that the offender would be almost sure to violate them (confronting the court, with unacceptable frequency, with the dilemma whether to punish the violations or revoke the noncustodial sentence itself).

Experience says that judges (and prosecutors) simply will not treat seriously the violation of a sentence condition by an offender whose violation is not itself a crime and whose worst-case mischief would be something less than serious harm. When an offender poses a risk that is less than "serious," it is unwise to put the court's credibility on the line with a preventive or incapacitating sentence condition whose violation the court cannot or will not punish—particularly when the probability of violation is high or when the condition is not likely to prevent the harm itself. Worse, when it becomes commonly understood that the conditions imposed through some noncustodial sentences will not be enforced, it is harder to believe that the court really intends to enforce the conditions imposed in cases where the conditions are "real"—where they are designed to reduce the risk of more serious harm.

High Probability/Grave Harm

It may be difficult to imagine a sentence other than a substantial term of imprisonment for a felony offender who is thought likely to do substantial harm if given the chance. But, in the context of the current discussion, it should be useful to examine the period after release from whatever term of imprisonment might be imposed. It should be useful for the reason, among others, that truth-in-sentencing jurisdictions increasingly are requiring specification of postconfinement supervision conditions at the time of sentencing. See Smith and Dickey (1998) for an extended discussion of how correctional resources might be deployed best to manage public safety risks in the places to which risky offenders are returned, from prison or court.

Take, for example an eighteen-year-old female who stands convicted of four armed robberies.[10] Her lover and codefendant on all charges is four years older. From early childhood until she ran away at age fifteen, her parents neglected and abused her emotionally and physically. Her father sexually abused her for years; she was taken into foster care briefly and returned to suffer further sexual abuse. She dropped out of school in her midteens, never has been employed, and since running away from home has been attached to one abusive male after another. She credibly claims to have done the armed robberies because, if she refused, her lover would beat her or leave her or both. But four times, over a period of several weeks, she entered convenience stores while he waited in the car. She put a loaded pistol in the face of a clerk, and she took the money from the till.

In most jurisdictions, her crimes expose her to sentences totaling 200 years or so—more than enough to serve all conceivable sentencing purposes. Some will say she deserves twenty years in prison, some say more, and some less. But for almost anyone, her dependency on abusive men, her codefendant's manipulation of her, and the virtual absence of a family life that might have socialized her bear on the question of how deserving she is of extended punishment. And unless she is confined substantially beyond the term she deserves, she will be a very substantial threat to public safety when she is released from her prison term.

What conditions of supervision might make the risk at that time manageable? Perhaps, on account of her characteristics and circumstances, she should be imprisoned for substantially less time than she ordinarily might be thought to deserve. Because of the threat she would pose at the conclusion of any deserved prison term, it might be better to reduce it and to craft conditions for a substantial period of postconfinement supervision along the lines of "quality foster care with a fence." The gravity of the harm she could cause, the high probability that she would cause it (for there are others like her codefendant with whom she surely would partner, both in women's prison and upon her release), leads inexorably to rehabilitation as an essential (but not sole) penal strategy in her case. It is the only way public safety can be protected from her in the period after she has been punished as much as she deserves. This suggests a short period of prison or jail confinement (with a substantial period of confinement held in reserve if the conditions of her supervision upon release are not met). This should be coupled with conditions of supervision that provide the socialization she did not get at home while coming as near as possible to assuring that for a long time she will not be at liberty to wander about in search of another partner like the last.

Conclusion

Guideline grids have brought some order to the imposition and execution of sentences. But what is required to bring law to bear is for a lawful purpose of the sentence to be clearly specified, along with the strategy by which that purpose is to be pursued and the penal measures to be employed. Justice requires that when state force is applied to individuals—even individuals convicted of crimes—the purpose should be a lawful one, the strategy for achieving it should be at least plausible, and the particular penal measures should be at least more likely to advance that strategy than available alternatives.

While for many today a retributive rationale for imposing sentences satisfies the requirement of lawful purpose, it does not capture the public safety purposes that legislators, judges, and corrections agents have in mind when authorizing (or mandating), imposing, and executing sentences. Justice is offended if the purpose for exercising state power over an individual is not clearly articulated and linked, by a strategy that is plausible under the circumstances, to the characteristics, facts, and circumstances of the particular offender.

For it to be likely that the public safety will be served by a particular sentence, it is necessary for the court to find and make inferences from those characteristics and circumstances of an offender that are relevant to the penal strategy by which it intends its purpose to be achieved. And if penal power is to be justly exercised and is not to be misdirected and wasted, it is necessary to couple that individualization of sentences with specificity, clarity, and parsimony in each of the choices the court makes in reasoning toward the sentence. If judges were required to sentence this way (and if, as might be expected, they in turn demanded advocacy from counsel and information from community corrections personnel of the kind they would need to do it) we could break free of grid-guidelines and have real "rule-of-law sentencing."

This prescription calls for imagining performance at a very high level by judges, lawyers, and community corrections personnel. It is a level of performance not routinely delivered today—perhaps unknown today. Thus, this author is speculating about possibilities for improvement, as perhaps Judge Marvin Frankel was when, a little more than twenty-five years ago, he sketched the idea of a sentencing commission (Frankel, 1973). If this author's speculations are to have any force at all in shaping the future of this field, he would be wise, as Judge Frankel has been, not to expect early on that high level of performance (Frankel, 1992).

Endnotes

[1] The core argument and illustrations presented here first were offered in a paper presented to a group of judges and academics convened by the Edna McConnell Clark Foundation, to consider possible effects of the then freshly minted federal sentencing guidelines (Smith, 1987). This author developed some of the themes further in an article for the *Federal Sentencing Reporter* (Smith, 1991). Since the presentation of this paper at the IARCA conference in 1995, the author has recast the argument for discussion in a Roundtable on Structured Sentencing at the 1997 Law and Society Meeting in St. Louis, and for recent collaborative work on the role of corrections in creating and preserving public safety (Smith and Dickey, 1998). This painfully slow evolution of simple thoughts should come to rest, for a while, with their forthcoming appearance in article form, in *Law and Policy*. In recognition of evolutionary developments since 1995, the author has amended this conference paper by inserting some more recent thoughts, where the need was most apparent.

[2] This feature of imprisonment leads some offenders to prefer a period of confinement to the rigors and risk of violation that follow from imposition of demanding noncustodial conditions—if they know that they will be held accountable for compliance with them.

[3] It is simple only by comparison with actually sentencing a human being to the sentence one of the numbers represents—or so the author came to believe from talking with his judicial colleagues on the New York State Sentencing Guidelines Committee when we were putting numbers in the grid; it is disturbing because it was so easy to do.

[4] This is not to say that imprisonment has not had powerful reformative effects on individual offenders. Rather, the net effect of imprisoning those who may be improved by the experience and those whose socialization is interrupted, or worse, does not make prison or jail a promising instrument for pursuit of rehabilitative sentencing objectives.

5   This would not be true if a judge thinks the offender deserves less time than deterrence requires—a low-visibility problem, so long as judges really do not know what deterrence requires and so long as there is a widespread feeling that offenders deserve relatively harsh treatment.

6   The author intends a distinction between the "purpose *at* sentencing" and what are conventionally termed "the purposes *of* sentencing." The latter (retribution or desert, incapacitation, general deterrence, specific deterrence, and rehabilitation) may be an exhaustive list of permissible purposes for the state's imposition of penal measures. The former is the objective that is sought—or might permissibly be sought—by the state at the point in a criminal prosecution when guilt has been established and the judiciary is poised to exercise state power. For centuries, we have been accustomed to the idea that the exercise of the power to punish can be justified by any or all the purposes *of* sentencing. It is a harder question, whether a sentencing judge expects and intends the exercise of that power actually to accomplish any one or more of those purposes in a particular case. We (and our sentencing judges) have become more accomplished at explaining how a given sentence *can be justified* by any permissible purpose than we are at assessing what *should and could be accomplished* through sentencing power in particular cases.

7   If we think a commitment to equality demands that the residentially fortunate be removed to the hostel, perhaps the hostel is too unpleasant for its principal intended purpose—incapacitation. If so, justice and economy suggest we invest in making hostels more like homes, rather than expanding the number of unpleasant hostels so as to incapacitate those who already have homes to which they could be confined.

8   By this, the author is referring not to the "risk factors" used to predict an offender's risk of failure on probation or parole. An offender's "propensity" for causing harm inheres in the situation of which the offender is a part, not in the offender—it is not a quantifiable characteristic of the offender (*see* Popper, 1990, 10-16). An offender's circum- stances may be rich with vulnerable victims and starved of naturally occurring guardians for them, or it may be devoid of either or both; the places where persons or property are found that are vulnerable to the offender may or may not have naturally occurring guardians upon which community corrections personnel might rely. These circumstances interact with various offender characteristics (which tend to be more stable) to shape whatever threats to public safety warrant supervision of an offender in the community (*see* generally, Smith and Dickey, 1998). Whatever the situation of which an offender is part, we should expect it—and its propensity for harm—to be changing all the time. For that reason, we should expect changes over time in the nature and likelihood of the harm against which we seek protection through community supervision of an offender, and we should expect community corrections agents to work at manipulating, directly and indirectly, the offender circumstances which, together with his or her characteristics, define the propensity for harm.

9 This may not go down well with the day treatment program staff who expect the court to help them keep their adolescent charges in line. They are concerned about risks to the integrity of their program, and some of the most interesting and difficult tussles in alternative sentencing arise when a community-based program wants a court to use its power to help enforce its rules (violate him!) while the court wants to conserve its power for risks it gauges as more serious (go back to that program . . . and be good!).

10 This scenario is drawn from a real case, adapted for use in sentencing seminars at the University of Wisconsin Law School, which for the past few years, has brought a handful of judges, corrections officials, prosecutors, and defense attorneys together with this author's students, to search for an effective way to bring sentencing within the rule of law.

References

Cook, P. J. 1980. Research in Criminal Deterrence: Laying the Groundwork for the Second Decade. In N. Morris and M. Tonry, eds. *Crime and Justice: A Review of Research*. Chicago: University of Chicago Press.

El Nasser, H. 1995. Crime-weary Public Scoffs at "Service" as Punishment. *USA Today*. 6 July, 6A.

Frankel, M. E. 1973. *Criminal Sentences: Law Without Order*. New York: Hill and Wang.

————. 1992. Sentencing Guidelines: A Need for Creative Collaboration. *Yale Law Journal*. 101:2043-2051.

Hillsman, S. T. and J. Greene. 1988. Tailoring Criminal Fines to the Financial Means of the Offender. *Judicature*. 72:38-45.

MacDonald, D. 1989. *Punishment Without Walls: Community Service Sentences in New York City*. New Brunswick, New Jersey: Rutgers University Press.

Morris, N. and M. Tonry. 1990. *Between Prison and Probation: Intermediate Punishments in a Rational Sentencing System*. New York: Oxford University Press.

Popper, C. R. 1990. *A World of Propensities*. Bristol, U.K.: Thoemmes Antiquarian Books.

Smith, M. E. 1984. Will the Real Alternatives Please Stand Up? *New York University Review of Law and Social Change*. 12:171-197.

————. 1987. Notes on the Purposes of Sentences and their Relation to the Construction of Guideline Sentencing Schemes. Unpublished paper.

————. 1991. Designing and Implementing Noncustodial Penal Sanctions: What Purposes Will Real Alternatives Serve? *Federal Sentencing Reporter.* 4 (1):27-29.

————. 1995. "Public Safety and the Criminal Justice System" in Temporary State Commission on Constitutional Revision. In *Effective Government Now for the New Century: A Report to the People, the Governor, and the Legislators of New York*, edited by Rockefeller Institute of Government. Albany: Rockefeller Institute of Government.

Smith, M. E. and W. J. Dickey. 1998. What If Corrections Were Serious about Public Safety? *Corrections Management Quarterly.* 2(3):12-30.

Zimring, F. E. 1973. *Deterrence: The Legal Threat in Crime Control.* Chicago: University of Chicago Press.

Zimring, F. E. and G. Hawkins. 1996. *Incapacitation: Penal Confinement and the Restraint of Crime.* New York: Oxford University Press.

SECTION 2:

THE DIFFUSION OF RESEARCH INNOVATION

TOWARD THE STRATEGIC MANAGEMENT OF CORRECTIONAL INNOVATION: PUTTING "WHAT WORKS" INFORMATION TO WORK

5

Alan T. Harland, L.L.M., Ph.D.

Wayne N. Welsh, Ph.D.

Department of Criminal Justice
Temple University
Philadelphia, Pennsylvania

Introduction

As we understand it, the central issue raised by the organizers of this, the third conference on "what works" in community corrections, is how to apply and extend the significant body of theoretical and empirical knowledge on that question, of the type summarized and discussed at the two earlier meetings,[1] in ways that will optimize its impact in the development and implementation of successful policy and practice changes in the future. Put somewhat differently, a modification of Mark Moore's statement in his introductory paper for this conference asks:

> How do we handle the growing body of theory and research information about "what works," in ways that will spur the rate of successful innovation in corrections in the future?

Under either formulation, the implicit task remains one of extending perhaps the most important theme of the conference series: how to build bridges between the scholars and evaluators producing and disseminating the research and theoretical information, and the planners, policy makers, administrators, and individual-case decision-makers who must put that information to its best use.

The importance and difficulty of the challenge cannot be overstated, whether in the context of improving the actual performance of community corrections, or from the related standpoint of cleaning up its very tarnished image in the eyes of the public and many professionals in other parts of the criminal justice system. Community supervision is estimated to include no more than 1 contact per month with a probation officer for 3 out of 5 felony probationers nationwide, and average caseloads are approaching 150:1 for probation and 80:1 for parole.

Even these numbers, however, would seem very small to many beleaguered chiefs in some larger metropolitan areas such as Los Angeles, where recent estimates place 60 percent of all probationers in the category of computer-only supervision, with no contact at all with an officer (Petersilia, 1995; Langan, 1994; U.S. Advisory Commission, 1993). If community corrections is to marshal the integrity and popular and professional support that would facilitate successful innovation in the immediate and longer-term future, doing business-as-usual obviously cannot be the path.

Knowledge about "what works" may not be enough to elevate the war against crime above the ideological posturing and information-vacuum in which it is so typically waged. Ignoring or being indifferent to it, however, surely must condemn us to a future of more of the same, or worse.

Although a wide variety of specific reasons for the problem can be found, the relative neglect of "what works" information is tied significantly to the bigger failure of jurisdictions and agencies to invest seriously in broad-based processes of strategic management of criminal justice innovation in the same way that is taken for granted in commercial enterprises in the private sector. At all levels of decision-making, whether at a policy, program, or case level, there is clearly a need for improved forums and processes for identifying, assessing, and communicating effectively, the information necessary to spur innovation and facilitate rational choices by policy makers, program developers, and sentencing authorities.

This paper discusses a number of general action-research approaches and specific tools for addressing the foregoing need. The authors argue that one of the main advantages of creating the types of information-processing mechanisms discussed is that they are likely not only to improve the probability that the best sources of information appropriately are brought to bear on decisions about correctional options, but also that they are likely to stimulate, indeed demand, the production of ever higher quality and clearly communicated additional information in the future.

"What Works" Revisited: Understanding the Question

Before addressing directly the challenge of how to make better use of "what works" information, it is important to remember that questions about what is successful can be categorized and answered in a variety of different ways, depending on how the terms "what" and "works," respectively, are defined. The former, for example, may mean punitive sanctions (specific deterrence) or treatment measures (rehabilitation) designed to reduce an offender's proclivity to reoffend; "what" also may refer to restraints designed to reduce the offender's opportunity to reoffend (incapacitation); or it might signify punishments intended to reduce the inclination of the public as a whole to engage in criminal conduct (general deterrence) (Cullen, Wright, and Applegate, 1996; Gendreau, 1996; Palmer, 1996). Because most "whats" of this kind are likely to involve differing combinations of ingredients on each of the foregoing dimensions, and others of importance to any assessment of their relative merit, such assessment only can proceed on the basis of extensive descriptive information specifying in detail the exact nature and scope of the option under consideration (Harland, 1996a).

"What" also can include a variety of clinical and statistical diagnostic mechanisms (risk/needs assessments) and monitoring and evaluation information systems to make sure those interventions are being applied to appropriate target populations (Bonta, 1996; Jones, 1996). In addition, it might embrace a variety of program management and adaptation strategies and techniques, aimed at maximizing the probability that any particular innovation will be adopted and successfully implemented (Harris and Smith, 1996; Moore, this volume).

Decision-makers in a policy- or program-development setting, or at an individual case level, who must make judgments about whether any of the foregoing "whats" are considered to "work" obviously will need to look to quite different sources and types of information, depending on the particular option they are considering. For each one, moreover, the determination of whether it "works" will depend, in turn, on any combination from a variety of criteria most salient to the key decision-makers involved. These may begin with general concerns about effectiveness, efficiency, and fairness, and devolve into more specific goals of impact on crime/recidivism, costs, disparity/equity, diversionary effects, degree of implementation, political and public support, and so on (Harland, 1996a; this issue is taken up in more detail in connection with the Rational Decision Matrix, discussed later in this chapter).

Without at all intending to diminish the central importance of data from individual studies, evaluation literature reviews, and meta-analyses of research into the recidivism impact of different sanctioning/intervention options, it is vital to be aware of the daunting range and complexity of additional substantive and process expertise and information that must be tapped if the rate of successful innovation in corrections is to be significantly increased. As will be discussed in more detail below, designing intervention programs or individual sanctions that are thought to reduce recidivism is only a narrow, albeit, critically important, aspect of a larger process of successful innovation. Knowledge about what reduces recidivism will be of little use to either sentencing authorities or policy and program developers, if any of the following conditions apply:

- The answer is beyond local fiscal, human, or technological resources.

- It is widely perceived as retributively or politically unpalatable.

- It does not respond to some other pressing felt need, say, to reduce jail crowding in the jurisdiction.

What is more important, program attributes often are less predictive of success than attributes of the implementation process and of the organizational setting within which even the most tightly designed program inevitably will have to be adapted to survive and succeed (Harris and Smith, 1996).

Case-Level Versus Policy and Program Level Answers

In a practical sense, the task of identifying and applying information about correctional options that work most typically occurs at two distinct but highly related levels of decision-making. Each ultimately involves selection from a menu of options intended to achieve an optimal balance in the effective, efficient, and fair disposition of criminal cases. First, at a policy and program development level, it is the task of court or correctional agency planners to incorporate the best available ingredients into the design of programs or interventions for inclusion on the menu in the first place.[2]

Ideally, this is done as part of a larger process of strategic management and program development with policymakers and administrators. Second, it is the task of the sentencing judge and other practitioners who control or provide input to making and operationalizing sentencing decisions on a case-by-case basis. At both of the foregoing levels of decision-making, it is an implicit and, in our experience, unassailable assumption of organizers of the present conference that the best available research and theory information currently is not being used to its maximum potential to spur and guide correctional innovation.

Sentencing decisions in many jurisdictions are constrained by inadequate options and resources (for example, not enough drug-treatment slots) available to the court. More critically, they continue be based on prosecution and defense recommendations, plea-bargains, or individual-judicial decisions that are unsupported by detailed and timely presentence information or analysis concerning the risk and needs of the offender or, consequently, about matching dispositional alternatives.

At the policy and program level, it is still too commonly the case that new approaches rarely are introduced on the basis of systematic assessment and application of the best theoretical and research information as it relates to the documented needs of local jurisdictions. Instead, more likely they are to be adopted because grant funds were available (the fiscal-opportunism approach to innovation), or because a judge or agency head was impressed after hearing about a "new" idea in the media or at a panel or site visit while attending a conference (the individual conversion or criminological-tourist approach innovation).

At both levels, there is clearly a need for improved mechanisms for assuring that the most appropriate sources of theoretical and empirical information are routinely and systematically identified, assessed, and communicated in ways most likely to spur innovation and facilitate rational choices by policymakers, program developers, and individual sentencing decisionmakers.

Explaining and Remedying the System's Tolerance of Information-deficient Decision-making

One way of thinking about how to give information about what works a more central role is to reflect for a moment on why it is that we do not do so already. Given the extensive body of knowledge about the technologies and advantages of locally developed and maintained risk and needs assessment instruments as means of guiding sentencing and classification decisions (Bonta, 1996; Jones, 1996), why is it that so few places have them at all, or have only outdated versions, or ones that were inappropriately adopted from another jurisdiction?

Similarly, given the amount of information about the differential effectiveness (or lack thereof) of various types of intervention, why is it that fad and fancy more than facts still seem to dictate development and imposition of sanctioning and noncoercive intervention options? And, given the overwhelming consensus about the importance of adequate monitoring and management-information systems in the design, implementation, and evaluation of correctional alternatives, why is it that so many jurisdictions continue to function at levels not far removed from the 3-by-5-cards-in-a-shoe-box-method of record keeping?

In each case, a key problem to be addressed must be the system's routine adherence, both at a policy and program level, as well as with respect to individual case dispositions, to decision-making practices that are characterized by remarkably deficient levels of information to satisfy even the minimum requirements of rational choice.

Explaining and counteracting the reasons why blatantly information-deficient decision-making by policymakers, program developers, and sentencing authorities is so much the norm and is so widely tolerated in our systems of criminal justice would appear to be an obvious first step in any effort to bring "what works" information more centrally into the picture.

Numerous specific reasons immediately spring to mind from the literature and from every professional's personal experience. One is that evaluation researchers often fail to invest sufficient energies in the effective communication of findings and recommendations, a process that must go well beyond the production of a final written report (Winberg, 1992). Another may be that decision-making in an information vacuum, with little more than present-charge categories and prior-record tallies, and indifference to evaluation information about effective correctional options, can be rationalized as acceptable, and even morally required, under simplistic interpretations of the demands of justice as indistinguishable from those of retribution.

The powerful political and professional influence of the advocacy of retributive sentencing models by thoughtful scholars such as Von Hirsch (1976) ironically but unquestionably has lent an added aura of legitimacy to such a mind-set over the last two decades. In addition to its obvious emotional congruity with baser vindictive sentiments, part of the practical appeal of a philosophy that requires choosing options that hurt against those that work is undoubtedly that the former generally will place fewer information demands on the system.

Development and processing of rich, reliable, and valid information as a prelude to choosing correctional options is rarely cheap or quick, and thus conflicts with system realities of tightening budgets, crowded caseloads, and corresponding pressures to process cases and develop quick-fix policies and programs as fast as possible. In addition, it is not simple, and the decisionmakers most likely to have ultimate authority to innovate are often lawyers, politicians, or administrators.

Yet, these individuals often are equipped very poorly by education, training, or experience to be able to evaluate knowledgeably and critically the complex kinds of information involved, or even to recognize the importance and value of it in the first place. This is not a gratuitous insult to colleagues in the legal profession, although it certainly would not hurt if even a few law schools in the country required at least basic social science methods and statistics courses. Rather, the authors argue that what is needed is far more assistance and guidance than currently is acknowledged or provided, in a decision-making task that is beyond any but the most polymathic individual, regardless of profession or primary disciplinary background.

Decisions at the Individual Sentencing Level

Even the most cursory reflection upon the nature and condition of the sentencing process nationwide inexorably leads to the conclusion that the need for more guidance remains as urgent a priority today as perhaps at any time in the past. Indeed, as the range and complexity of diagnostic and intervention options continue to increase, especially in the field of intermediate sanctions (Byrne, Lurigio, and Petersilia, 1991), it perhaps is surprising that the demand for structural assistance is not being voiced most forcefully of all from the bench and from others who are involved centrally in the day-to-day discharge of the sentencing function.[3]

For evidence of the need for improved levels of information, guidance, structure, and assistance to the key participants in the sanctioning process, consider the setting in which sentencing decisions routinely must be made. It frequently is characterized by the following features:

- Relative procedural informality is growing.[4]

- High-volume, time-pressured court dockets, especially in misdemeanor courts, are increasing.

- Unconstitutionally crowded jails and prisons and escalating construction costs force urgent consideration of community-based sanctions.

- A rapidly expanding range of new and relatively untested "intermediate sanctions" has grown dramatically, with no corresponding rise in guidance to decisionmakers on selection protocols that might give decisionmakers clear guidance on how, when, and why to use them. Increasing the number and type of community-based options available to the court also increases the complexity of the sentencing decision, and throws into question the continued validity of incarceration guidelines and forecasts based on historical sentencing practices observed prior to the proliferation of such alternatives.

- A high degree of media, public, and political scrutiny occurs in sensational cases.

- Input from multiple decisionmakers is fragmented, often with low visibility, extensive individual discretion, and largely without formally articulated and consistently monitored standards, rules, and procedures. This includes ultimately, the sentencing judge, but also, prosecutors and defense attorneys in plea negotiation and any sentencing memoranda and/or oral recommendations at the sentencing hearing. For the defense, such input is being supplemented extensively in a growing number of jurisdictions by client-specific planners or defense-based sentencing advocates (Yeager, 1992). It also includes probation officers preparing presentence reports and recommendations, a variety of public and, less commonly, private agencies and individuals who provide information and advice to the court, such as prior record and criminal-incident reports, drug testing, educational, employment, and other diagnostic and intervention-planning information. The process also includes victims through loss assessments for restitution purposes, or by way of more formal victim-impact statements.

- Most law schools and criminal justice agencies provide minimal formal educational or training emphasis on sentencing goals, options, and relevant decision-making skill and information requirements.

- There are grossly inadequate information systems for developing, implementing, monitoring, and evaluating sanctioning options.

Contrast the foregoing reality against idealized expectations that sanctioning decisions be made in an environment marked by adherence to the following types of broadly supported values and goals:

- Rationality with clear goal and policy basis, including choice from a full range of options and adequate information (for diagnosis, intervention planning, and monitoring)

- Accountability (to offenders, victims, and the public) based on reasoned decisions, visibility, broad-based input and the opportunity to challenge the prosecutor, defender/defendant, and the victim. There is also provision for questioning the sentencing advocate/client specific planner, and the probation presentence investigator.

- Fairness based on parsimony, equity, proportionality, legality, and constitutionality

- Effectiveness includes: making reparation to victims, reducing crime and recidivism, maximizing ancillary gains (such as offender potential through employment, education, and so forth)

- Efficiency which includes both cost consciousness and timeliness

- Humaneness and compassion which encompasses retributive sufficiency

Consider further that any serious attempt to begin to live up to the foregoing expectations suggests the need for a formidable amalgam of skills and knowledge to obtain and process information required for diagnostic and intervention planning and prognosis. Expertise is implied and assumed in areas as diverse as the following in the box.

Expertise is needed and expected in the following areas:

- Law—to assure procedural and substantive compliance with statutory and constitutional requirements and limitations.

- Social science methods and statistics—to be intelligent consumers of quantitative techniques for targeting appropriate offenders and sanctioning choices, including predicting: recidivism, risks and probabilities of risk, the stakes of choices, specific forms of dangerousness, and related offender-needs (diagnosis), and the evaluation methods upon which judgments about the strengths or weaknesses of different intervention programs or sanctioning options are made (intervention planning), as well as the likely consequences of imposing them on a particular defendant (prognosis).

- Psychology/psychiatry/pharmacology—to make comparable sense of clinical prediction and treatment options.

- Economics—to assure sanctioning measures imposed are the most cost-conscious options available, consistent with public protection and other important sanctioning goals and values.

- Public opinion—sensitivity to legitimate concerns of key constituencies, including the general public, professional and political groups, victim advocacy, and other special interest organizations.

- Philosophy—to assure balanced adherence to preventive, reparative, and retributive goals of sentencing, and related values of parsimony, equity, proportionality, and awareness of ethical concerns and related liability and other

> practical consequences of inaccurate decisions (for example, false positive or false-negative prediction errors).
>
> - System and community organization and resources—to assure optimal understanding and use of all available diagnostic and intervention options, and identification of deficiencies and needs for further development

What is immediately apparent from the partial listing in the box is that the task is obviously an interdisciplinary one. Yet, it is being handled predominantly by professionals with very much a single discipline background, the law. The ironies of this situation are multiple. First, many of the categories of information, such as those requiring understanding of research methods, statistics, psychology and psychiatry, and system and community program resources, are generally topics on which law school and continuing education courses for lawyers rarely focus.

Second, because of the clinical and adversarial nature of most legal practice, social science data and expertise are more likely to be seen as weapons to be manipulated or derided to achieve some case-specific advantage, than as a shared information-base upon which to forge consensus as to broader policy or program directions. Even the philosophical dimension of the decision is far less understood by members of the legal profession than they or the public typically assume. Most law school curricula do not dwell at length on legal philosophy at all, and not on sentencing philosophy, in particular. Certainly, beyond basic familiarity with the usual terminology, few practicing attorneys would claim to be well versed in the literature of sentencing theory, much less the empirical literature testing its underlying assumptions.

Ironically the law-related part of the decision, for which the most central participants in the process—judges, prosecutors, and defense attorneys—are trained, represents perhaps the most straightforward and least problematic aspect of the sentencing function. Making sure the sentence is within statutory limits and constitutional constraints rarely will pose much of a problem.[5]

It is obviously unreasonable, however, to expect a sentencing judge, or any other individual to possess complete mastery of all of the other various disciplines and issue areas outlined. As a result, it should be apparent to all but the most omniscient of judges and other sentencing officials that they need and deserve all the help and guidance they can muster, from each other and from all other relevant information sources. In short, it suggests an urgent need for interagency coordination and collaboration.

Such coordination and collaboration would be done to identify the most efficient and effective distribution of roles and responsibilities to get the many different parts of the sentencing task done as well as possible. Such a group also would aid in the development of formal rules, procedures, and guidelines, to assure consistency and integrity in the way relevant information is identified, communicated, and applied.

Improvements in such obvious targets as probation-based presentence reports, privately commissioned client-specific planning proposals, and defense-based and other forms of sentencing advocacy,[6] are all ways of responding to the need, highlighted earlier, for improved mechanisms for assuring that the most appropriate sources of theoretical and empirical information routinely and systematically are identified, assessed, and communicated in ways most likely to spur innovation and facilitate rational choices by individual sentencing decisionmakers.

However, although it is undoubtedly interesting and useful for the participants at this and similar conferences in the future to continue to explore such specific explanations and remedies for why information is so poorly used or underused in individual sentencing decisions, it is important to recognize that deficiencies at this level are largely a reflection of similar problems in the broader policy and program development environment in which they are rooted and perpetuated. The authors assume that organizational buy-in and successful improvements to information use at the individual case-level are more likely to be brought about and sustained if carefully planned and monitored within a broader, systematic process of policy and program development by the court, related agencies, or the system as a whole. The remainder of the paper will focus primarily upon the issue of enhancing the role of information on "what works" at this level.

Decisions at the Policy and Program Development Level

Once attention to the system's tolerance for information-deficient decision-making shifts from the case-level to the level of policy-making and program development, it is consistent with a recurrent and central theme of writers in the fields of organizational management and change to suggest the following: The relative neglect of "what works" information is tied significantly to the failure of jurisdictions and agencies to invest seriously in its generation and its application in broad-based forums and systematic processes of strategic management of criminal justice innovation that are taken for granted in the private sector.

Innovation that takes place outside such a systematic process (for example, an individual judge deciding to begin to impose community service sentences without any formal program structure) is not necessarily undesirable, per se. However, a strong case can be made for the proposition that we are unlikely to break the demoralizing cycle of failure of quick-fix, isolated, and crisis-oriented responses to the system's problems, unless we begin to define and tackle them from a systemwide perspective. This is one in which joint responsibility is accepted for the policies, programs, and processes that determine to a large degree the size, composition, and outcomes of case flow at different stages in the system; and one in which ownership of the problems and a stake in finding solutions that work are shared widely by all the key decisionmakers involved (Harland, 1991).

Consequently, providing a forum and a process designed to facilitate such an approach, and in which to take stock systematically of information about what works, and its likely fit with local problems and conditions, not only may be the most effective way of promoting information-based innovation, but also may be an important catalyst to the generation of more and better information in the future.[7]

Systematic Approaches to Policy and Program Development

In the United States, the National Institute of Corrections, with the support of other entities such as the State Justice Institute and the Edna McConnell Clarke Foundation, has been trying for several years to promote the creation of standing policy and related program development groups, involving community correctional agencies and multiple other court and governmental and private agencies, at the county, and, less often, at the statewide level. Although focused primarily in the area of intermediate sanctions, the lessons learned in the course of designing and delivering technical assistance and training to the many sites across the country, which have shown an interest in participating, extend readily into the broader realm of correctional innovation in general, including particularly the importance of an information-based approach to planned change.

More recently, state agencies, such as the Michigan Office of Community Corrections and the Pennsylvania Commission on Crime and Delinquency, also have provided similar technical assistance and training, as well as direct funding, for the development and support of similar strategic management teams in counties throughout their respective states. In each case, the immediate intent is to bring more of a policy-driven, information-based approach to county-level planning, implementation, and strategic management of community-based sanctions. As with the national level efforts of the National Institute of Corrections, however, the knowledge, tools, and skills involved are expected to translate into enhanced policy- and program-development capabilities of relevance to innovation in other aspects of the system as well.

At the policy level, details of the National Insitute of Corrections/State Justice Institute efforts in some two dozen jurisdictions are spelled out in the useful report: *The Intermediate Sanctions Handbook: Experiences and Tools for Policymakers* (McGarry and Carter, 1993). Figure 5.1 summarizes, in checklist form, some of the ingredients identified as most important to the success of such ventures.

FIGURE 5.1. Checklist of Steps for Developing Successful Policy for the Rational Allocation of Correctional Resources

1. A Coordinating Group/Policy Team

- Is organized with appropriate authority, leadership, and broad-based membership

- Has adequate staff support

- Has an approach to doing business that is characterized by frank and open communication

- Members have a sense of commitment, ownership, and incentive for the work

- Members and staff have energy and stamina to stay the course and handle the tasks to be done and the frustrations to be endured

2. Information Development—Definition of Problems and Prospects

- Describe the system—case processing and disposition options in the courts and corrections

- Describe the target population(s)—caseflow and population data at critical junctures

- Describe diagnostic/sanctioning/intervention alternatives [experience from past and other jurisdictions]

3. Consensus Building on Changes Desired/Policy to be Adopted

- What values and goals are to be served by sentencing and corrections?

- What policies expressly reflect those values and goals, and how will they be achieved?

- What are the short-term objectives for specific changes in agency and/or system policy and practice?

- What outcomes are desired for specific sanctioning options?

4. Adoption and Implementation of Change

- What internal agency changes and systemwide changes in policy and practice are needed?

- What changes in existing sanctioning options are necessary?

- What new sanctioning options are needed?

- What information system changes (diagnostic, monitoring, and evaluation) are needed?

- How can existing resources be reallocated, including personnel, and physical plant?

- What are the staff training and continuing education needs?

- What interagency cooperation is needed?

5. Outreach and Education—Marketing and Sales - How can you reach the following?

- Local legislative and executive officials?

- State legislative and executive officials?

- Key constituencies (such as, victim's groups, professional associations)

- Media?

- General public?

Although results of the National Institute of Corrections' investment in policy-team development have not been rigorously evaluated, it is safe to say that one of the more difficult and crucial ingredients of a successful venture of this type (whether at policy or program development level) is a group commitment, and provision of corresponding staff support and resources, to secure and communicate the information needed to sustain the decision-making process. Without adequate information-development resources, "what works" information is likely to continue to be underused and unappreciated, and the forums in which it is most needed are less likely to prosper and survive.

A Policy Forum Illustration

One site that has benefitted from both the National Institute of Corrections and the Pennsylvania Commission on Crime and Delinquency initiatives is Delaware County, Pennsylvania. The Delaware County Criminal Justice Advisory Committee offers a worthwhile case-study of how establishing an interagency forum, with appropriate authority structure and administrative and research support quickly can establish a broad-based "information-culture," within which innovation along numerous fronts appears to thrive.[8]

The Delaware County Criminal Justice Advisory Committee

The creation of the Delaware County Criminal Justice Advisory Committee stemmed in large part from Delaware County's involvement in two Pennsylvania Commission on Crime and Delinquency-sponsored sessions on team building and county community corrections plan development. After participating in these two meetings, county and court representatives were selected to become involved in a comparable national-level program, the "Intermediate Sanctions Project," run by the Center for Effective Public Policy in Washington, D.C., and sponsored by the National Institute of Corrections.

Under this project, beginning in the Fall of 1994, representatives of several court and county agencies participated in national, regional, and on-site meetings with National Institute of Corrections' staff and a variety of technical assistance experts. The aim was to explore the current use and potential for expansion and refinement of intermediate sanctions, referred to under Pennsylvania legislation as intermediate punishments. A special common interest of the sponsoring institutes and the Delaware County participants was the role of such sanctions in reducing the pressures on the county's overburdened prison.

To place discussion of the Delaware County Criminal Justice Advisory Commission in appropriate context, and to illustrate some of the reasons why state and county officials are so enthusiastic about its work and potential, it is necessary to describe its principal attributes.

First Steps in the Process

Then President Judge Toal in October 1994, after returning from a meeting of all sites involved in the National Institute of Corrections' project, convened an organizational meeting of selected county and court representatives. Another senior and widely respected member of the Common Pleas bench, Judge R. Barclay Surrick, agreed to chair subsequent monthly meetings. A subgroup of members of the committee and representatives of their staff served as a work team to provide logistical and informational support to the chair and to the committee between full-group meetings. The work team operates between each session of the committee and convenes approximately one week before the next meeting, to follow up on committee decisions, information requests, and other assignments, and to assist the chair in preparing agenda items and maintaining a record of the proceedings. Additional information development activities between the full group meetings of the advisory committee are the responsibility of a number of more ad hoc subcommittees.

At a second meeting in November 1994, participants developed a mission statement and a standard agenda format and approved inviting representatives of several additional agencies to serve as members of the committee. The committee continues to meet on a monthly basis.

To provide logistical support and, more importantly, research and data analysis assistance essential to stimulate and inform the advisory committee's decision-making, consulting services were made available during a six-month start-up period, with funding through the National Institute of Corrections/Center for Effective Public Policy project, and subsequently through the Pennsylvania Commission on Crime and Delinquency. One of the authors of this paper, Dr. Harland, has served as the primary advisor to the committee on both process and research issues since its inception. The basic elements of the Delaware County Criminal Justice Advisory Committee are summarized in Figure 5.2.

FIGURE 5.2 Summary Fact Sheet
Delaware County Criminal Justice
Advisory Committee

Initiated

- October, 1994

Composition

- Chair: Honorable R. Barclay Surrick, Court of Common Pleas Judge

- Committee: Leaders of key court and county government agencies

- Work team/Subcommittees: Selected committee members +/or senior associates

Support Services

- Administration: Designated staff of agencies represented on the committee

- Research: Court/county data specialists, local university faculty, and students

Operational Procedures

- Monthly committee meetings (reports on activities from represented agencies, special information briefings, discussion and decision/recommendation period)

- Work team and subcommittee meetings and research and information-development activities (for example, prison population study, system mapping, county resources inventory)

Process Aims

- Regular and open communication and dialog among major stakeholders

- Cooperation and collaboration among key court and county decision-makers

- Systemwide action-research process of:
    - Identifying problems/opportunities for change

— Assessing alternative options for improvement (policies, programs, technologies, information, staff, facilities)

— Making decisions to recommend/take appropriate action

- Coordinated data-based approach to criminal justice policy/ program planning

- Cost-conscious allocation of prison and other resources of the court and county

- Expanded continuum of sanctions under Intermediate Punishment Laws

Impact Goals

- Measurable improvements to the county criminal justice enterprises:

— Effectiveness (for example, public safety, victim reparation)

— Efficiency (for example, reduction of delay/crowding/cost)

— Fairness—reduce disparity

- Increased system accountability (to public, victims, defendants)

- Improved public perception of county system

Change Strategies

- Unilateral change within individual agencies represented on the committee

- Cooperative agreements among agencies represented on the committee

- External advocacy (for example, to change state policy)

In short, the intent is to bring together key decisionmakers in a routine and systematic forum for sharing and discussing ideas, issues, and problems concerning the administration of criminal justice. By opening and sustaining communication and dialog between key stakeholders, the aim is to assure thorough and balanced input to defining problems, exploring options for change, and making data-informed recommendations and decisions that will improve the effectiveness, efficiency, fairness, and accountability of the county's criminal justice system. A particular concern is to bring the most broad-based expertise and viewpoints to the task of designing and implementing a full range of intermediate sanctions under the state's intermediate punishment laws, and otherwise to the development of sound policies, programs, technologies, information, staffing, and other resources that will assure the optimal use of county prison space.

Conceptual Framework

Pursuing improvements to the criminal justice system through the very systematic strategy that the advisory committee employs involves essentially a process of identifying problems and opportunities for change, considering alternative methods of improvement, and making decisions to recommend and take appropriate action. The success of any such *process of rational decision-making* generally is considered to depend heavily upon the presence of three essential elements: clearly defined *goals*, thorough consideration of *options* for achieving them, and adequate *information* to allow confidence that the options chosen are those most likely to achieve the goals desired (Gottfredson and Gottfredson, 1988).

Goals

Although the list of different members' specific goals and hopes for the advisory committee is lengthy and constantly changing, important common ground exists in the group's shared interest in exploring changes in the criminal justice system that might have significant potential for the following four goals: (1) greater effectiveness (for example, lower recidivism, fewer supervision failures, increased victim reparation); (2) greater efficiency (for example, less delay, lower costs, less crowding); (3) greater fairness (for example, more equity, less disparity, more parsimony); and (4) greater accountability (for example, better monitoring and evaluation information systems).

Options

Driven by these goals, members of the advisory committee and other stakeholders have voiced ideas about problems and *options for change* (additions, cuts, and reallocations) that might be made in all of the following areas: laws, administrative policies, programs, technologies (for example, information systems and diagnostic tools and intervention tools), personnel, and physical space or facilities.

Whether the options identified are short-term or long-term prospects, they can be categorized further as changes that can be made through the following: unilateral internal action by leaders of specific agencies or programs, individual practitioner changes in approach, interagency agreement and cooperation among agencies within the county, and external lobbying (for example, changes in federal or state law or practice).

To make informed recommendations or decisions to take action in any of the foregoing directions, discussions by the committee and work-team members have identified an interest in information that would allow each major option to be evaluated and prioritized according to its merit on at least the following criteria:

- High-consensus—Does it have broad support within the committee (for example, reductions in processing delays that do not involve differences of opinion at a value level)?

- Otherwise quick and straightforward—Can it be done without major professional disruption or resource investment?

- Public safety—Is it likely to reduce crime or recidivism, or, given other important benefits, at least not produce any unacceptable increased risk to public safety?

- Prison-bed savings—Is it likely to produce significant savings in the number of prison bed days through reducing admissions or through reducing the length of stay?

- Unintended consequences—Is it likely to contribute to delay, crowding, or other system problems? For example, reducing prison crowding may exacerbate probation crowding.

- Cost savings—Is it likely to produce significant financial savings to the county?

- Public support—Is it likely to be understood and accepted by the general public?

Discussion

In addition to the extensive amount of time and effort that different members have invested in establishing and participating in the advisory committee/work team process, progress has been made on a number of substantive fronts in the four years since the committee was first convened. The committee has explored changes and in almost every possible category discussed in the conceptual framework for the committee's activities (policy, program, staffing, and so forth). Those activities have included:

Research and Planning: The Delaware County Criminal Justice Advisory Committee has generated more than thirty ministudies, reports, and decision-briefs, covering issues as diverse as a profile of the prison population, a prison-design needs assessment, a day reporting center planning study, studies of the sheriff's transportation and courthouse activities, probation and parole violation practices, district justice arraignments, community service for driving under the influence of alcohol offenders, good-time policies at the prison, costs of summary appeals, use of courthouse space, restitution-processing fees, and fast-tracking and prompt transfer of state-sentenced inmates. In addition, the Pennsylvania Commmission on Crime and Delinquency approved the committee's grant proposal to support a variety of Delaware Criminal Justice Advisory Commission activities, including funding for some of these studies and projects to reengineer the court's pretrial services and to implement a comprehensive program of intermediate punishment for substance-abusing defendants.

Outreach: Members of the committee have made presentations on the Delaware County Criminal Justice Advisory Committee at national conferences sponsored by the National Institute of Corrections, and to the local bar association (in cooperation with the State Sentencing Commission), to the Pennsylvania Commission on Crime and Delinquency's statewide community corrections conferences and to the 1996 State Trial Judges Association Conference in Philadelphia. Dr. Harland has presented papers at the Delaware County Criminal Justice Advisory Committee professional conferences in Canada, New Zealand, Britain, and the United States. The work of the committee has been featured in numerous articles in local newspapers as well as in the statewide Pennsylvania Commission on Crime and Delinquency criminal justice newsletter. Most recently, it was the subject of a half-hour cable network television show.

Videoconferencing: Based on the committee's planning and recommendations, the court has begun and is continuing to explore the wider use of videoconferencing technologies for a variety of hearings from the county prison. This not only reduces scheduling and hearing delays, but cuts down on transport costs for the sheriff and on security risks at the courthouse and the prison. Videoconferencing has been introduced for arraignment, and for bail, habeas, extradition, and juvenile detention hearings, as well as for interviews with defendants by public defenders, private attorneys, and staff from probation, drug and alcohol, and psychological assessment. A variety of other possibilities are under active consideration, including pretrial conferences, postconviction-relief hearings, interviews for bail hearings at the district justice level, and some civil applications such as depositions from witnesses in other states.

Integrated Justice Information Systems Development: Based on repeated observations by members that there is a critical need for an integrated justice information system to support planning, case-management, and monitoring and evaluation of the criminal process, the committee brought in representatives of nationally prominent companies to advise on a suitable strategy. Thanks largely to the strong initiative of the county executive, a supportive and vitally important member of the Delaware County Criminal Justice Advisory Committee recently approved a large-scale investment in contracts with consultant firms to begin the process of assessing and meeting the county's information and technology needs. The county's commitment to the considerable expense and long-term nature of this process is perhaps the most telling indicator of the success of the Delaware County Criminal Justice Advisory Committee in promoting the value and necessity of adequate and accessible information in the strategic management and planning of justice reforms.

Prison Population Management and Reduction: Through a number of carefully planned and monitored policy and program innovations designed to minimize delay in processing detainees and to reduce the incidence of avoidable admissions to the county prison, the committee has played an important role in safely reducing jail crowding and the corresponding costs of local incarceration to the taxpayers. These include faster transfer of state-sentenced inmates out of the Delaware County Prison to a state institution; expedited hearings and release-processing due to videoconferencing; expansion of pretrial and probation and parole supervision options, such as electronic monitoring, new halfway house facilities, and a community service program in lieu of weekend sentences; standardized good-time policy at the Delaware County Prison; and changes in sentencing and negotiation practices to reduce the incidence of state-sentenced offenders serving time in the Delaware County Prison.

Revenue Generation: Revised fee structures have been implemented in a number of areas ranging from standard court costs to community service fees, and the Board of Judges recently approved a Delaware County Criminal Justice Advisory Committee proposal to add a restitution processing fee to the list. This ties into parallel activity expanding the use of credit cards at both common pleas and district justice levels to improve collection rates for fines, costs, fees, and restitution for crime victims.

Court Administration and Docket Management: Because the number of judges and related court personnel has not kept pace with the increase in caseloads for many years, a number of initiatives have been taken to streamline procedures and otherwise to try to relieve pressure on the common pleas docket. In addition to videoconferencing and other changes already mentioned, refinements also have been made to expand the Accelerated Rehabilitation disposition (pretrial diversion) process; to develop additional sentencing alternatives in the district justice courts; use a master instead of common pleas judge to handle bail and habeas hearings and *Gagnon II* hearings for selected probation and parole violators; and grant funding to support a criminal case-management project ("gatekeeper project") to assist the court in early identification and appropriate processing of cases eligible for intermediate punishment, especially those with drug and alcohol dependencies.

Other Works in Progress: Following extensive planning work by the Day Reporting Center Subcommittee, a satellite probation office/day reporting center opened in Upper Darby early in 1997. This adds a major program option for handling cases at the pretrial, sentencing, and violation stages of the process. A second day reporting center recently has been added in the City of Chester, which, together with Upper Darby, accounts for a large percentage of all criminal cases in the county.

Through still another Pennsylvania Commission on Crime and Delinquency-funded project, work is underway towards developing a computerized manual that lists and provides standardized information fields about all diagnostic and intervention resources available to the court in Delaware County. This includes criminal justice system resources, other government resources, and resources in the private sector, and is intended as a tool to assist all decisionmakers in the criminal process.

Impact Assessment

As Mark Moore has noted at this conference, strategic management starts with accountability of systems and participants to each other and to funding and political oversight agencies as well as to the public. This requires ongoing monitoring and evaluation of the implementation and impact of innovations. Due perhaps to the staunchly Republican tradition of Delaware County, changes initiated as a result of action by the Delaware County Criminal Justice Advisory Committee routinely are viewed as "investments" for which it is important to be clear about the costs, risks, and anticipated returns, and to monitor their performance record carefully and make adjustments, if necessary (boost investment if better, reduce if worse than expected). Consequently, all of the changes introduced as a result of Delaware County Criminal Justice Advisory Committee activity are monitored as closely as possible to assess their impact in both the short and longer term (see Figure 5.3). Perhaps of most immediate interest to the taxpayers, the combined cost savings and revenues attributable to the Delaware County Criminal Justice Advisory Committee initiatives so far conservatively may be estimated in the millions of dollars, largely due to savings in jail-bed costs at the county prison.

FIGURE 5.3: Delaware County Criminal Justice Advisory Committee Activity and Impact Data Record

ACTION NUMBER:	Sequentially assigned number to track total number of changes
DATE:	Date change implemented
ACTION:	Brief description of the action/change undertaken
TYPE OF CHANGE:	For example, policy, program, procedure, technology, staff, other
AGENCIES:	Agencies centrally involved in implementing change
IMPACT FOCUS:	For example, reduce admissions, length of stay, other benefits
IMPACT THEORY:	Logic of expected reduction/benefit (such as reduce decision-delays)
IMPACT SIZE:	Size of estimated/documented impact (for example, jail bed days saved)

COST ITEMS:	Cost items associated with change [staff, and so forth]
COST AMOUNTS:	Dollar estimate
SOURCE OF FUNDS:	For example, None, PCCD, Federal grant, county grant, other

Sustaining Momentum

As the focus of the committee continues to expand and the impact of many of its ongoing efforts in other areas begin to be felt, the benefits of the hard work that all of its participants have invested in the Delaware County Criminal Justice Advisory Committee process to this point undoubtedly will continue to register on all of the dimensions of effectiveness, efficiency, and fairness on which improvements are being sought. Although it has operated for four years now, there is full agreement on the committee that its successes to date are only the tip of the iceberg in terms of the potential for further change and innovation that can be achieved in the coming months and years.

The intuitive value of the type of process outlined here is not hard to grasp; the potential payoff of systematically attempting to harness the collective will, imagination, and extensive expertise of the system's most influential actors, to the task of system improvement is self-evidently appealing. What is generally less appreciated is the fact that initiating, managing, and sustaining such an endeavor requires no less of a political and financial commitment, especially in its start-up period, than any other project aimed at reducing crowding or otherwise improving the system. This is especially important in the early phases, when information development tasks that later may become much more routine tend to be more resource- and time-intensive as they are tackled the first time (Harland, 1991).

For purposes of the main inquiry at the present conference, an exciting aspect the Delaware County Criminal Justice Advisory Committee approach is the overriding emphasis that it places on systematically seeking and using the best available information to guide its activities in all of the broad senses of "what" and "works" outlined earlier in this chapter. This includes interest in learning more about the way the system is doing business currently, to develop an informed and shared understanding of the nature of existing problems and opportunities; learning more about the availability, feasibility, and likely impact of other options worth trying; and drawing lessons from organizationa management theory and research useful in sustaining and enhancing the performance of the forum itself and the likely adoption and implementation of the innovations it promotes.

Equally significant is the impetus and pressure that the Delaware County Criminal Justice Advisory Committee's example provides for generating a similar "information culture" and commitment to comparable value and policy-driven leadership and management approaches within the individual agencies participating. This is critical because, within the global policy framework and climate for innovation established by entities such as the Delaware County Criminal Justice Advisory Committee, it is at the individual agency level that specific program development and individual case-management improvements will ultimately flounder or flourish.

A Systematic Approach to Program Development

Paralleling their work in the policy area, the National Institute of Corrections also has supported related initiatives over the last several years designed more narrowly to improve the rate and quality of program development within community corrections agencies throughout the United States. Employing a team-building approach comparable to its work with intermediate sanctions policy groups, emphasis in this narrower context has been on finding ways to spur successful correctional program innovation through a hands-on collaboration between national technical assistance and training experts and agency planning, research, administrative, and line staff, applying best general principles to the assessment and improvement of local program-development capabilities and products.

One of the National Institute of Corrections' program development projects, from 1992 to 1994, involving teams from six sites in five different states, was directed by a group of Temple University faculty, consisting of the authors of the present paper and others. One of the early needs we identified was for an economical way to distill the sizable literature on program development and organizational management and change into a practical training and technical assistance tool that would serve at least two purposes. First, as an instructional aid, it should summarize succinctly the main ingredients of what might be considered a model program development process. Second, in more of a technical assistance function, it should serve as a diagnostic tool for consultants and site personnel themselves, to identify strengths and weaknesses in the agency's or jurisdiction's approach to program development in general, and where they stand with respect to any specific program development activity they happen to be engaged in at a particular point in time. A product of this challenge is the grid of program development "Phases and Tasks" in Figure 5.4.

For purposes of our present discussion, the program development model outlined in Figure 5.4, and explained in more detail in the narrative description of each cell, reproduced as Appendix A, at the end of this chapter, is instructive in several ways. First, the range and complexity of the various activities it encompasses mirror the conclusion drawn earlier with respect to the difficulty of individual sentencing decisions; it is an interdisciplinary and multifaceted undertaking, in which information about which particular correctional interventions may or may not reduce recidivism constitutes only one, albeit critical, piece of the puzzle.

Second, it reinforces the foregoing point by isolating the conceptually discrete phase of program design, represented by Column 3 of the model, and during which information about what programs or program components seem likely to "work" most obviously will be relevant guideposts, from the far broader context of program development, represented by Figure 5.4 in its entirety.

Significant errors or omissions in any of the other phases may affect the likelihood of successful adoption and implementation, as much as or more than failure to factor the best sources of "what works" information into decisions about matching the target population defined in the first cell of the program design column with the various selection, intake, intervention, staffing, and other design features in the rest of the column.[9] That said, however, the quality of each of those features, and of the innovation as a whole, obviously cannot help but be improved to the extent that decisionmakers in charge of making choices in this phase of the process become more accustomed to doing so on the basis of the best available sources of "what works" information.[10] This is more likely, in turn, the more they are empowered to do so by being afforded access and training as to the necessary knowledge, skills, and tools for the job.

Structuring the Choice of Options that Work[11]

One such tool is the Correctional Program Assessment Inventory (CPAI) discussed by Don Andrews (*see* Chapter 6). Although still in the development stage, it represents a significant step forward in meeting a need for what the author describes as "psychometrically sound and practically useful approaches to the assessment of the potential of particular

FIGURE 5.4: A Systematic Approach to Program Development (Phases and Tasks)

1 Define Problem	2 Set Goals and Objectives	3 Design Program	4 Develop Action Plan	5 Develop plan for Monitoring Program Implementation	6 Develop Outcome Evaluation Plan	7 Initiate the Program Plan
Describe history of problem	Write goal statements	Define target population	List resources and cost projections	Design monitoring instruments	Develop outcome measures	Initiate action plan
Identify stakeholders	Seek participation in goal statements	Define client selection procedures	Describe resource aquisition or reallocation plan	Assign responsibility for data collection, storage and analysis	Specify research design	Coordinate activities
Document need for change	Write outcome objectives for each goal	Describe intake procedures	Specify dates by which implementation tasks will be accomplished	Develop information system capacities	Identify potential confounding factors	Begin monitoring
Analyze the data	Specify an impact model	Define program components	Assign responsibility for implementation tasks	Develop mechanisms to provide feedback to staff, clients, and stakeholders	Identify users and uses of evaluation results	Make adjustments to program plan
Examine causes	Identify needs and opportunities for interagency collaboration	Describe sequence of activities	Develop mechanisms of self-regulation		Reassess entire program plan	Examine prerequisites for evaluation
Examine previous interventions		Write job descriptions	Specify plan to maintain support base			Collect and analyze evaluation data
Identify barriers and supports		Define staff skills and training needs	Anticipate resistance and develop responses			Reassessment—ongoing for life of program
← Review	← Review	← Review	← Review	← Review	← Review	

interventions in terms of their ability to reduce the chances of reoffending" (Andrews, 1995, 2).

A related tool for decisionmakers who must choose between contending correctional options is presented in Figure 5.5. Although obviously considerably cruder than the Correctional Program Assessment Inventory, it has the advantage of structuring the assessment along a broader array of criteria than simply the dimension of rehabilitative potential. It is a working tool that can be used by individuals or in groups, to structure decision-making at the individual case level, or for program or policy development purposes. It is designed around the premise that decisions most commonly reduce to a matter of choice between a couple of leading contenders, about which decisionmaker(s) will have at least a general understanding going into the assessment and selection process. The choices usually will include a reform or innovation option (styled Option A in Figure 5.5) versus the status quo, or problem option (Option B in Figure 5.5).[12]

To use the instrument in Figure 5.5 as a basis for making choices about sanctioning options, participants in the assessment begin by listing, in Column I, the major goals against which they think the soundness of their decision most fairly should be evaluated. In one sense, this will be no more than specifying the immediate problems facing the decisionmaker(s) involved, such as preventing recidivism or reducing crowding of correctional facilities.

At another level, it requires reflection upon other important goals within which such immediate objectives must be pursued. These often may be spelled out in an agency's broader mission statement, or derive from similarly general goals of the system as a whole, such as operating within acceptable limits of public safety (crime and recidivism risks), justice for offenders and for victims, cost-conscious management of resources, and so on.

Although not intended to be an exhaustive listing, the criteria included in Figure 5.5 are representative of the most common dimensions of concern from the justice literature. Their generality and importance have been confirmed repeatedly by participants in a variety of training and conference settings over the last several years. Consequently, although different cases, problems, or change situations obviously will generate their own lists of goal statements, as will different decisionmakers, in all probability, they will tend towards some variant of the illustrative factors in Figure 5.5.

FIGURE 5.5: Rational Assessment Matrix: Choosing Between Correctional Options

SECTION ONE — Goal or Impact Measure on Which Comparison of Options is Being Made	SECTION TWO — Rank Order of Importance Assigned to Goal [1, 2, 3, 4, etc.]	SECTION THREE — Comparative Rating — Option A: _____ versus Option B: _____						SECTION FOUR — Row subtotal for each goal listed [+2 to -2]
		Option A is Much Better [+2]	Option A is Some-what Better [+1]	A and B are About Equal [0]	Option B is Some-what Better [-1]	Option B is Much Better [-2]	Unsure Need More Info [0]	
Crime reduction (general deterrence)								
Recidivism reduction (rehabilitation/incapacitation/specific deterrence)								
Appropriate level of retribution ('fit' with crime seriousness)								
Reduce disparity/increase equity								
Reduce delay—expedite processing								
Reduce jail population levels (admissions/length of stay)								
Victim benefits (restitution; other)								
Offender benefits (employment; education; etc.)								
Legality/constitutionality								
Reduce financial costs to system								
Satisfy key constituent opinion (public/professional/political)								
Other (specify _____)								

Source: New York Times, May 12, 1996

Preliminary discussion should focus on developing a shared sense of the meaning of the goals listed, whether from the examples in the table, or additions entered in the empty rows. Participants also may wish to assess separately any subcomponents of the measures already specified (for example, rehabilitative versus incapacitation impact in the "recidivism reduction" row; or employment, education, other gains, in the "offender-assistance" row). To the extent possible, each goal should be operationally defined as early as possible, by specifying in advance the most appropriate measurable indicators of its achievement. In practice, this step may occur later in the process, after a clearer definition of the problem and response options has been developed.

Step two in the assessment exercise requires consensus building around the rank order of importance attributed to each goal. The results of this discussion are entered in Column II, with the most important criterion assigned a value of 1, the next a 2, and so forth. Tied rankings are not fatal to the exercise, but should be broken wherever possible by further discussion.

Step three is perhaps the most deceptive and time-consuming part of the exercise summarized in Figure 5.5, requiring a detailed description (definition) of the two options to be compared. This will include the main actors and intervention measures involved, ideally requiring thorough mapping of processing routes, time-frames, and attendant resource and cost allocations for each option under assessment. Based on this detailed understanding of what each option entails, step four then involves identifying and applying the best logical and empirical evidence available, to make a judgment about which of the two options will rate better than the other on each of the criteria listed in Column I.

Starting with the goals ranked highest, participants enter a check mark, row by row, in one of the columns in section III. If the leading reform candidate (Option A) is judged to look "much better" than existing practice (Option B), in terms of likely impact on jail populations, for example, a check would be marked in the column headed A++ on the row in which that goal is listed; a check under the column head A+ would indicate an assessment that Option A was "better" than Option B on that dimension; the "About Equal" column would be checked for those criteria on which the conclusion is that one option is likely to be as good or bad as the other; column B+ would be checked if Option B looks "better"; column B++would be checked if Option B looks "much better"; and, very importantly, the column headed 'don't know' should be checked if the available theoretical and empirical information simply is not adequate to make a decision on anything other than blind faith or unexplicated instinct.

Next, participants can enter in column IV the numerical scores corresponding to the check mark on every row (A++ = 2; A+ = 1; About equal = 0; B+ = -1; B++ = -2; and Don't know = D/K). These scores give at a glance an indication of the number of dimensions on which the proposed innovation (Option A) fares better and worse than its competition, and a rough indicator for each criterion of how much better or worse. Obviously, if column IV ends up being filled with positive scores of 2 on every measure, the case for proceeding to adopt the new option appears very strong. If it scores well on many of the criteria, but poorly on one or more ranked as being highly important, however, the decision is less clear.

One advantage of the admittedly crude-scoring technique is that any negative scores for an innovation that otherwise is judged to fit well with a majority of the goals identified, need not be taken necessarily as grounds for rejection. Rather, they can be used to identify dimensions on which design revisions might be considered at the outset, to strengthen the original conception of what the reform option would look like, and directly address the weaknesses that caused it to score poorly on a particular measure in the first analysis. Entries in the D/K column obviously highlight areas in which further information might be collected and/or where early monitoring and evaluating of the data ought to be emphasized if a decision is taken to proceed in advance of obtaining such information.

The framework for assessing decision options encapsulated in Figure 5.5, is designed to be useful at two levels. First, it is intended to capture as succinctly but as comprehensively as possible the most crucial elements of what is required to satisfy the minimum standards of rational decision-making—clarity of goals, options, and information linking the two.

Second, it is a tool that may be used as a sort of worksheet to guide those engaged in actual decision situations, whether to adopt, continue, modify, or reject a particular option, and whether as a disposition in an individual case, or as a matter of choice between one criminal justice program or policy and another. It may be used by decisionmakers seeking to hold themselves accountable to the intellectual and scientific rigor of such a process, and to challenge others who would impose their own options for perhaps more ideological, emotional, or purely political reasons.

In each instance, the instrument serves as a reminder of the major conceptual stages in the decision process, and of the complexity of goals, value judgments, and theoretical and empirical information that must be weighed in selecting the most rationally compelling course of action. It highlights the importance of clarifying and prioritizing goals, and of identifying and defining target populations and other baseline details of the principal options for achieving them. Insofar as it exposes inconsistencies or lack of fit between important goals and aspects of a program or policy being assessed, the instrument also helps to pinpoint design weaknesses and corresponding areas for reformulation and improvement. In addition, by explicitly and precisely recognizing gaps in our knowledge about the relative ability of either option to deliver on the assumptions and expectations underlying the major goal statements, the instrument exposes deficiencies in available evaluation data and information systems that must be remedied in order to inspire any confidence that a truly informed choice has been made.

Finally, and perhaps most importantly, by emphasizing the significance of measurably defined objectives and evaluation standards, and the corresponding role of demonstrably relevant performance and outcome information, the instrument demonstrates the vital need for close and ongoing collaboration between the key decisionmaker(s) and the research scientist under a rational decision-making approach (Harland and Harris, 1984, 1987). This type of collaborative, group process approach to program or policy development and evaluation generally is known as the action-research model.

Propounded almost half a century ago by Kurt Lewin (1947), it has been described as involving a sequence or circle of problem analysis, fact-finding, conceptualization, development, selection, and execution of action responses, more fact-finding or evaluation, and then a repetition of this whole circle of activities (Sanford, 1970). It is an approach reflected in the program development phases and tasks summarized in Figure 5.4. In the long run, it may be the best response not only to the central question asked at the outset of this conference—how to maximize the use of "what works" information to spur correctional innovation—but to the still more pressing need to assure the continued and improved development of such information in the first place.

Endnotes

[1] Earlier conferences took place in 1993 and 1994 in Philadelphia and Seattle, respectively.

2 Program design is only one phase of a much larger process of program development. It is an increasingly voiced belief in the planned change literature that overall program success or failure may be influenced as much or more by how systematically and well each phase of that process is tackled than by any particular strength or weakness in the program concept itself. The process of policy and program development, or more generally, a systematic approach to innovation, is discussed at length later in this paper.

3 The explanation for the absence of a unified judicial voice complaining about this problem as well as others that individual judges, almost to a person, always can be counted on to raise—such as mandatory sentencing and mechanistic sentencing guidelines—may be that judges less than perhaps any other "agency" in the system rarely function as a policy or program development "team." Except for jurisdictions with a strong administrative president or judge, they meet casually and are not used to functioning as policy groups; individual discretion is the rule of the day. This has implications for discussion later in this paper of policy and program development teams, especially within single agencies.

4 "Although the criminal trial on the issue of guilt is strictly a formal procedure, the determination of what is to be done with a convicted offender is often a rather informal one" (President's Commission on Law Enforcement 1967, 141-150).

5 Although not often a problem, especially since recent Supreme Court decisions seem virtually to have emasculated the doctrine of proportionality as a constraint on state sentencing power (*see*, for example, *Harmelin v. Michigan,* 1991), constitutional problems in community- based sentences might occur, for example, if a Jewish offender were required to perform community service for a Catholic charitable organization.

6 Less-obvious reforms of the sentencing process that bring a more dynamic quality to the case-specific task are various approaches emerging within the "restorative justice" movement, including victim-offender mediation sessions, and fascinating extensions of that idea in indigenous people's tribunals such as "circle sentencing" practiced in parts of Alaska (Stuart, 1996). These latter practices, because of an expanded emphasis on situational and community causes and responsibilities in responding to crime, seem particularly promising mechanisms for combining case-specific information development to spur thinking and action about more policy and program-level changes to prevent and respond to similar offending in the future (*see* generally, Galaway and Hudson, 1996).

7 Although the present discussion focuses on the use more than the generation of "what works" information, there is obviously still a daunting amount of work to do in the latter area. For a detailed and ambitious proposal of the heavy investment that it will take if we are ever to develop a more definitive body of "what works" information in the field of correctional intervention, *see* Palmer (1995).

[8] Delaware County was selected as the jurisdiction with which, as a consultant to National Institute of Corrections and Pennsylvania Commission on Crime and Delinquency, the paper's lead author has had most extensive and recent opportunity to observe in depth. Other sites with which we have had similar although less intensive experience in the past, however, undoubtedly could provide equally rich case studies. A particularly impressive statewide example of a strategic management forum in which the role and value of research and evaluation information is also well in evidence is to be found in the work over a number of years of the Colorado Criminal Justice Commission, in Denver, Colorado.

[9] It should be obvious that the approach outlined in Figure 5.4 is not intended to imply a rigid sequence of phases and activities, proceeding from the top left to the bottom right of the grid. Aspects of the process may take place simultaneously, and, as the arrow-loops at the foot of each column indicate, many of the individual tasks may have to be revisited based on the outcome of another part of the process. Rather, the Phases and Tasks summary is intended to convey an overall image of the key ingredients in the process, and to serve as a mechanism for identifying and remedying omissions and errors that may jeopardize program success, regardless of the order or timing of their occurrence.

[10] This point may sound self-evidently unhelpful, until it is realized how many of the components of correctional programs in agencies all over the country were developed in other ways, such as because they happened to be a favorite, or perhaps because they were the only approach known to a senior treatment staff member involved in the design process.

[11] This section of the paper is adapted from Harland (1996b).

[12] The term *incarceration guidelines* is a far more accurate description of extant efforts to structure judicial discretion than the broader idea of sentencing guidelines. While the former focuses upon the in, out, and length of incarceration issues, the latter must contend with the additional question of out-under-what-conditions, or the choice among multiple levels and types of community sanctions. Although the former has been the subject of extensive scholarly and practitioner attention (for an excellent although self-proclaimed partisan review, *see* Gottfredson and Gottfredson, 1984). The latter remains relatively unexplored except for very preliminary commentaries on the need to develop a guidelines approach to intermediate sanctions (Knapp, 1988; Von Hirsch, 1992).

References

Andrews, D. A. 1995. *Assessing Program Elements for Risk Reduction: The Correctional Program Assessment Inventory*. Paper presented at the Research to Results Conference of the International Community Corrections Association, October, Ottawa, Ontario.

Bonta, J. 1996. Risk-needs Assessment and Treatment. In A. T. Harland, ed. *Choosing Correctional Options that Work: Defining the Demand and Evaluating the Supply*. Thousand Oaks, California: Sage Publications.

Byrne J., A. Lurigio, and J. Petersilia, eds. 1991. *Smart Sentencing: The Emergence of Intermediate Sanctions*.Thousand Oaks, California: Sage Publications.

Cullen, F. T., J. P. Wright, and B. K. Applegate. 1996. Control in the Community: The Limits of Reform? In A. T. Harland, ed. *Choosing Correctional Options that Work: Defining the Demand and Evaluating the Supply*. Thousand Oaks, California: Sage Publications.

Galaway, B., and J. Hudson, eds. 1996. *Restorative Justice: International Perspectives*. Monsey, New York: Criminal Justice Press.

Gendreau, P. 1996. The Principles of Effective Intervention with Offenders. In A. T. Harland, ed. *Choosing Correctional Options that Work: Defining the Demand and Evaluating the Supply*. Thousand Oaks, California: Sage.

Gottfredson, M. R. and D. M. Gottfredson. 1984. Guidelines for Incarceration Decisions: A Partisan Review. *University of Illinois Law Review*. 2:801-827.

―――. 1988. *Decision-making in Criminal Justice: Toward the Rational Exercise of Discretion*. New York: Plenum Press.

Harland, A. T. 1991. Jail Crowding and the Process of Criminal Justice Policy Making. *Prison Journal*. 71:77-92.

―――, ed. 1996a. *Choosing Correctional Options that Work: Defining the Demand and Evaluating the Supply*. Thousand Oaks, California: Sage.

―――. 1996b. Correctional Options that Work: Structuring the Inquiry. In A. T. Harland, ed. *Choosing Correctional Options that Work: Defining the Demand and Evaluating the Supply*. Thousand Oaks, California: Sage.

Harland, A. T., and P. W. Harris. 1984. Developing and Implementing Alternatives to Incarceration: A Problem of Planned Change in Criminal Justice. *University of Illinois Law Review*. 2:319-364.

―――. 1987. Structuring the Development of Alternatives to Incarceration. In S. Gottfredson and S. McConville, eds. *America's Correctional Crisis*. Westport, Connecticut: Greenwood.

Harris, P. W., and S. Smith. 1996. Developing Community Corrections: An Implementation Perspective. In A. T. Harland, ed. *Choosing Correctional Options that Work: Defining the Demand and Evaluating the Supply*. Thousand Oaks, California: Sage.

Jones, P. R. 1996. Risk Prediction in Criminal Justice. In A. T. Harland, ed. *Choosing Correctional Options that Work: Defining the Demand and Evaluating the Supply*. Thousand Oaks, California: Sage.

Knapp, K. 1988. Assistance for Structured Sentencing Projects. Next Step: Non-imprisonment Guidelines. *Perspectives*. 12:8-10.

Langan, P. 1994. Between Prison and Probation: Intermediate Sanctions. *Science*. 264:791- 794.

Lewin, K. 1947. Group Decisions and Social Change. In T. M. Newcomb and E. L. Hartley, eds. *Readings in Social Psychology*. New York: Holt, Rinehart, and Winston.

McGarry, P., and M. M. Carter, eds. 1993. *The Intermediate Sanctions Handbook: Experiences and Tools for Policymakers*. Washington, D.C.: National Institute of Corrections.

Palmer, T. 1995. Programmatic and Nonprogrammatic Aspects of Successful Intervention: New Directions for Research. *Crime & Delinquency*. 41:101-131.

———. 1996. Programmatic and Nonprogrammatic Aspects of Successful Intervention. In A. T. Harland, ed. *Choosing Correctional Options that Work: Defining the Demand and Evaluating the Supply*. Thousand Oaks, California: Sage.

Petersilia, J. 1995. A Crime Control Rationale for Reinvesting in Community Corrections. *Prison Journal*. 75:479-496.

President's Commission on Law Enforcement and the Administration of Justice. 1967. *The Challenge of Crime in a Free Society*. Washington, D.C.: U.S. Department of Justice.

Sanford, R. 1970. Whatever Happened to Action Research? *Journal of Social Issues*. 26:4-19.

Stuart, B. 1996. Circle Sentencing: Turning Swords into Ploughshares. In B. Galaway and J. Hudson, eds. *Restorative Justice: International Perspectives*. Monsey, New York: Criminal Justice Press.

U.S. Advisory Commission on Intergovernmental Relations. 1993. *The Role of General Government Elected Officials in Criminal Justice*. Washington, D.C.: U.S. Advisory Commission on Intergovernmental Relations.

Von Hirsch, A. 1976. *Doing Justice: The Choice of Punishments*. New York: Hill and Wang.

———. 1992. Scaling Intermediate Punishments: A Comparison of Two Models. In J. Byrne, A. Lurigio, and J. Petersilia, eds. *Smart Sentencing: The Emergence of Intermediate Sanctions*. Thousand Oaks, California: Sage.

Winberg, A. Effective Communication. 1992. In J. Hudson, J. Mayne, and R. Thomlison, eds. *Action-oriented Evaluations in Organizations: Canadian Practices.* Toronto, Ontario: Wall and Emerson, Inc.

Yeager, M. G. 1992. *Survey of Client-specific Planning of Programs and Their Feasibility as an Alternative to Incarceration in Canada.* Ottawa, Ontario: Canada Solicitor General.

Appendix A
Narrative Overview to Figure 5.4
A Systematic Approach to Program Development:
Phases and Tasks

PHASE 1: Defining the Problem

** (a) Describe the history of the problem:

List critical events leading up to the agency's perception of the problem and its definition of the problem. What is the history of this problem and what attempts have been made to address it?

(b) Identify stakeholders:

Who are the key people in the agency, in other agencies in the community, in government, and so forth, who have an interest in this problem and may make attempts to change it? Are there different definitions of the problem, or what should be done about it?

(c) Document the need for change:

Where is the problem and how big is it? Collect data or examine existing data (own agency's or others) to determine the incidence, prevalence, and location of the problem. Identify characteristics of those affected by the problem. Types of data include the following: interview key informants (interview experts and stakeholders), consider social indicators (examine statistics), conduct and review needs assessments (conduct surveys), use a community forum (invite community members to share ideas).

(d) Analyze the data:

What patterns and relationships emerge? Do the data suggest different causes of the problem? Different solutions? Who are the proposed targets of the intervention? Begin defining characteristics of the target population (who will be reached or affected by the program?).

(e) Examine the causes of the problem:

What are the potential causes of (contributors to) the problem? How do different causal factors relate to one another? Types of causes may be individual, group, organizational, community, or social structural.

(f) Examine previous interventions:

What types of interventions have been tried to address this problem? What did they do? How effective were they? Has the agency considered different options before deciding on a particular course of change? Sources may include the following: experts or key participants, personnel in similar agencies, research and evaluation reports, government reports, and research journals

(g) Identify potential barriers and potential supports of change:

Consider a wide range of factors (physical, social, economic, educational, and political): who or what will support your proposal; who or what will present barriers? Formulate options for decreasing resistance and building support.

PHASE 2: Setting Goals and Objectives

(a) Write goal statements for the program: what is the broad mission of the program? What kind of change is expected? Goals provide direction for change; they organize different constituents around a common purpose.

(b) Seek participation in goal setting. Is there disagreement regarding the goals of the intervention? If so, who differs? Sources: stakeholders, community, potential targets, agency staff, interagency personnel, and research reports and publications

(c) Write outcome objectives for each goal. Outcome objectives refer to specific results (a change in the problem) that the program will try to achieve. Objectives should include four criteria: (1) a time frame by which the intended results are expected; (2) specification of the intended targets of change; (3) key result intended: clear specification of behavioral or attitudinal change expected, direction of change (up or down), and the magnitude of the change (how much?); and (4) criterion: a specific measure of the key result intended.

(d) Specify an Impact Model. Describe (1) the problem and the change expected, (2) the primary causes identified, and (3) the intervention (program). Are these three elements consistent with one another: program (intervention), specific causes (s) of the problem, and change(s) in the problem?

(e) Identify needs and opportunities for interagency collaboration: Consider the agency's external environment when attempting any kind of change. Where are the opportunities for collaboration? Examples: political support, shared information, exchange of services, joint intake and assessment, referrals, and cross-referrals.

*Review stage 1 and make any needed adjustments to the problem definition.

PHASE 3: Designing the Program (Writing the Blueprint)

Clients

(a) Define the characteristics of the target population (for example, age, sex, location, criminal record, employment, and so forth). These are people who are eligible for the program.

(b) Define the client selection procedures. How will targets be selected or recruited for participation in the program (for example, agency lists, advertising, referrals, and so forth)?

(c) Describe the intake procedures. How will clients be assessed and placed? How are clients introduced to the program? How can we be sure the program is taking the clients intended?

Service Delivery

(a) Define the component parts of the program (for example, counseling, vocational training, employment assistance, tutoring, and so forth).

(b) Describe the sequence of activities of the program: who does what to whom, in what order, and how much?

Staff

(a) Write job descriptions of staff; define major activities and responsibilities of each staff person.

(b) Define qualifications, training, and skills required for each staff position.

*Review phases 1-2 and make any necessary adjustments to the problem definition and objectives.

PHASE 4: Develop an Action Plan

Once the program design is complete, develop an action plan that specifies all the tasks that need to be completed to implement the design. For example, this might include: locating space, hiring and training staff, designing client forms, purchasing equipment and supplies. Then, set dates and assign responsibility for completion of each task.

(a) Identify resources needed: both human (program staff and supporting staff) and physical (salaries, equipment, rental space, supplies, and so forth). Make cost projections; estimate the amount of each resource required. Is the allocation of resources to different program components in balance with the priorities defined in the goal statement for the program?

(b) Plan to acquire and/or reallocate resources. You will need to acquire new resources and/or reallocate existing ones. Identify possible resource providers (for example, local businesses, government agencies, private granting agencies). Identify possible options for reallocating human or physical resources within the agency and invite participation from staff and managers in different departments.

(c) List all implementation tasks that need to be accomplished (hiring and training staff, designing client forms), and specify dates by which implementation tasks will be accomplished. List each task that needs to be completed, and set a realistic date for completion. Pay careful attention to the timing of each task (for example, intake forms are ready to go when the first clients arrive).

(d) Assign responsibilities for carrying out tasks of implementation. Assess the skills and expertise within your agency (and perhaps other agencies) and assign explicit responsibility to certain individuals to complete each of the tasks on the list by the specified date.

(e) Develop self-regulation and self-control mechanisms to ensure that staff follow program design procedures (for example, holding staff meetings, using legitimate authority, providing enabling resources, providing incentives, or specifying sanctions for noncompliance).

(f) Specify a plan to maintain the support base for the program. Continue to inform stakeholders of program progress and seek constructive criticism. Make plans to continue ongoing communication.

(g) Anticipate resistance and conflict (both intra-agency and inter-agency) and formulate strategies to respond.

*Review phases 1-3 and make any necessary adjustments to problem definition, objectives, or program design.

PHASE 5: Develop a Plan for Monitoring Program .Implementation

Develop a plan for collecting information to find out whether the program design (blueprint) is being carried out as planned (review phase 3). Identify gaps between the program on paper and the program in action, and make adjustments.

(a) Design instruments to collect monitoring data. Key questions:

- Clients—is program reaching the intended clients? Why or why not? How are they responding to the program?

- Staff—are staff adequately trained and qualified? Are they following job descriptions? Why or why not?

- Service delivery—are all the program services or components actually being administered as planned? Why or why not?

Four types of data can be used: (1) observational data, (2) service record data (program documents, client information,and so forth), (3) service provider data (staff perceptions), and (4) participant data (client perceptions)

(b) Locate expertise and designate responsibility for data collection, storage, and analysis. Who is good with data? Computers?

(c) Develop information-system capacities: estimate and locate the human and physical resources required to create, maintain, and adapt an effective information system for the program.

(d) Design mechanisms to provide feedback to clients, staff, and stakeholders about progress toward objectives.

*Review phases 1-4 and make any necessary adjustments to problem definition, objectives, program design, resource plan, or implementation.

PHASE 6: Develop a Plan for Evaluating Outcomes

Develop a research design for measuring program outcomes (intended change in the problem). Note that all planning, including formulation of an evaluation plan, precedes the actual start-up of the program.

(a) Develop outcome measures for each objective. Consider: validity (does the instrument measure what it is intended to measure?) and reliability (is the measure consistent?).

(b) Specify the research design:

- When will measures be collected, and how often? Will this be pre or post design? longitudinal design?

- What kind(s) of comparison group will be used? For example, will it be random assignment or nonequivalent control groups?

(c) Identify potential confounding factors (something other than the program which affects the outcome). Examples: biased selection (program clients differ from control subjects), biased attrition (clients drop out at higher rates than controls), or history (unanticipated events which bias outcome measures).

(d) Identify users and uses of evaluation results. Who will be interested in the results of the evaluation, and how will they use the information? If the evaluation is to be useful, it should serve the information needs of the agency and its stakeholders. Develop plans and assign responsibility for packaging and communicating evaluation results to different users.

(e) Reassess entire program plan before actually initiating the action plan

*Review phases 1-5 and make any necessary adjustments to problem definition, objectives, program design, resource plan, implementation, and/or monitoring.

PHASE 7. Initiating the Program Plan

(a) Initiate the plan: put the action plan into effect (phase 4 plan).

(b) Coordinate activities: integrate and orchestrate program components. Maintain consistency between written procedures and behavior; develop clear lines of communication with staff; pay attention to timing of tasks (phases 3 and 4 plans).

(c) Begin monitoring (phase 5 plan).

(d) Make adjustments to the program plan. As gaps are found between the program on paper and the programming action, plan to make necessary adjustments (for example, demand for services exceeds supply; resources prove inadequate, and so forth). All programs go through a growth stage; adjustments to the program design should be informed by data and carefully planned (phase 5 plan).

(e) Examine two prerequisites before beginning evaluation:

- Objectives must be clear, specific, and measurable (phase 2 plan).

- The program must have been sufficiently well-implemented to ensure that its critical elements have been carried out (phase 5 plan).

(f) Collect and analyze evaluation data (phase 6 plan).

(g) Provide feedback to users and stakeholders (phases 5 and 6 plans).

(h) Reassessment—continue to monitor the implementation of the program. Good programs need continuous reevaluation and readjustment.

Assessing Program Elements for Risk Reduction: The Correctional Program Assessment Inventory

6

Donald A. Andrews, Ph.D.
Department of Psychology
Carleton University
Ottawa, Ontario

Introduction

This report is concerned with the structured assessment of the crime-reduction potential of criminal justice and correctional interventions with offenders. The particular assessment instrument reviewed is the Correctional Program Assessment Inventory (CPAI) (Gendreau and Andrews, 1994). The CPAI approach is best understood in the context of what has been established to date from controlled studies of the effects on reoffending of different interventions with groups of individual offenders. To better understand the findings of the controlled outcome studies, an appreciation of research on the predictors of criminal behavior is helpful. Thus, a description of the Correctional Program Assessment Inventory is preceded by overviews of the prediction and intervention research literatures.

Prediction of Criminal Behavior

The systematic and quantitative risk/need assessment of offenders is now widely practiced and accepted in criminal justice and corrections. With some practical, ethical, and theoretical limitations of offender-based risk/need assessment acknowledged (Jones, 1994), there is now an unprecedented consensus in regard to several issues such as the following (Andrews and Bonta, 1994):

(1) The best-validated of the major risk/need factors include antisocial attitudes and cognitive-emotional states, antisocial associates, a history of antisocial behavior, indicators of an antisocial personality pattern, along with problems in the areas of home, school/ work, leisure, and substance abuse.

(2) The predictive accuracy of risk/need assessments increases with the number and variety of major risk factors assessed (as the major risk/need factors were noted above), use of multiple sources of information (for example, interviews and review of records), an extended follow-up (opening the window wider for the detection of reoffending by high-risk cases), and reassessment to detect changes in risk/need.

(3) The major risk factors are acknowledged within a number of the most empirically defensible theories of crime (for example, social learning perspectives) and the weaker theoretical perspectives (such as anomie, labeling, and deterrence approaches) are being reformulated to accommodate the wealth of empirical support for the major risk factors.

(4) The predictive validity and practical value of risk/need assessments are appreciated across a wide variety of correctional and forensic settings (institutional and community) and across a diverse correctional and forensic clientele.

(5) Many issues remain to be explored, including maximizing predictive accuracy and utility; however, predictive accuracy rates in the area of 75 to 85 percent are typically way above what could be expected by chance and are highly meaningful (albeit not 100 percent).

The impressive validities of offender-based risk/need assessment, however, should not deflect attention away from the matter of the importance of the type and quality of correctional treatment services delivered to offenders. Although minor compared to the thousands of studies of offender-based risk/need factors, the published research literature has more than 500 controlled studies of the effects of criminal justice and correctional interventions. These studies suggest that type and quality of criminal justice/correctional interventions may contribute to reduced reoffending in a way that is related to offender-based risk/need. The intervention studies also reveal that some very popular prevention and rehabilitation strategies (for example, deterrence-based interventions) actually increase crime relative to the clear crime-reduction achievements of alternative programs that are sensitive to risk and criminogenic need (for example, cognitive-behavioral programs focusing on the major risk/need factors). We now turn to an overview of the effectiveness literature.

Overview of Effective Correctional Treatment

There is a new appreciation of the state of the criminal justice and correctional intervention literature (*see* chapters one through four in the collection edited by McGuire, 1995; *see* reviews sponsored by IARCA such as Gendreau, 1994), and that appreciation makes it possible to speak seriously of an evidence-based approach to effective correctional practice. Evidence-based practice, by definition, will develop and change in accordance with the growing body of research on criminal conduct. At the same time, practice will be informed and guided by legal, ethical, sociocultural, and political-economic considerations, along with developments in related fields of service and science, and with evaluated applications of informed hunches and visions. For now, however, what do the systematic reviews of the controlled outcome literature have to say about effective approaches to reduced reoffending? First, we take a broad look at the outcome literature:

(1) Simply on the basis of the large number of controlled outcome studies now available, it is reasonable to expect that some evidence-based guidelines can be derived. There is a substantial number of controlled outcome studies in the research literature with more than 500 written in the English language and perhaps as many as an additional 250 in Europe alone (Losel, 1995).

(2) The overall average effect of interventions generally is agreed to be in the area of .10 (*see* Andrews, 1994; Losel, 1995). This suggests that when the overall base rate of reoffending is 50 percent, the recidivism rate in the treatment group would be 45 percent compared to 55 percent in the comparison group: that is, a 10 percent difference suggesting lower

recidivism among treated offenders (or an average effect size of .10). Thus, in terms of both the overall number of studies and the overall positive (albeit mild) average effect of treatment, it is reasonable to anticipate some guidance toward evidence-based practice.

(3) There is great variability from study to study in both the magnitude and the direction of estimates of effect size. While the average effect size suggests that the "treated" offenders are recidivating at a rate 10 percent lower than the "untreated" offenders, in some studies the difference in recidivism rates favorable to treatment is much greater than 10 percent and in some studies the "treated" cases even are found to be reoffending at higher rates than the "untreated" cases. Some of this variability may be due to methodological factors (for example, sample size or random assignment). Some may be due to setting conditions (for example, community versus prison). Some may be due to differences in the cases treated (for example, risk levels), and some may be due to differences in type of treatment (for example, official punishment versus human service or cognitive-behavioral service versus psychodynamic treatments). Once again, this time because of the variability found in the magnitude and direction of the outcomes, there is good reason to expect guidance from the research literature on evidence-based effective practice.

(4) Our focus is on treatment-related factors, so let us get the methodological/design issues out of the way for now (although we will return to research issues with the Correctional Program Assessment Inventory). There is no doubt that some of the differences in outcome may be traced to study characteristics other than treatment (Andrews et al., 1990; Lipsey, 1990; Losel, 1995). Still, however, every major quantitative review of the outcome literature that has addressed the issue, agrees that effects of treatment continue to be found even with statistical controls for methodological/research design considerations. Very positively then, some of the variation in more or less positive outcomes and in more or less negative outcomes found in the literature may be traced to aspects of intervention that are within the range of influence of legislators, policymakers, police, judges, program funders, program designers, program managers, program supervisors, and program workers.

Characteristics of Promising Correctional Treatments

What are the characteristics of promising correctional treatments as they may be derived from the existing controlled outcome literature? In positive terms, what characteristics of correctional treatment are associated with average effect sizes greater than that overall average of 10 percent? In negative terms, but equally important, what are the characteristics of intervention programs that actually increased rather than decreased reoffending? Evidence-based practice with an interest in reduced reoffending would want to introduce the positive and reduce use of the negative. Following is a sample of the characteristics of effective programs which, as will be shown, shaped the content and style of the Correctional Program Assessment Inventory:

(1) Human-service delivery in the context of criminal sanctions (official punishment)

Average reductions in recidivism are much greater in studies of human service in diversionary, community, and custody settings than are the average effects of variation in type or severity of official punishment in the absence of treatment (which, in fact, tend to be negative). In brief, apart from short-term incapacitation effects, the action in regard to reduced reoffending resides not in the criminal sanction but in the delivery of human service under a variety of setting conditions that may be established by the criminal sanction.

(2) Risk classification

To whom do we offer more intensive human service? When actually explored within studies—as done by Andrews et al. (1990), and in the Carleton University extended databanks—lower risk cases do as well or better with minimal service, while reduction of the recidivism of higher risk cases is enhanced with more intensive human service. Interestingly, Lipsey (1990) and the Carleton University group with their expanded databank also found that the same effect when reports that did not differentiate between risk groups within their samples were coded as involving samples that were lower versus higher risk cases (for example, according to prior record). The risk effect now is considered obvious by even the most sophisticated researchers in the field (for example, by Lipsey, 1995). How could we find large reductions in recidivism rates among lower-risk cases when the chances of recidivism initially are slight? Yet still, researchers such as Antonowicz and Ross (1994), on the basis of a highly selected sample of studies and an unspecified definition of risk, conclude that the effects of treatment are equal for lower and higher risk cases. Open to whatever the research findings on this issue ultimately show, this point should be clear: It is the higher-risk cases which account for the vast amount of recidivistic crime, and more intensive treatment for higher risk cases promises much greater crime control than does intensive treatment for those of lower risk! However, there continues to be no evidence of reduced recidivism on the part of high risk/need offenders who are also very egocentric.

(3) Criminogenic need

What are the more appropriate intermediate targets if an ultimate objective is reduced reoffending? Criminogenic needs are dynamic risk factors, risk factors on which people may change, and change is associated with subsequent variation in reoffending. Elsewhere (Andrews and Bonta, 1994) we list more promising and less promising intermediate targets according to the prediction, treatment, and theoretical literature. As suggested in our brief review of the prediction literature, we know something about the major dynamic risk factors: antisocial cognitions and emotional states, antisocial associates, indicators of antisocial personality such as weak self-control and problem solving skills, a behavioral repertoire that is weak in the area alternatives to antisocial behavior, weak and problematic ties in the areas of home, school/work and leisure, and substance abuse. In brief, for enhanced reduction of reoffending, match the intermediate targets of human service with the dynamic-risk factors revealed by systematic assessments of criminogenic need.

(4) General responsivity principle (a positive statement)

What styles and modes of service are most promising for cases identified as higher risk through whatever combination of particular criminogenic needs? To an overwhelming degree, in every systematic quantitative review but one that was seriously flawed, the most effective styles and modes of service used behavioral and cognitive behavioral strategies of influence that focused on skill development in a variety of areas of life. In brief, higher-risk cases may present with more than one criminogenic need, and these needs are best addressed by methods that make systematic use of reinforcement, graduated practice, modeling, and cognitive restructuring.

(5) General responsivity principle (a negative statement)

What styles and modes of service are best avoided? In contrast to the cognitive-behavioral strategy described above, the least-effective interventions were narrow in focus, concentrated on punishment (for example, deterrence and just desert-based programs), followed widely disseminated models based on clinical sociology (for example, nonservice oriented programs based on labeling, anomie, subcultural and nonbehavioral differential association perspectives); and/or followed classic psychodynamic, nondirective, relationship-oriented and evocative models. In brief, and once again in more positive terms, use styles and modes of service that are not only appropriately targeted but are matched with the learning styles of functioning human beings rather than the depersonalized conceptions of people represented in social location and social reaction theories that deny individual differences.

(6) Specific responsivity considerations

As described elsewhere (Andrews and Bonta, 1994), interpersonally and cognitively immature clients require structured services while the more psychologically mature client may respond to more evocative styles of service; interpersonally anxious clients, in particular, respond poorly to highly confrontational services; other specific considerations also may be applicable for some subtypes of offenders. Age, gender, ethnicity, psychopathy, and motivational considerations are additional high priority research issues in the domain of responsivity.

(7) Therapeutic integrity

Involvement of the researcher in the design and delivery of the evaluated service is an important source of enhanced reductions in reoffending. More than simply experimenter bias, this factor primarily reflects integrity of treatment delivery as indicated by the training and clinical supervision of the service deliverers as well as monitoring of service process and intermediate gain.

(8) Other treatment-relevant factors

Other factors associated with enhanced success include community rather than custodial settings, adequate dosage, as well as additional factors based more on clinical wisdom than large-scale research validation.

The documented ability to sort people into lower- through higher-risk categories, the documented validity of dynamic risk (or "need") factors, and the finding that some interventions are effective while others are ineffective combine to underscore our responsibility to begin to assess the risk-reduction potential of prevention and rehabilitation programming as seriously as we assess offender-based risk/need. It is no longer sensible for prevention programs and programs offered under the rubric of protection of the public from recidivistic crime to be designed or delivered without reference to what is known about both risk/need and effective and ineffective correctional treatment.

The author is not arguing against rationales for intervention based on just desert, restorative justice, incapacitation, or even general deterrence except where those rationales also imply that the imposition of just, retributive or restorative sanctions will protect the public from recidivistic crime. The Correctional Program Assessment Inventory (Gendreau and Andrews, 1994) is our response to the clear promise of an assessment instrument that was sensitive to the risk/need research and would serve to assist in identifying the recidivism-reduction potential of ongoing or planned interventions.

The Correctional Program Assessment Inventory is still in the developmental stage and its shape and content is still under study. Studies of the reliability and validity of the Correctional Program Assessment Inventory are minuscule compared to the number and quality of psychometric studies of offender-based risk/need assessment instruments. For all of that, our pilot work with the Correctional Program Assessment Inventory has attracted a tremendous amount of interest in an issue which Paul Gendreau and this author feel is crucial both to the development of an empirically defensible theoretical criminology and to the reduction of antisocial behavior through prevention and correctional programs. Thus, the remainder of this paper describes the Correctional Program Assessment Inventory, including its underlying rationale and the specifics of its particular items.

Overview of the Correctional Program Assessment Inventory

The Correctional Program Assessment Inventory, in the 1992 version (the version that has been subjected to the most intensive study), was composed of 9 sections with a total of 56 scorable items. The sections were as follows:

1. Program description/demographics

2. Program implementation (11 items)

3. Client preservice assessment (7 items)

4. Program characteristics (4 items)

5. Therapeutic integrity (9 items)

6. Relapse prevention (6 items)

7. Staff characteristics (9 items)

8. Evaluation (6 items)

9. Other (4 items)

Each of the scorable items, which are reviewed below, is scored as not applicable ("na"), not known ("nk"), "0" (element absent), or "1" (element present). (A few exceptions to this approach are not worth discussion here). Then, each subtotal may be summarized in terms of the percentage of elements judged present relative to the total number of elements assessed. This also may be done to yield an overall total CPAI score, an overall CPAI treatment score (subtotals "3" through "7"), or any other combination of interest to users.

Readers familiar with offender-based risk/need assessments such as the LSI-R (Andrews and Bonta, 1995) will recognize how similar it is to the scoring of the Correctional Program Assessment Inventory. Essentially, the best-validated of the offender-based risk/need assessment instruments tabulate the number and variety of major risk factors present for particular cases. The CPAI tabulates the number and variety of the best-validated elements of effective correctional programs present for particular programs.

Just as in the case of offender-based assessments of risk/need, the sources of information used in scoring the CPAI may be very influential. To date, site visits, file reviews, interviews, and responses to structured questionnaires have been used in the scoring of the CPAI. To date, no conclusions have been drawn regarding the differential and/or incremental validity of the multiple sources of information on the CPAI items.

Subsections of the Correctional Program Assessment Inventory are as follows:

(1) Program Description/Demographics

This section provides the opportunity for a narrative description of the program and includes the obvious factors of program name, contact persons, address, setting (diversion, probation, parole, group home, prison, and so forth), budget, number of cases served, number of staff, and program philosophy. This, of course, is the typical type of program description with which most of us are familiar and, apart from setting and the incidentals that may be pulled from statements of philosophy, is largely irrelevant to assessments of rehabilitative potential. We do not score this section because for the most part, the typical designations of programs as educational/vocational, skill building, family counseling, individual counseling, group counseling, milieu therapy, and so forth, are not sufficient to assess the chances of that program successfully reducing reoffending. In other words, the principles of risk, need, responsivity, and therapeutic integrity apply across a variety programs labeled as educational, familiar, group, or personal.

(2) Program Implementation

This section too, although scorable, is not that relevant to assessments of rehabilitative potential. In this section, the Correctional Program Assessment Inventory essentially is surveying characteristics of the program designer ("2A") and the conditions of program implementation ("2B") that have to do with chances of the program surviving for any length of time. Here Paul Gendreau and this author, with the findings of Margaret Lederman's thesis in hand, suggest that certain conditions of implementation are more favorable than others. The eleven items, scored favorable, include initiation by the designer and the host agency (as opposed to imposed by "head office"), program champions within the agency, cost-effectiveness and sustainability, and some internal funding (as opposed to a totally externally funded demonstration project). The items are as follows:

2A) Designer

01. Qualified through a university degree in one of the helping professions with some courses in correctional/forensic/legal area

02. Previous experience with some correctional treatment program

03. Selection and training of staff is a direct responsibility of program designer

04. Involved through direct service and/or direct supervision staff

05. Currently involved in direct service or direct supervision of staff

2B) Program

> 06. Literature review conducted to identify relevant program content and materials
>
> 07. Need for program assessed systematically prior to introduction
>
> 08. Value congruency exists between program and host agency and between program and broader community
>
> 09. Judged cost-effective by administration and line staff
>
> 10. Judged sustainable in terms of adequate funding and resources
>
> 11. Program piloted before formal introduction

(3) Client Preservice Assessment

With this section we enter the domain of scorable items that are judged directly relevant to the program's potential for recidivism reduction. The seven items in this section are numbers 12-18, as follows:

> 12. Appropriate clients according to program people
>
> 13. Rational exclusions: not all programs need accept all clients but a program may be expected to state a rational clinical or other basis for excluding some types of cases
>
> 14. Reasonable attempt to address risk, need and/or responsivity without requiring that the assessments be empirically validated
>
> 15. Risk assessments of demonstrated psychometric quality are employed
>
> 16. Risk levels are assigned in accordance with useful levels such as low, moderate, high, which translate into meaningful differential action such as less versus more-intensive service
>
> 17. Need assessments with psychometric quality are employed
>
> 18. Responsivity assessments with psychometric quality are employed

(4) Program Characteristics

> 19. Criminogenic needs are set as intermediate targets (the majority of targets must fall within the dynamic risk-factor set)

20. Noncriminogenic needs are not emphasized, even though they may be addressed

21. Effective treatment methods are employed (for example, cognitive-behavioral methods)

22. Printed treatment manuals are available

(5) Therapeutic Integrity

In future editions, this section will be reformulated somewhat but here we are looking for indicators of service quality.

23. Program participants are separated from the rest of the population

24. High level of involvement, at least 40 percent of time in treatment activity

25. More intensive service for higher-risk cases

26. Matching according to responsivity

27. Matching staff and client

28. Client has some input into program structure and specifics (with approval of program supervisor)

29. Ratio favors rewards over punishment

30. Variety of rewards available

31. Program addresses criminal sentiments in structured manner

(6) Relapse Prevention

This section may be renamed "structured follow-up" in future editions.

32. Monitor training

33. Rehearsal of plans/alternatives

34. Practice in increasingly difficult situations

35. Booster sessions

36. Advocacy/brokerage

37. Train significant others in supportive roles

(7) Staff Characteristics

This section surveys education, training, and supervision issues.

38. Educated: 75 percent with a BA, 10 percent of staff with advanced degree

39. Related training: education, nursing, psychology, social work, or specialized fields such as addictions

40. Relevant experience: 75 percent of staff have worked in correctional treatment programs for at least one year

41. Appropriate personal characteristics, such as relationship skills, firm but fair

42. Stability/length of stay: 50 percent of staff on job for at least two years

43. Clinical skills assessed and clinical supervision received

44. Formal training in specific theory and practice

45. Staff have input regarding the program

46. Advisory board available to staff and managers

(8) Evaluation

47. Management audit, including file reviews

48. Consumer satisfaction survey (at least once a year)

49. Outcome evaluation studies completed

50. Postprogram follow-up outcome evaluations completed

51. Process evaluation including objective and standardized assessment of service-delivery process and intermediate outcomes

52. External evaluator involved at some point

(9) Other

53. Ethical guidelines recorded and practiced

54. Positive changes in the program planned or underway

55. Funding situation is positive and stable

56. Community support is positive and stable

Paul Gendreau and this author currently are involved in modifying some items, changing the content and labels of some sections, and generally attempting to make the Correctional Program Assessment Inventory a more useful and valid instrument. Even now, however, certain conclusions may be drawn with some degree of confidence. These conclusions follow:

(1) The Correctional Program Assessment Inventory may serve as a major incentive and vehicle for programs to articulate what they are about. In this sense, we have found many program representatives who appreciate concrete assistance with (a) describing their program in terms of constructs such as the preservice client characteristics of risk, need, and responsivity and/or with (b) describing their program in terms of the level, targets, or style/mode of service. Thus, a major role of the Correctional Program Assessment Inventory has been to assist programs with what is often called "evaluability assessment." Without knowledge of who is served, with what intent, in what ways, and with what intermediate changes, a program is simply not open to a reasonable and helpful evaluation. An incidental, but not unimportant, bonus here is that program people may be brought into contact with well-validated efforts similar in structure and intent to theirs.

(2) The Correctional Program Assessment Inventory is not a substitute for a formal controlled-outcome evaluation. It, however, is clearly a way in which a program may gain a quick sense of where it fits in terms of evidence-based effective practice. The simple fact is that formal-controlled outcome evaluations, as valuable as they may be, do not provide programs with useful feedback in a timely fashion.

(3) The best of the formal-controlled outcome evaluation studies also include attention to service process variables such as specific intervention strategies and the monitoring of particular intermediate outcomes. The Correctional Program Assessment Inventory may assist in the assessment of service process.

(4) The Correctional Program Assessment Inventory provides a concrete means of stimulating service-relevant research in service settings. Its content, for the most part, obviously is relevant to the activities of

managers and staff, and thus the general issues of case assessment and service process become natural concerns for ongoing research.

(5) The Correctional Program Assessment Inventory now has been employed in several large-scale surveys of correctional programs (for example, Gendreau, Coggin, and Annis, 1990; Hoge, Leschied, and Andrews, 1993). These surveys certainly located a large number of active service settings with caring and enthusiastic personnel. We also have uncovered some programs that score very high on the elements of effective programming. The overall findings, however, suggest that for all of the activity, very few programs incorporate many of the effective elements. For example, within a recent survey of programs for young offenders, fewer than 10 percent of the programs had even 50 percent of the elements of effective programming. The areas in which programs had the lowest scores were therapeutic integrity and relapse prevention. Interestingly, from a systemwide perspective, the government department responsible for young-offender programs responded with the introduction of systematic risk/need assessment and training of staff in cognitive-behavioral intervention techniques.

(6) One point must be stressed here. Remember, for effective correctional practice, not all programs need score high on all of the elements surveyed by the Correctional Program Assessment Inventory. Low-intensity, low-contact interventions are appropriate for the lowest-risk cases.

Conclusions

There now is a human science of criminal conduct. There are theories of criminal conduct that are empirically defensible and that may be helpful in designing and delivering effective service. The literature is reasonably strong and supports vigorous pursuit of ethical, decent, humane and cost-efficient approaches to prevention and rehabilitative programming for higher risk cases under a variety of conditions of just sanctioning. The active and effective human service agency may contribute to a still more powerful knowledge base by building assessment, reassessment, and research into the agency.

A major issue, one on which research only is beginning, is how to make use of what works—research on the dissemination, implementation, and ongoing development of effective programming (Andrews and Bonta, 1994, 236).

A major element of dissemination and program development is the availability of accurate summaries of that knowledge base. There are now available many summaries of this knowledge base; hence, it is no longer the case that the knowledge is difficult to access. In addition to the journal articles and books already cited in this paper, there are exceptional compilations prepared and distributed by the National Institute of Corrections, International Community Corrections Association, Correctional Services of Canada, and the National Parole Board of Canada.

Paraphrasing Andrews and Hoge (1995), it is time for evidence-based practice in correctional treatment service and correctional management. Sole reliance on models of radical nonintervention, deterrence, control, and just desert are no longer justifiable on moral or utilitarian grounds. An active interventionist agenda is indicated, and the Correctional Program Assessment Inventory is a developing tool to assist in the assessment of those interventions.

References

Andrews, D. A. 1994. An Overview of Treatment Effectiveness: Research and Clinical Principles. Paper prepared for the Treatment Programming: An Element of Offender Risk Management, National Institute of Corrections Community Corrections Seminar, offered in cooperation with the National Institute of Corrections Academy, Longmont Colorado.

————. 1995. The Psychology of Criminal Conduct and Effective Treatment. In J. McGuire, ed. *What Works: Reducing Reoffending*. Chichester: John Wiley.

Andrews, D. A. and J. Bonta. 1994. *The Psychology of Criminal Conduct.* Cincinnati: Anderson.

————. 1995. *LSI-R: The Level of Service Inventory, Revised.* Toronto: Multi-health Systems.

Andrews, D. A. and R. D. Hoge. 1995. The Psychology of Criminal Conduct and Principles of Effective Prevention and Rehabilitation. *Forum on Corrections Research.* 7:34-36.

Andrews, D. A., I. Zinger, R. D. Hoge, J. Bonta, P. Gendreau, and F. T. Cullen. 1990. Does Correctional Treatment Work? A Clinically Relevant and Psychologically Informed Meta-analysis. *Criminology.* 28:369-404.

Antonowicz, D. and R. R. Ross. 1994. Essential Components of Successful Rehabilitation Programs for Offenders. *International Journal of Offender Therapy and Comparative Criminology.* 38:97-04.

Gendreau, P. 1994. The Principles of Effective Intervention with Offenders. Paper prepared for the IARCA Consensus Conference.

Gendreau, P. and D. A. Andrews. 1994. *The Correctional Program Assessment Inventory*, 4th edition. Saint John, New Brunswick: University of New Brunswick.

Gendreau, P., C. Coggin, and H. Annis. 1990. Survey of Existing Substance Abuse Programs. *Forum on Corrections Research.* 2:608.

Hoge, R. D., A. Leschied, and D. A. Andrews. 1993. *An Investigation of Young Offender Services in the Province of Ontario.* Toronto: Ministry of Community and Social Services.

Jones, P. R. 1994. Risk Prediction in Criminal Justice. Paper prepared for the IARCA Consensus Conference.

Lipsey, M. W. 1990. Juvenile Delinquency Treatment: A Meta-analytic Inquiry into Variability of Effects. Report to the Research Synthesis Committee of the Russell Sage Foundation, New York, New York.

———. 1995. What Do We Learn from 400 Research Studies on the Effectiveness of Treatment with Juvenile Delinquents? In J. McGuire, ed. *What Works: Reducing Reoffending.* Chichester: John Wiley.

Losel, F. 1995. The Efficacy of Correctional Treatment: A Review and Synthesis of Metaevaluations. In J. McGuire, ed. *What Works: Reducing Reoffending.* Chichester: John Wiley.

McGuire, J., ed. *What Works: Reducing Reoffending.* Chichester: John Wiley.

SECTION 3:

THE PRINCIPLES OF NEEDS AND RESPONSIVITY

ASSESSMENT METHODS IN CORRECTIONS

7

Larry Motiuk, Ph.D.

Correctional Service of Canada
Ottawa, Ontario
Canada

Introduction

In practice, the analysis of offender risk serves to structure many of the decisions we make with respect to custody or security designations, temporary and conditional release, supervision requirements, and program placement (Leis, Motiuk, and Ogloff, 1995). The cornerstone of any effective risk-management program is to make decisions after having considered all of the available information. However, the capacity to conduct formalized risk assessments is directly related to the number of resources a correctional agency has at its disposal. It is not surprising, therefore, to find that objective assessment procedures for classifying criminal offenders have proliferated throughout North America (Austin, 1986; Clements, 1996; Van Voorhis, 1988).

Most assessment instruments being used today originally were crafted during the late 1970s and early 1980s. Some examples include: the Salient Factor Score (Hoffman, 1983), the Client Management Classification Strategies (Lerner, Arling, and Baird, 1986); the Level of Supervision Inventory (Andrews, 1982); and the Statistical Information on Recidivism Scale (Nuffield, 1982).

All of these instruments use objective scoring techniques and scientific approaches. Although better than chance predictions can be made using any one of these risk instruments, the fact remains that the amount of variance left unexplained in the prediction of correctional outcomes continues to outweigh that which can be explained by these tools. This reality has led the current generation of risk assessors in corrections to view offender assessment as an integrated process that incorporates a variety of assessment methodologies (Leis, Motiuk, and Ogloff, 1995).

Faced with the correctional challenges of the 1990s, one can use multimethod and multipredictor assessment techniques and systematic reassessment (Andrews and Bonta, 1994; Motiuk, 1991) to advance risk-management practices. This situation is particularly true for the Correctional Service of Canada, which undertook an ambitious correctional strategy in 1990. Basically, this initiative put forth a framework for establishing program priorities, implementing programs, and allocating resources to best meet the needs of offenders. Insofar as an emphasis is placed on the safe reintegration of offenders into the community, the Service recognized the need for a comprehensive and integrated process to assess federal offenders (those serving sentences of two years or more) at intake. The Offender Intake Assessment process exemplifies this direction.

Before elaborating on the Offender Intake Assessment model, it is important to reflect upon the service's breakthrough in the implementation of systematic offender risk/needs assessment in the community. This achievement was instrumental in providing the conceptual foundation and impetus for an offender risk/needs assessment process for admission to federal custody. Overall, the strategy for risk management is to conduct formalized assessments upon admission to prison and link them in meaningful ways (using the same language and cues) with reassessments conducted during conditional release.

Community Risk/Needs Management Scale

Previous research on the predictive value of offender risk/needs assessments has found that criminal-history factors are strongly related to outcome on conditional release (Glaser, 1987; Gottfredson and Tonry, 1987); that a consistent relationship exists between the type and number of needs that offenders present and the likelihood of their reoffending (Bonta and Motiuk, 1985,1987,1990; Motiuk, 1993) and, most importantly, that combined assessment of the level of both risk and needs significantly improves our ability to predict who is likely to reoffend and who will not (Motiuk and Porporino, 1989a).

In October 1988, as part of the field testing of new standards for conditional release supervision (Motiuk and Porporino, 1989b), case management staff of the Correctional Service of Canada were required to use a systematic approach to assess the needs of offenders, the risk of reoffending, and any other factors that might affect successful reintegration to the community. In keeping with this standard, a Community Risk/Needs Management Scale was designed, developed, and implemented to provide case-specific information on criminal history and a critical set of case-need dimensions for the classification of federal offenders while they were on conditional release.

Design

The Community Risk/Needs Management Scale clearly was intended to be used to focus supervision resources (such as frequency of contact) and monitor changes in the offender's behavior, attitudes, and circumstances while under supervision. However, its design and development purposely had followed the Case Management Strategies (CMS) approach to assessing offender needs (Lerner, Arling, and Baird, 1986), which uses a protocol called the Force-field Analysis of Needs. The case-management strategies approach to offender assessment had been developed in the midwestern United States for youthful probationers and was adopted by the Correctional Service of Canada for assessing the individual case needs of federally sentenced adult prisoners. While the force-field analysis of needs provided a way to make parole officer/manager judgments of offender risk and needs more objective and systematic, it did not take into account the context (community versus institution) or changes across time and settings. As a result, the Community Risk/Needs Management Scale was designed, which essentially put into practice a simple scheme that would allow parole officers to classify offenders under supervision.

To assess risk (of reoffending) systematically and consistently, parole officers use the Statistical Information on Recidivism Scale (SIR)

(Nuffield, 1982), which has been officially adopted by the National Parole Board in Canada as a release risk scoring system. The SIR scale involves an extensive review of an individual's official criminal record to complete fifteen risk-related items (such as age, number, and variety of criminal convictions, breaches of trust, and so forth). In addition, parole officers use two other sources of information so that the level of criminal history could be determined in an objective, reliable, and accurate way. These include the National Parole Board's overall assessment of risk (low versus not low) and their own judgment of criminal-history risk, which is based on a thorough review of an offender's criminal record.

The need areas selected for this component of the Community Risk/Needs Management Scale are typical of those included in most other need assessment instruments used in various jurisdictions (Motiuk and Porporino, 1989b). A total of twelve need areas are covered: academic/vocational skills, employment pattern, financial management, marital/family relationship, companions/significant others, living arrangements, behavioral/emotional stability, alcohol usage, drug usage, mental ability, health, and attitude. Although each area of need is rated (factor seen as an asset to community adjustment, no current difficulties, some need for improvement, considerable need for improvement) according to specified guidelines, an overall rating of need is given simply by compiling case manager judgments into one of three needs levels: low, medium, or high.

The appropriate frequency of contact for parole supervision is determined by linking the two types of assessments—static factors (criminal history) and dynamic factors (case needs)—in a matrix format (such as high-risk/high need) shown in Table 7.1.

TABLE 7.1. Risk/Needs Level and Minimum Frequency of Contact

Static Factors Criminal History Risk	Dynamic Factors Case Needs		
	Low	Medium	High
Low	1/month	2/month	4/month
High	4/month	4/month	4/month

To ensure that the Community Risk/Needs Management Scale would accommodate the community-supervision needs of certain special categories of offenders (such as sexual offenders and offenders with mental disorders), two additional special-needs categories were included. A special needs category of "other" is reserved for those who do not meet the aforementioned criteria but are viewed by parole officers as meriting a higher rating.

Development

The field test of the Community Risk/Needs Management Scale found that parole officers in the community easily could differentiate among federal offenders (n = 453) as to the nature and level of risk and needs they presented, and these offender risk/need assessments consistently were related to conditional-release outcome (Motiuk and Porporino, 1989b). By simply combining case-manager assessments of criminal history risk with global ratings of case needs (see Table 7.2), as many as 47.5 percent of offenders who had been assessed as being high-risk and high-need were suspended within six months of their initial assessment.

On the other hand, substantially fewer offenders assessed as low-risk and low-need were suspended (5.1 percent) while on conditional release. Of particular interest, this low-risk and low-need group was the largest category among the risk/need level groupings that were identified (representing one-third of the total sample of cases that were assessed). Therefore, reducing the frequency of supervision for these lower-risk cases had important implications for reallocating and refocusing of community resources (Andrews, Bonta, and Hoge, 1990).

TABLE 7.2. Field Test Distribution and (Suspension Rates) by Risk/Needs Levels

Criminal History Risk	Case Needs		
	Low	**Medium**	**High**
Low	34.4% (5.1%)	9.7% (13.6%)	5.7% (26.9%)
High	16.8% (22.4%)	20.3% (41.3%)	13.0% (47.5%)

Analyses were conducted using a variety of scoring mechanisms of the need areas (simple tallies of identified needs, scaled ratings, weighted ratings based on the strength of the relationship between each need area and likelihood of reoffending) to provide an overall rating of case needs (Motiuk and Porporino, 1989b). While the "weighted-ratings" method yielded only slight improvements in precision, the disadvantage was that parole officers perceived summing and calculating to be too mechanistic and clerical in nature. Therefore, global ratings of each of the twelve separate need areas coupled with an overview became the scoring method of choice.

The early pilot work also explored the distributions of the twelve need dimensions of the Community Risk/Needs Management Scale. The purpose of the test was to learn more about each factor in terms of managing cases.

TABLE 7.3. Outcome on Conditional Release for Cases with Identified Needs

Need Dimension	n (%) with identified need	Suspended within six months (%)	Significant statistical relations
Academic/vocational skills	94 (20.8)	35.1	**
Employment pattern	158 (35.0)	36.1	***
Financial management	167 (37.0)	37.1	***
Marital/family relations	150 (33.2)	37.3	***
Companions/significant others	182 (40.4)	40.7	***
Accommodation	70 (15.5)	45.7	***
Behavioral/emotional stability	157 (34.8)	34.4	***
Alcohol usage	84 (18.6)	46.4	***
Drug usage	71 (15.7)	39.4	***
Mental ability	39 (8.7)	28.2	ns
Health	41 (9.1)	14.6	ns
Attitude	112 (25.1)	40.2	***

Note: ns=nonsignificant; ** p < .01; *** p < .001.
Identified need = some need and considerable need for improvement combined.

The field research showed the proportion of offenders suspended (supervision was interrupted by a parole officer for a breach of conditions) within six months and other statistically significant relationships between specific need dimensions and the likelihood of suspension (*see* Table 7.3). Statistical analysis revealed that only two of the twelve need areas assessed did not significantly relate to failure on conditional release. The two need dimensions found not to be significant were mental ability and health.

Implementation

To proceed with the full implementation of new national standards for conditional release supervision, a training team conducted a series (a total of seventeen) of one-day professional development workshops across the Correctional Service of Canada. It is estimated that more than 550 individuals participated in these professional-development workshops. While the majority of those who participated in the training were Correctional Service of Canada staff, there were also trainees from other organizations (such as provincial jurisdictions, service agencies, and halfway house associations). The training workshops included the following: background to the project; history of frequency of contact; research findings from the field test of the Community Risk/Needs Management Scale; an overview of the new standards for conditional-release supervision; clarification of exemptions and exceptions to the standards; Section 5 of the standards (Offender Assessment, Classifi-cation, Frequency of Contact); hands-on training with the risk/needs assessment tool; and feedback on results of assessment training.

In the hands-on training exercises, we were attempting to establish an acceptable level of agreement among community case managers for frequency of contact decisions. For each of the workshops, this entailed two types of training exercises or two different approaches. One was an individual assessment of a practice case and the other was a group assessment of a different case. It was expected that the individual-practice approach would equip the parole officers with a thorough understanding of the Community Risk/Needs Management Scale assessment device. Then, by following this up with a group assessment, there would be not only a reinforcement of prior understanding but also a pooling of the available on-site professional expertise in assessing a particular case.

The hands-on training exercises confirmed the ability of community case managers to apply the Community Risk/Needs Management Scale as a systematic method for assessing the needs of offenders, the risk of reoffending, and any other factor that might affect the successful adjustment of an offender into the community. The results of practice case assessments demonstrated acceptable levels of agreement among parole officers when assessing the same case for the first time using the Community Risk/Needs Management Scale with respect to frequency of contact considerations. The variability in case needs level ratings at the different training sites also pointed to a need for ongoing clarification of the various needs dimensions being assessed with training and reference to guidelines. Further, a combination of individual and group-practice exercises can result in improved levels of agreement among parole officers for risk/needs ratings.

A postimplementation follow-up of the Community Risk/Needs Management Scale was made possible by means of an Offender Population Profile System. Through the Offender Population Profile System, the overall risk/needs levels gathered since scale implementation systematically were being stored and subsequently retrieved to provide monthly snapshots. Table 7.4 shows a national overview of the risk/need levels of the conditional-release population over the first three years of implementation.

TABLE 7.4. National Overview of the Conditional Release Population: Percentage Distribution of Risk/Needs Levels

Risk/Needs Levels	Time				
	End-of-year 1 (7,023)	Middle-of-year 2 (7,800)	End-of-year 2 (8,169)	Middle-of-year 3 (8,453)	End-of-year 3 (8,666)
Low-Low	31.6	30.3	28.2	26.6	27.0
Low-Medium	26.0	24.9	24.9	26.0	24.9
Low-High	2.4	2.4	2.8	2.5	3.0
High-Low	3.0	2.7	2.2	1.6	1.5
High-Medium	11.8	9.5	8.9	7.8	7.5
High-High	25.3	30.3	33.2	35.4	36.1

According to the Offender Population Profile System, there was a steady decline of the proportion of cases assessed as being low-risk and low-need (31.6 percent to 27.0 percent) as opposed to the steady increase in the proportion of cases assessed as being high-risk and high-need (25.3 percent to 36.1 percent). While the definitive answer to this change remains unclear, it may represent drift in risk assessment over time. That is, parole officers may be overestimating the level of risk. This may be somewhat akin to the phenomenon of overclassification that is found in many institutional populations (Bonta and Motiuk, 1992). In any event, this kind of information told us how field staff had been responding to the conditional-release population over time. For certain, if frequency of contact guidelines were being adhered to strictly, then a substantially larger proportion of offenders on conditional release were being supervised much more closely after implementation of the supervision standards than ever before.

Another feature of our postimplementation follow-up was a closer examination of an early cohort of 7,023 assessed cases systematically tracked over a two-year period. In Table 7.5, we see the percentage distribution of cases across four separate six-month follow-up periods. We note that less than one-third of the original cohort were still under community supervision at the end of the follow-up.

Once identified, we grouped the early cohort of supervision cases according to their respective frequency of contact requirement. That is, "low" (low-risk, low-needs), "moderate" (low-risk, medium-needs) and "high" (low-risk, high-needs; high-risk, low-needs; high-risk, medium-needs, high-risk, high-needs). We then tracked this cohort over a two-year period. As expected, higher-risk/need offenders were more likely to be suspended than lower-risk/need offenders. More importantly, this finding was most robust in the early phases (within six months) of follow-up. Further, it points to the utility of dynamic assessment methods in the case supervision of offenders in the community.

TABLE 7.5. Distribution of Supervision Cases Across Follow-up Periods

0 to 6 months	7 to 12 months	13 to 18 months	19 to 24 months
5,404 (76.9%)	4,088 (58.2%)	2,905 (41.4%)	2,049 (29.2%)

TABLE 7.6. Suspension Rates by Overall Risk/Needs Level

Follow-up Period	Base Rate	Overall Risk/Needs Level		
		Low	Moderate	High
0-6 months	18.3% (991/5,404)	5.7% (109/1,911)	17.4% (239/1,370)	30.3% (643/2,123)
7-12 months	10.2% (417/4,088)	4.5% (90/1,992)	9.8% (115/1,174)	17.0% (212/1,244)
13-18 months	8.9% (288/3,232)	5.2% (96/1,833)	11.2% (83/738)	16.5% (109/661)
19-24 months	6.5% (151/2,307)	4.3% (65/1,508)	10.3% (44/429)	11.4% (42/370)

In advancing further the concept of dynamic assessment methodology (Motiuk, Bonta, and Andrews, 1990), it is also not surprising that when offender risk/need levels increase so does the likelihood of failure while under community supervision (see Tables 7.6 and 7.7). More specifically, offenders showing an increase in overall risk/needs level were more likely to be suspended than those who had either a decrease in risk/needs level or no change at all. Once again, this finding was particularly robust within the first six months of follow-up.

Application

Presently, the Community Risk/Needs Management Scale (now called the *Community Intervention Scale*) is administered and readministered systematically to federal offenders under community supervision by parole officers across Canada. It provides an efficient system for recording criminal history risk and case needs, level of risk and need, required frequency of contact, and related background information on each offender (such as release status, and sentence expiration). While the Community Risk/Needs Management Scale first was implemented in hardcopy form, the computerized version has been in use for several years.

Of particular interest from both an organizational and risk-management perspective, there exists a computerized means to monitor offender

TABLE 7.7. Suspension Rates by Changes in Overall Risk/Needs Level

Follow-up Period	Base Rate	Overall Risk/Needs Level		
		Decrease	No Change	Increase
6-12 months	9.3% (288/3,112)	8.8% (38/431)	9.0% (230/2,553)	15.6% (20/128)
13-18 months	7.5% (160/2,121)	6.3% (22/350)	7.7% (127/1,642)	8.5% (11/129)
19-24 months	6.5% (100/1,534)	6.8% (12/176)	6.2% (79/1,268)	10.0% (9/90)

risk/needs levels by using the Offender Management System (OMS). Using the Offender Management System, the overall risk/need levels that have been gathered since implementation of the Community Risk/Needs Management Scale are being stored systematically and can be retrieved to provide caseload snapshots.

As expected, the ability to produce an offender risk/needs profile of an entire conditional-release population has proven to be extremely useful for raising awareness about community supervision, providing basic statistics with respect to risk/needs levels, and estimating resource implications with respect to frequency of contact considerations. The ability to monitor the risk levels of the Correctional Service of Canada's conditional-release population has moved the organization closer toward an effective risk-management program.

New Research

Today, the automated version of the Community Risk/Needs Management Scale can produce a distribution of identified needs for the entire community supervision population (*see* Table 7.8). This case-based information is representative of some 600 parole officers spread across Canada, reflecting their collective experience and knowledge of the cases that they have under their direct supervision. The distribution of identified needs indicates that employment, financial, marital/family, and behavioral/emotional problems are frequent among the community

TABLE 7.8. Distribution of Offenders with Identified Needs by Gender (in percentage)

Need Dimension	Male offenders (5,271)	Female offenders (175)	Significant statistical relations
Academic/vocational skills	1,929 (36.6)	60 (34.3)	ns
Employment pattern	2,334 (44.2)	76 (43.4)	ns
Financial management	2,038 (38.6)	63 (35.8)	ns
Marital/family relations	1,455 (27.7)	60 (34.3)	ns
Companions/significant others	1,482 (28.2)	50 (29.1)	ns
Accommodation	597 (11.4)	27 (15.5)	ns
Behavioral/emotional stability	2,072 (39.4)	77 (43.8)	ns
Alcohol usage	794 (15.1)	19 (10.9)	ns
Drug usage	837 (15.9)	18 (10.3)	*
Mental ability	255 (5.0)	8 (4.6)	ns
Health	896 (17.0)	41 (23.3)	*
Attitude	558 (10.6)	14 (8.1)	ns

Note: ns=nonsignificant; * $p < .05$
Identified need = some need and considerable need for improvement combined.

supervision population. Statistical analyses revealed gender differences for only two of the twelve need dimensions. Male offenders were more likely than female offenders to experience drug problems while in the community. In contrast, female offenders were more likely than male offenders to have health problems.

To examine differences in case needs across each phase of conditional release, we collapsed the caseload snapshot of 5,286 male offenders into three groups: 0 to 6 months, 6 to 12 months, and 12 months or over (*see* Table 7.9). Some interesting, yet different patterns emerge across the various phases. As expected, offenders who have been in the community twelve months or longer have a much reduced level of need on all dimensions (due to adjustment in the community) relative to their more recently released counterparts.

TABLE 7.9. Distribution of Offenders with Identified Needs by Phase (in percentage)

Need Dimension	0 to 6 months (1,403)	6 to 12 months (1,555)	12 months or more (2,313)	Significant statistical relations
Academic/vocational skills	50.9	44.2	22.8	***
Employment pattern	59.9	49.6	31.0	***
Financial management	53.7	44.4	25.7	***
Marital/family relations	38.3	30.0	19.6	***
Companions/significant others	46.1	32.5	14.5	***
Accommodation	13.2	11.6	10.1	*
Behavioral/emotional stability	56.8	46.2	24.2	***
Alcohol usage	27.3	16.4	6.8	***
Drug usage	29.0	18.4	6.4	***
Mental ability	5.7	6.0	3.6	***
Health	15.5	16.8	18.1	ns
Attitude	14.7	11.9	7.4	***

Note: ns=nonsignificant; * $p < .05$; *** $p < .001$.
Identified need = some need and considerable need for improvement combined.

Table 7.10 presents the correlations between each need area and suspension of conditional release (within six months of being assessed using the Community Risk/Needs Management Scale) across the three separate phases of release. The majority of case needs, when present, were found to be significantly associated with community supervision failure. A consistent pattern emerged when looking at the relationship between identified need and failure across all three phases of release for academic/vocational skills, employment pattern, marital/family relations, companions/significant others, and drug usage. In fact, the magnitude of these relationships became stronger with time out on supervision. This has important implications for risk prediction. We know from previous studies that static variables, like criminal history, probably have more predictive power than needs at the early stages of release. There is, however, a good explanation for this, in that over time, if an offender is going to manifest recidivism, it is the dynamic variables (such as employment status, marital/family situation, addictions) that begin to drive the likelihood of recidivism. One should be cautioned when interpreting seemingly low or deflated correlations as not significant. Such correlations simply may be a reflection of parole officers intervening when necessary, thereby reducing variation in correctional outcome measures being predicted (such as reductions in suspension rates).

Using regression analysis, one can explore the most important assessment variables determining outcome on conditional release. To do this, age, criminal history risk level, case needs level, and identified needs were entered into a stepwise-regression equation. For male offenders, the

TABLE 7.10. Relationship Between Identified Needs and Outcome by Phase

Need Dimension	0 to 6 months	6 to 12 months	12 months or more
Academic/vocational skills	.07**	.11***	.11***
Employment pattern	.09***	.08**	.11***
Financial management	.04	.09***	.08***
Marital/family relations	.06*	.08**	.12***
Companions/significant others	.08**	.12***	.12***
Accommodation	.07**	.05	.12***
Behavioral/emotional stability	.02	.10***	.11***
Alcohol usage	.05	.05	.15***
Drug usage	.10***	.08**	.14***
Mental ability	.01	.06*	.02
Health	-.01	.01	.03
Attitude	.06*	.03	.04

Note: ns=nonsignificant; * p < .05 **p<.01; ***P<.001
Identified need = some need and considerable need for improvement combined.

variables that came into play for predicting outcome (in order of magnitude) included needs level, risk (static) level, age, and drug use. For female offenders, drug use and marital family relations were the most important predictors. This finding clearly demonstrates the shift in emphasis that has occurred over the last five years. It appears that with the assessment of dynamic factors or criminogenic needs, a subset of overall risk is driving community-supervision practices.

The Offender Intake Assessment Process

The Offender Intake Assessment process represents the latest generation of risk-assessment technology (Motiuk, 1997). It integrates information gathered from a variety of sources using many techniques. While the mechanics of the whole-intake assessment process are beyond the scope of this paper, a quick look at the Criminal Risk Assessment (static factors) and Case Needs Identification and Analysis (dynamic factors) domains should serve to tell more about our ability to assess offender risk and need.

Case Needs Identification and Analysis

Under the auspices of the 1991 Correctional Strategy initiative, it was decided that an offenders' needs should drive programming, and that service delivery should focus primarily on successful reintegration into the community. At the time, however, only the force-field analysis of needs was being used to conduct assessments upon admission to federal corrections. A national working group concluded that the force-field analysis of needs was an inadequate tool for the expressed purposes of the correctional strategy (such as profiling offender needs). Consequently, a scheme was crafted for case-needs identification and analysis.

Development of the new instrumentation purposefully followed, and expanded on, the Case Management Assessment Interview, the force-field analysis of needs, and the Community Risk/Needs Management Scale. The intention was to capitalize on existing information-gathering practices, retain essential outputs (such as case-management strategy groupings) and build on staff training to date. As a result, the new Case Needs Identification and Analysis protocol collapsed the twelve need areas of the Community Risk/Needs Management Scale into seven need dimensions or target domains. These include employment, marital/family, associates/social interaction, substance abuse, community functioning, personal/emotional orientation, and attitude.

Rating guidelines are available for each of the seven case-need dimensions. In rating each need area during intake assessment (factor "seen as asset to community adjustment" through to "considerable need for improvement"), the offender's entire background is considered. This includes personal characteristics, interpersonal influences, situational determinants, and environmental conditions. An overall rating of needs is the compilation of professional judgments derived from the results of an initial assessment (medical, mental health, and suicide risk) and the observations (such as degree or severity of need) on each of the seven need areas. In addition, each case need area has a list of indicators, which reflect problems or deficits. For example, among the thirty-five indicators grouped under the "employment" domain are the following: "has no high school diploma," "unstable job history," and "has difficulty with supervisors."

After an initial version of the Case Needs Identification and Analysis protocol was drafted, additional assessment domains (*see* Table 7.11, below) were added to augment and complete the Offender Intake Assessment process.

TABLE 7.11. Offender Intake Assessment Domains

1) Postsentence Community Assessment (linked to 7 case need areas)	4) Case Needs Identification and Analysis (employment, marital/family, associates, substance abuse, community functioning, personal/emotional, attitude)
2) Initial Assessment (security, mental health, suicide risk, and so forth)	5) Psychological Assessment
3) Criminal Risk Assessment (criminal history record, offense severity record, sex offender history, Statistical Information on Recidivism Scale)	6) Supplementary Assessment(s) (education, employment, substance abuse)

Criminal Risk Assessment

At intake to federal corrections, a rating of criminal risk for every federal offender is based on the following: the criminal history record, the offense severity record, the sex offense history checklist, whether detention criteria are met, the result of the Statistical Information on Recidivism Scale, and any other risk factors, as detailed in a criminal profile report. The criminal profile report provides details of the crime(s) for which the offender is currently under sentence.

By systematically reviewing the offender's file, which includes police reports, court transcripts, and criminal records, an overall rating of criminal risk is the compilation of professional judgments derived from the results of the criminal history record [based on previous offense(s), the number and type of convictions, youth court dispositions, adult court sanctions, and crime-free periods], offense severity record (based on the type of conviction(s), sentence length, the number and types of victim(s), the degree of force used on victim(s), and the degree of physical and psychological harm to victim(s), and sex offense history checklist [based on sex-offender status, type of sex offense (current sentence), type of sex offense (past sentences), victims, serious harm, assessment, and treatment history]. In addition, the results of the Statistical Information on Recidivism Scale and any other risk factors are taken into account.

The Offender Intake Assessment process was implemented across the Service in 1994. While it was developed principally for assessing offender needs upon admission to federal custody, it has resulted in efforts to streamline the scope of the Community Risk/Needs Management Scale. Because the individual ratings for both "criminal risk" and "case need" levels as well as for each need area were kept at intake, it is possible to align the community-based version of risk/need assessment with the prison intake version. Consequently, the capacity now exists to assess offenders at admission in a comprehensive, integrated, and systematic fashion and reassess them routinely thereafter.

As for the community supervision population, the Service also has the ability to produce an offender risk/needs profile for the entire institutional population. For example, a distribution of identified needs (assessed at admission) among the institutional population is shown in Table 7.12. This offender information is representative of all inmates in federal institutions across Canada. The distribution of identified needs at admission to federal custody indicates that personal/emotional, employment, and substance abuse problems are frequent among the institutional population.

TABLE 7.12. Distribution of Identified Needs at Admission (in percentage)

Need Dimension	Institutional Population (13,126)
Employment	9,950 (75.5%)
Marital/family	8,524 (64.9%)
Associates	9,677 (73.7%)
Substance abuse	9,904 (75.5%)
Community functioning	8,954 (68.2%)
Personal/emotional	11,969 (91.2%)
Attitude	8,529 (65.0%)

Note: Identified need = some need and considerable need for improvement combined.

Conclusion

In sum, it is clear that by using a systematic assessment and reassessment approach, we have more information about offenders in correctional institutions and under community supervision than we did previously. This dynamic assessment method serves to instruct us about those with whom we are dealing, where they are, what they are like, and what kind of problems not only they faced out in the community before they arrived in prison, but also what they experience when released into the community and while under supervision. A meta-analytic review of criminal history and case needs has confirmed these as robust predictor domains of adult offender recidivism (Gendreau, Little, and Goggin, 1996). While targeting key areas (such as employment and substance abuse) for service delivery has been found to have considerable merit, the kind of intervention strategies one envisages to respond to offender needs continues to be the real challenge.

References

Andrews, D. A. 1982. *The Level of Supervision Inventory: The First Follow-up.* Toronto: Ontario Ministry of Correctional Services.

Andrews, D. A. and J. Bonta. 1994. *The Psychology of Criminal Conduct.* Cincinnati: Anderson.

Andrews, D. A., J. Bonta, and R. D. Hoge. 1990. Classification for Effective Rehabilitation: Rediscovering Psychology. *Criminal Justice and Behavior.* 17:19-52.

Austin, J. 1986. Evaluating How Well Your Classification System is Operating: A Practical Approach. *Crime & Delinquency.* 32:302-322.

Bonta, J., D. A. Andrews, and L. L. Motiuk. 1993. *Dynamic Risk Assessment and Effective Treatment.* A paper presented at the annual meeting of the American Society of Criminology, Phoenix, Arizona.

Bonta, J. and L. L. Motiuk. 1985. Utilization of an Interview-based Classification Instrument: A Study of Correctional Halfway Houses. *Criminal Justice and Behavior.* 12:333-352.

————. 1987. The Diversion of Incarcerated Offenders to Correctional Halfway Houses. *Journal of Research in Crime and Delinquency.* 24:302-323.

————. 1990. Classification to Correctional Halfway Houses: A Quasi-experimental Evaluation. *Criminology.* 28:497-506.

————. 1992. Inmate Classification. *Journal of Criminal Justice.* 20:343-353.

Clements, C. B. 1996. Offender Classification: Two Decades of Progress. *Criminal Justice and Behavior.* 23:21-143.

Gendreau, P., T. Little, and C. Goggin. 1996. A Meta-analysis of the Predictors of Adult Offender Recidivism: What Works! *Criminology. 34:575-607.*

Glaser, D. 1987. Classification for Risk. In D. M. Gottfredson and M. H. Tonry, eds. *Prediction and Classification: Criminal Justice Decision Making.* Chicago: University of Chicago Press.

Gottfredson, D. M. and M. H. Tonry. 1987. *Prediction and Classification: Criminal Justice Decision Making.* Chicago: University of Chicago Press.

Hoffman, P. 1983. Screening for Risk: A Revised Salient Factor Score. *Journal of Criminal Justice.* 11:539-547.

Leis, T., L. L. Motiuk, and J. Ogloff. 1995. *Forensic Psychology: Policy and Practice in Corrections.* Ottawa: Correctional Service Canada.

Lerner, K., G. Arling, and S. C. Baird. 1986. Client Management Classification: Strategies for Case Supervision. *Crime & Delinquency.* 32:254-271.

Motiuk, L. L. 1991. *Antecedents and Consequences of Prison Adjustment: A Systematic Assessment Reassessment Approach.* Doctoral dissertation, Carleton University.

————. 1993. Using the LSI and Other Classification Systems to Better Predict Halfway House Outcome. *IARCA Journal on Community Corrections.* 5:12-13.

————. 1997. Classification for Correctional Programming: The Offender Intake Assessment (OIA) Process. *Forum on Corrections Research.* 9 (1):18-23.

Motiuk., L. L. , J. Bonta, and D. A. Andrews. 1990. Dynamic Predictive Criterion Validity in Offender Assessment. Paper presented at the Canadian Psychological Association Annual Convention, Ottawa, Ontario.

Motiuk, L. L. and S. Brown. 1993. *The Validity of Offender Needs Identification and Analysis in Community Corrections.* Report No. 34. Research and Statistics Branch, Correctional Service of Canada.

Motiuk, L. L. and F. Porporino. 1989a. *Offender Risk/Needs Assessment: A Study of Conditional Releases.* Report No.1. Research and Statistics Branch, Correctional Service Canada.

————. 1989b. *Field Tests of the Community Risk/Needs Management Scale: A Study of Offenders on Caseload.* Report No. 6. Research and Statistics Branch, Correctional Service Canada.

Nuffield, J. 1982. *Parole Decision-making in Canada: Research Towards Decision Guidelines.* Ottawa: Communication Division, Correctional Service of Canada.

Van Voorhis, P. 1988. A Cross Classification of Five Offender Typologies: Issues of Construct and Predictive Validity. *Criminal Justice and Behavior.* 15:109-124.

Stages of Change Approach to Treating Addictions with Special Focus on Driving While Intoxicated (DWI) Offenders[1]

8

James O. Prochaska, Ph.D.
Cancer Prevention Research Center
University of Rhode Island
Kingston, Rhode Island

Introduction

The vast majority of people with substance abuse problems never seek professional help (Sobell et al., 1996; Veroff, Douvan, and Kulka, 1981). Of those who do, about half drop out of treatment quickly and prematurely (Wierzbicki and Pekarik, 1993). Of those who complete treatment, about one-quarter are abstinent at a twelve-month follow-up (Hunt, Barnett, and Branch, 1971). If we multiply enrollment (25 percent) times retention (50 percent) times efficacy (25 percent), we find that on a population basis, professional treatment programs impact upon only about 3 percent of substance abuse problems. One of the consequences of the minimal impact of current clinical services is that substance abuse usually goes untreated until crises occur, such as arrests for driving while intoxicated or other criminal offenses.

Startled by such poor impacts of clinical services, behavioral interventionists have taken addiction treatment and prevention programs into communities, work sites, and schools. In the Minnesota Heart Health project, for example, 40 million dollars was spent with five years of intervention in four communities totaling 400,000 people. There were no significant differences between treatment and control communities on smoking, diet, cholesterol, weight, blood pressure, and overall risks for cardiovascular disease (Luepker et al., 1994).

What went wrong? The investigators speculate that maybe they diluted their programs by targeting multiple behaviors. But the COMMIT (1995) trial had no effects with its primary target of heavy smokers and only a small effect with light smokers. Similarly, the largest work-site cessation programs produced no significant effects (Glasgow et al., 1995). In the largest school-based prevention program ever conducted, the DARE program, the results are similarly discouraging—minimal effects on substance abuse (Ennett et al., 1994).

A closer look at participation rates can account for some of the dismal results. In the Minnesota study, nearly 90 percent of smokers in both the treatment and control communities had processed media information about smoking in the past year (Lando et al., 1995). But only about 10 percent had physicians intervene. And only about 3 percent had participated in the most powerful behavioral programs, such as individualized and interactive clinics, classes, and contests. We cannot have much impact on the health of our communities if we only interact with a small percentage of populations at high risk.

There is an old intervention rule that reads, if we do not like how our clients or our communities are acting, we need to change our behavior. We cannot continue to offer only action-oriented treatment and prevention programs and expect the results to be better. We need to shift from an action paradigm to a stage paradigm if we are to have impact on a much higher percentage of populations at risk.

The Stage Paradigm

The stage paradigm construes behavior change as a process involving progress through six stages: precontemplation, contemplation, preparation, action, maintenance, and termination. Action is seen as one of the six stages, and it becomes integrated as part of the process of individual, community, or population change.

Precontemplation is the stage in which people are not intending to take action in the foreseeable future, usually measured as the next six months. People in this stage are often defensive and resistant, particularly against programs and persuasions designed to have them take action. They also can be demoralized by previous failures, and as a result, they tend to avoid reading, viewing, listening, or talking about their unhealthy habits. They certainly are not ready to enroll in action-oriented programs. Historically, we labeled such individuals as unmotivated, resistant, or not ready for therapy. The reality is we were not ready for them, and we were not motivated to match their needs. Without planned interventions, people in precontemplation can remain stuck in this stage for years.

In the contemplation stage, individuals are intending to take action in the next six months. They are more aware of the benefits of changing, but they also acutely are aware that change costs. The profound ambivalence they often experience can keep them contemplating for years. Chronic contemplators tend to substitute thinking for acting. In one sample, we found that less that 50 percent quit smoking for twenty-four hours over twelve months even though all had initially intended to quit smoking for good in the next six months (Prochaska et al., 1993).

In the preparation stage, people are ready to participate in action-oriented interventions, since they are intending to take action in the next month and have taken some action in the past twelve months. They are more convinced that the pros outweigh the cons of quitting. These are the more motivated members of a population, though we prefer the concept of preparation over motivation. People often perceive motivation as something that happens to them, like hitting bottom, while preparation is more under personal control.

Action involves overt behavioral modification, such as stopping abusing, and is one of the reasons that change was equated with action. Action is the stage in which people work the hardest and apply the largest number of processes of change most frequently. In our research, we found people having to work hard for about six months before they could ease up (Prochaska and DiClemente, 1983). One problem is the public expects the worst to be over in a few weeks or a few months and ease their efforts too quickly. Such poor preparation is one of the reasons so many people relapse so quickly.

After about six months of concentrated action, people enter the maintenance stage. They continue to apply particular processes of change but they do not have to work nearly as hard to prevent relapse. During maintenance, the most common risks for relapse are times of emotional distress, such as times of anger, anxiety, boredom, depression, and stress. People need to be prepared adequately to cope with such distress without resorting back to their unhealthy habits.

How long does the maintenance stage last? For some, it is a lifetime of maintenance. Others can terminate their unhealthy habits totally and experience zero temptations across all high-risk situations and have 100 percent confidence that they never again will resort back to their unhealthy habit. Let us examine how this stage of the paradigm can be applied to five of the most important phases of planned interventions.

Participation

Recall that action-oriented treatment programs fail in this first phase of intervention. Table 8.1 reports results that can help explain such failures. Across four different samples, it can be seen that 20 percent or fewer of smokers are in the preparation stage (Velicer et al., 1995). In a study of fifteen high risk behaviors in 20,000 people, we found that a 40, 40, 20 rule held quite well across the problem behaviors: 40 percent of the population is in precontemplation, 40 percent is in contemplation, and 20 percent is in preparation (Rossi, 1992). When we provide action-oriented programs, we are explicitly or implicitly targeting less than 20 percent of a population. The other 80 percent plus are left on their own.

In one of the Minnesota Heart Health studies, smokers randomly were assigned to one of three recruitment methods for home-based cessation programs (Schmid, Jeffrey, and Hellerstedt, 1989). These announcements generated 1 to 5 percent participation rates, with a personalized letter doing the best.

TABLE 8.1. Distribution of Smokers by Stage Across Four Different Samples

Characteristic	Precontemplation	Contemplation	Preparation	Sample Size
Random digit dial	42.1%	40.3%	17.6%	4,144
Four USA work sites	41.1%	38.7%	20.1%	4,785
California	37.3%	46.7%	16.0%	9,534
RI high schools	43.8%	38.0%	18.3%	208

In two home-based programs with 5,000 smokers in each study, we reached out either by telephone alone or by personal letters followed by telephone calls if needed, and recruited smokers to stage-matched interventions. Using these proactive recruitment methods and stage-matched interventions, we were able to generate participation rates of 82 to 85 percent, respectively (Prochaska, Velicer, Fava, Rossi, Laforge, 1996). Such quantum increases in participation rates provide the potential to generate unprecedented impacts with entire populations of smokers.

Impact equals participation rate times efficacy or action. If a program produced 30 percent efficacy (such as long-term abstinence), historically it was judged to be better than a program that produced 25 percent abstinence. But a program that generates 30 percent efficacy but only 5 percent participation has an impact of only 1.5 percent (30 percent times 5 percent). A program that produces only 25 percent efficacy but 60 percent participation has an impact of 15 percent. With intervention programs, this would be 1,000 percent greater impact on a high-risk population.

The stage paradigm would have us shift our outcomes from efficacy to impacts. To achieve such high impacts, we need to shift from reactive recruitment, where we wait and react when people reach us, to proactive recruitments where we reach out to interact with all potential participants.

But proactive recruitment alone will not work. In the most intensive recruitment protocol to date, Lichtenstein and Hollis (1992) had physicians spend up to five minutes with each smoker just to get them to sign up for an action-oriented cessation clinic. If that did not work, a nurse spent ten minutes to persuade each smoker to sign up, followed by twelve minutes with a videotape and health educator and even a proactive counselor was called, if necessary. The base rate was 1 percent participation. This proactive protocol resulted in 35 percent of smokers in precontemplation signing up. But only 3 percent showed up, and 2 percent finished up, and zero percent end up better off. With a combination of smokers in contemplation and preparation, 65 percent signed up, 15 percent showed up, 11 percent finished up, and some percent ended up better off. In a group of 151 driving while intoxicated (DWI) offenders identified as problem drinkers, assigned to an alcohol counselor, only 27 percent of the sample contacted their counselor and 18 percent completed counseling (Flores, 1982).

To optimize our impacts, we need to use proactive protocols to recruit participants to programs that match their stage. In the Midlands Region of England, for example, 3,500 physicians, nurses, and allied-health professionals have been trained in the paradigm stage that proactively reaches out to all of their patients with alcohol, drug, and nicotine abuse problems. Such proactive and interactive interventions for substance abusers in all stages of change have much greater potential to treat problems before they result in crises like driving while intoxicated or other criminal offenses.

Retention

One of the skeletons in the closet of psychotherapy and behavior-change interventions is their relatively poor retention rates. Across 125 studies, the average retention rate was only about 50 percent (Wierzbicki and Pekarik, 1993). Furthermore, this meta-analysis found few consistent predictors of which participants would drop out prematurely and which would continue in therapy. One of the rare predictors was that addicted patients drop out more often. In studies on smoking, weight control, substance abuse, and a mixture of DSM III disorders, stage-of-change measures proved to be the best predictors of premature termination.

In three groups of psychotherapy participants: the pretreatment-stage profile of the entire 40 percent who dropped out prematurely as judged by their therapists was that of patients in precontemplation. The 20 percent who terminated quickly but appropriately had a profile of patients in action. Using pretreatment stage related measures, we were able to classify correctly 93 percent of the three groups (Medeiros and Prochaska, 1996).

We simply cannot treat people with a precontemplation profile as if they were ready for action interventions and expect them to stay with us. Relapse-prevention strategies would be indicated with addicted clients who are taking action. But those in precontemplation are likely to need drop-out prevention strategies.

The best strategy we have found to promote retention is matching our interventions to the individual's stage of change. In four smoking-cessation studies using such matching strategies, we found we were able to retain smokers in the precontemplation stage at the same high levels as those who started in precontemplation (Prochaska, 1994a).

If we compare patients in mandated treatment to those voluntarily in therapy, we can see more clearly the importance of providing programs that match the needs of patients in the precontemplation stage. O'Hare (1996) found that in a sample of voluntary clients, 44 percent were in the precontemplation stage at the start of treatment. In the same clinics, he found that 72 percent of court-ordered clients were in the precontemplation stage. In many, if not most, treatment programs, DWI offenders are much more likely to be court-ordered into treatment than to be there voluntarily. Knowing how to provide counseling to people in precontemplation should become an essential part of DWI-treatment programs, especially with offenders who are mandated or pressured into treatment.

Progress

The amount of progress participants make following health promotion programs is directly related to the stage they were in at the start of the interventions. This stage effect is illustrated in Figure 8.1 where smokers initially in precontemplation show the smallest amount of abstinence over eighteen months, and those in the preparation stage progress the most (Prochaska, DiClemente, and Norcross, 1992). Across sixty-six different predictions of progress, we found that smokers starting in contemplation were about two-thirds more successful than those in precontemplation at six, twelves, and eighteen month follow-ups.

FIGURE 8.1. Point-prevalent Abstinence in Percentage by Stage of Change

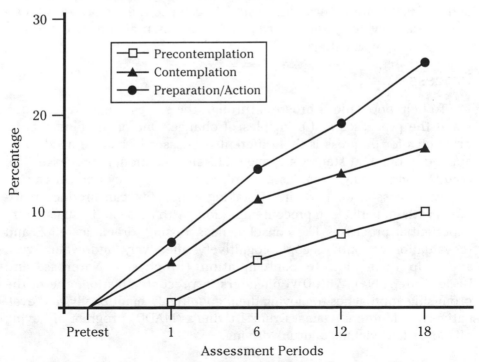

Similarly, those in preparation were about two-thirds more successful than those in contemplation at the same follow-ups (Prochaska, Velicer, Fava, Rossi, and Laforge, 1996).

In Project MATCH (1996), the largest alcohol-treatment study ever conducted, a variety of demographic, problem severity, psychopathology and personality variables were used to predict posttreatment success. In the outpatient groups randomly assigned to three different therapies, stage of change was the best predictor of successful outcomes over the course of fifteen months of follow-up.

These results can be used clinically. A reasonable goal for each therapeutic intervention with substance abusers is to help them progress one stage. If over the course of brief therapy they progress two stages, they will be about two and two-thirds times more successful at longer term follow-ups.

This strategy is being taught to nurses and physicians' assistants in Britain's National Health Care System. One of the first reports is a marked improvement in the morale of such professionals intervening with all patients who abuse alcohol, drugs, and tobacco (Burton, personal communication). These professionals now have strategies that match the needs of all of their patients, not just the minority prepared to take action. Furthermore, these professionals can see the majority progressing where previously they saw most failing when action was the only measure of movement.

Process

To help populations progress through the stages, we need to understand the processes and principles of change. One of the fundamental principles for progress is that different processes of change need to be applied at different stages of change. Classic-conditioning processes like counterconditioning, stimulus control, and contingency control can be highly successful for participants taking action but can produce resistance with individuals in precontemplation. With these individuals, more experiential processes like consciousness raising, dramatic relief, and reevaluation can move people cognitively, affectively, and evaluatively, and help them shift to contemplation (Prochaska, Norcross, and DiClemente, 1994). With DWI offenders in precontemplation, one of the promising approaches to moving them cognitively, emotionally, and evaluatively, is Mothers Against Drunk Driving's (MADD) program of having offenders face victims of drunk driving.

We have reported in detail which processes are best matched to each stage (Prochaska, Norcross, and DiClemente, 1994). Space limitations permit only a couple of examples of progress principles. Figure 8.2 presents the pros and cons of changing across the stages of change for twelve different behaviors from ten different populations (Prochaska et al., 1994).

FIGURE 8.2. Point-prevalent Abstinence in Percentage by Stage of Change

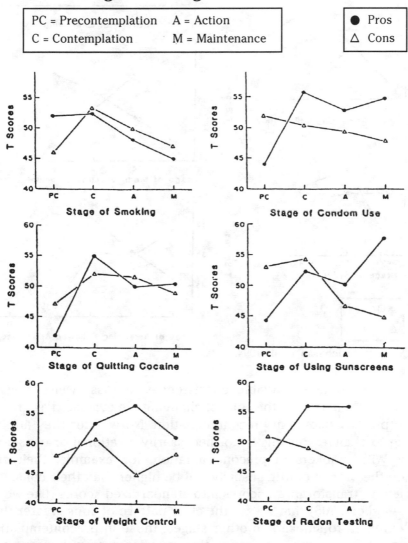

(continued)

FIGURE 8.2. (continued)

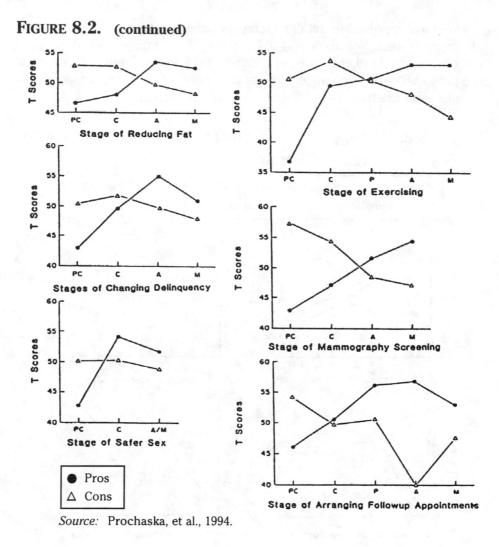

Source: Prochaska, et al., 1994.

There are some remarkable consistencies across twelve diverse behaviors. With all twelve, the cons of changing are evaluated as greater than the pros by people in precontemplation. No wonder they are not intending to change. But this is not necessarily a rational or conscious process. With smokers in precontemplation, for example, their raw scores on the pros of quitting usually will be higher than their cons. It is only when we transform raw scores into standardized scores (like we do on the MMPI or WAIS) that we see the clear pattern of cons greater than pros. Compared to smokers in other stages, those in precontemplation are underestimating the pros of quitting, overestimating the cons and probably are not conscious of the process. No wonder we need to apply consciousness-raising techniques, like feedback, to help them progress.

With all twelve problems, the pros are higher in contemplation than precontemplation, but there is no consistent pattern with the cons. With some behaviors, the cons of change increase as people begin to think seriously about taking action. So, one principle of progress is that the pros of changing must increase for people to move from precontemplation to contemplation.

With all twelve problems, the cons are lower in action than in contemplation. A second principle of progress then, is that the cons of changing must decline as people move from contemplation to action.

We can be even more mathematical. Across all twelve behaviors we discovered a strong principle of progress that states:

$$\text{Precontemplation} \longrightarrow \text{Action} \cong 1 \text{ S.D.} \uparrow \text{Pros}$$

That is, to progress from precontemplation to action, the pros of changing increase approximately one standard deviation (Prochaska, 1994b).

We also discovered a weak principle that states:

$$\text{Precontemplation} \longrightarrow \text{Action} \cong .5 \text{ S.D.} \downarrow \text{Cons}$$

To progress from precontemplation to action, the cons of changing must decrease .5 standard deviations. One application of these principles would be to place twice as much emphasis on increasing the appreciation of the pros of changing than on decreasing the cons.

In a sample of 230 cocaine and heroin addicts in action-oriented drug treatment, we found the same pattern of relationships between stage of change and the pros and cons of quitting drugs (Tsoh, Prochaska, and Rossi, 1996). Furthermore, we found the same pattern for the pros and cons of substance-abuse treatment. Using standardized scores, clients in precontemplation rate the cons of therapy as dramatically greater than the pros. Those in preparation and beyond had the opposite pattern with the pros markedly higher than the cons. Finally, we found that the addicts in precontemplation saw themselves as being in treatment more because of coercion than because of choice. Those in preparation and beyond perceived therapy participation as due much more to choice than coercion. No wonder the majority of substance abusers do not seek therapy or complete therapy.

Outcomes

Research on therapeutic interventions on different problem areas tends to follow a common historical path. First, the emphasis is on trying to demonstrate that therapies are effective for a particular problem like driving while intoxicated. Then, comparative therapy studies are done to see which therapy or therapies are most effective. Next, a more sophisticated matching question is asked: which therapies are most effective with which type of DWI offenders?

This has been the history of outcome research in the DWI field. Up through the mid 1980s, the field was struggling to demonstrate that therapeutic interventions could enhance outcomes beyond what legal interventions already were producing. Compared to effectiveness studies in other problem behavior areas, the DWI field faced some serious limitations. First, in many studies, random assignment to different treatments was not feasible and/or possible. Second, true control groups were often not viable because of the perceived need to treat and/or punish most if not all offenders. Third, DWI offenders were a much more heterogeneous group than is the case for most problem areas. DWI offenders include relatively well-adjusted social drinkers, problem drinkers with criminal histories, young thrill-seeking drivers with a range of traffic offenses, older drivers with serious marital problems, and so forth.

It is not clear that any single therapy effectively could treat all the different problems that appear under the domain of DWI offenses. Another major problem is the relatively low base rate for DWI arrests—typically less than 10 percent a year. With recidivism as the main-outcome measure there can be a floor effect that is hard to outperform. With addiction-treatment outcomes, for example, relapse rates are in the range of 80 percent in the first year, so there is considerable room for improvement. No wonder after years of evaluation, the outcomes research was inconclusive as to the effectiveness of therapeutic interventions for driving while intoxicated.

For example, Holden (1986) found in a randomized clinical trial that there were no differences in DWI arrests or other arrests for social drinkers assigned to no treatment, education classes, probation, or probation plus education. But the DWI arrest rates per year for the control group of social drinkers was less than 6 percent—a measure with such a floor effect that it could be impossible to outperform. With problem drinkers, Holden found no differences in DWI arrests for no treatment controls compared to therapy alone, probation alone, and probation plus therapy. Again the base rates were low (less than 10 percent of the arrests per year). For other types of arrests, the two probation-supervision groups did outperform the no-treatment and therapy only groups.

In contrast, Nickel (1990) in Germany used a quasi-experimental design and found that no-treatment comparison group did worse (18.8 percent recidivism) than did the three combined therapy groups (13.4 percent recidivism). This was true even though the no-treatment group would be expected to do better since their alcohol, driving, and other problem histories were better than those assigned to treatment.

The most common conclusion from services of DWI rehabilitation outcome research is that there is a small beneficial effect on the drinking behaviors of DWI offenders (Mann, Leigh, Vingilis, and DeGenova, 1983; Peck, Sadler, and Perrine, 1985; Wells-Parker, Landrum, and Topping, 1990). There are reviewers of the research who conclude that the more rigorous the design of the outcome research, the less support there is for effectiveness of rehabilitation programs (for example, Holden, 1986; Jacobs, 1989; and Nichols et al., 1981).

One reason that the effectiveness of therapies can be difficult to establish in literature reviews is that poor treatments get mixed in with good treatments. If enough studies assess poor treatments or weak treatments, then the potential effectiveness of good treatments can be watered-down or overwhelmed by ineffectiveness of poor or weak therapies. The next step in research then is to carry out comparative-outcome studies to identify which are the best therapies and which are the worst.

The most common outcome when comparing alternative therapies for the same problem behavior is a grand tie (Smith, Glass, and Miller, 1980). It is very difficult to demonstrate that one therapy outperforms an alternative therapy for the same problem. Such a tie was found in the National Institute of Mental Health's largest depression study when cognitive therapy, interpersonal therapy, and drug therapy produced common outcomes (Elkin et al., 1989).

With the largest treatment study ever done on alcohol abuse and alcoholism, common outcomes were found for both outpatients and aftercare patients randomly assigned to cognitive-behavior therapy, motivational-enhancement therapy, and 12-step therapy (Project MATCH, 1996). With one of the largest comparative treatment evaluation studies done with DWI offenders, common outcomes were found for group-behavior therapy, group individual psychology therapy, and group dynamics therapy (Nickel, 1990).

How can we improve the effectiveness of interventions when very diverse therapies produce such common outcomes? Matching treatment to the type of patient was seen as one of the most promising areas of research in the past decade. Cluster analyses on samples of DWI offenders clearly demonstrated that there are different types of offenders (for example, Donovan and Marlatt, 1982; Steer, Fine, and Scoles, 1979; Wells-Parker et al., 1990; Wieczorek and Miller, 1992; and Wilson, 1991). The types range from the relatively well-adjusted offenders with low psychopathology and alcohol abuse to those with moderately high psychological and alcohol problems, to those with the most severe psychopathology and alcoholism. This type of typology based on severity of problems finds that the relatively well-adjusted offenders make up 30 to 45 percent of the DWI population. The high severity group accounts for about 30 to 40 percent of DWI samples. Typologies can be based on other sets of variables such as demographics, motivational level, treatment history, and so forth.

The hope is that different treatments will have their greatest effects with different types of offenders. If, for example, 12-step treatments were found to work best with more chronic offenders, and motivational-enhancement therapy with less-motivated offenders, and cognitive-behavior therapy with more criminal offenders, then DWI programs could match the therapy to the type of offender and thereby maximize outcomes.

The DWI research on matching to date has all been post hoc analyses (Wells-Parker, Landrum, and Topping, 1990). After a comparative treatment study is completed, analyses are done to determine if one treatment performed better with certain types of offenders and another treatment did better with other groups. Since there is always variance in any study, such post hoc analyses can maximize on chance outcomes. Post hoc analyses are scientifically acceptable for generating hypotheses but not for confirming hypotheses.

A priori predictions are needed to confirm hypotheses. There has been only one study designed to date to test a priori predictions on matching hypotheses. Project MATCH tested ten matching variables based on post hoc analyses of comparative treatment research with alcoholism and alcohol abuse (Project MATCH, 1996). Some of the patients in Project MATCH were DWI offenders referred by courts but unfortunately they were not analyzed separately.

The matching variables that were tested were divided into ten categories: (1) alcohol severity; (2) cognitive impairment; (3) conceptual level (simple versus complex); (4) gender; (5) meaning seeking (spiritual orientation); (6) motivation; (7) psychiatric severity; (8) sociopathy; (9) support for drinking; (10) typology (consisting of Type A, representing low genetic vulnerability and low severity; and Type B, representing high vulnerability and severity of alcohol dependence). The treatments that were compared (12-step therapy, cognitive-behavior therapy, and motivational-enhancement therapy) all were provided as individual therapy. The two groups tested were outpatients and patients in aftercare following a minimum of seven days of residential care.

Out of thirty-two matching hypotheses tested across the three treatments and two groups, only one was significant. In the outpatient group, clients low in psychiatric severity had more abstinent days after 12-step treatment than after cognitive-behavior therapy. The basic conclusion is that each of the three different therapies produced common outcomes not only for the overall samples, but for each of the ten subtypes as well.

One of the most promising hypotheses of the past decade for alcoholism treatment generally and DWI offenders specifically received practically no support from this outstanding scientific study. Where are we to search next for the impacts of our programs?

Most of the research on matching has been done on group matching; match one group (for example, type) of patient to one type of therapy, and hopefully better outcomes will result. In our stage approach, we advocate individual matching: tailoring the intervention to the individual's needs as much as possible. We assess each individual on the fifteen dynamic variables that are the best predictors of progress across the stages. We then interact with each individual around their particular profile and provide individualized feedback about what they are doing right, what processes and principles they are underutilizing, and which they are overutilizing.

Rather than applying only three manuals of therapy, this approach allows us to deliver more than 20,000 different treatment interactions. Let us examine what we have discovered to date when applying interactive interventions matched as much as possible to the needs of each individual.

In the computer portion participants completed by mail or telephone, forty questions that were entered in our central computers generated feedback reports. These reports informed participants about their stage of change, their pros and cons of changing, and their use of change processes appropriate to their stages. At the baseline, participants were given positive feedback on what they were doing correctly and guidance on which principles and processes they needed to apply more in order to progress.

In two progress reports delivered over the next six months, participants also received positive feedback on any improvement they made on
any of the variables relevant to progressing. Thus, demoralized and
defensive individuals could begin progressing without having to quit and
without having to work hard. Participants in the contemplation stage
could begin taking small steps, like delaying their first cigarette in the
morning for an extra thirty minutes. They could choose small steps that
would increase their self-efficacy and help them become better prepared
for quitting.

In the personalized condition, participants received four proactive
counselor calls over the six-month intervention period. Three of the calls
were based on the computer reports. Counselors reported much more
difficulty in interacting with participants without any progress data.
Without scientific assessments, it was much harder for both clients and

FIGURE 8.3. Point-prevalence Abstinence Rates of Four Treatment Groups

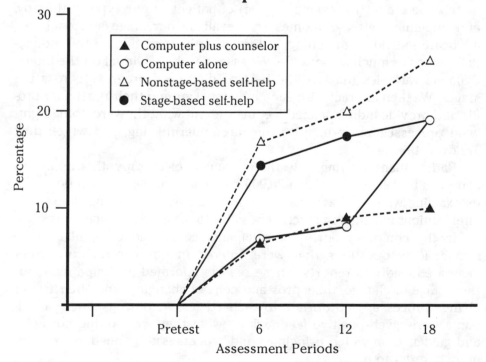

Source: Prochaska, et al., 1993.

counselors to tell whether any significant progress had occurred since their last interaction.

Figure 8.3 presents point-prevalence abstinence rates for each of the four treatment groups over eighteen months, with treatment ending at six months (Prochaska et al., 1993). The two self-help manual conditions paralleled each other for twelve months. At eighteen months, the stage-matched manuals moved ahead. This is an example of a delayed-action effect, which we often observe with stage-matched programs. It takes time for participants in early stages to progress all the way to action. Therefore, some treatment effects as measured by action will be observed only after considerable delay. But it is encouraging to find treatments producing therapeutic effects months and even years after termination.

The computer alone and computer-plus-counselor conditions paralleled each other for twelve months. Then, the effects of the counselor condition flattened out while the computer condition effects continued to increase. We only can speculate as to the delayed differences between these two conditions. Participants in the personalized condition may have become somewhat dependent on the social support and social control of the counselor calling. The last call was after the six-month assessment, and benefits would be observed at twelve months. Termination of the counselors could result in no further progress because of the loss of social support and control. The classic pattern in smoking-cessation clinics is rapid relapse beginning as soon as the treatment is terminated. Some of this rapid relapse could be due to the sudden loss of social support or social control provided by the counselors and other participants in the clinic.

In this clinical trial, participants were recruited reactively. They called us for help. How would their results compare to the participants that we called proactively to offer help? Most people would predict that those who called us for help would succeed more than those who we called to help.

Figure 8.4 shows the remarkable results of comparing individuals in a study who we called (reactive) (Prochaska et al., 1993) to those in a study that we called (proactive) (Prochaska, Velicer, Fava, and Rossi, 1996; Prochaska, Velicer, Fava, and LaForge, 1996). Both groups received the same home-based expert system computer reports delivered over a six-month period. While the reactively recruited subjects were slightly more successful at each follow-up, what is striking is how similar the results are.

FIGURE 8.4. Reactive and Proactive Individuals

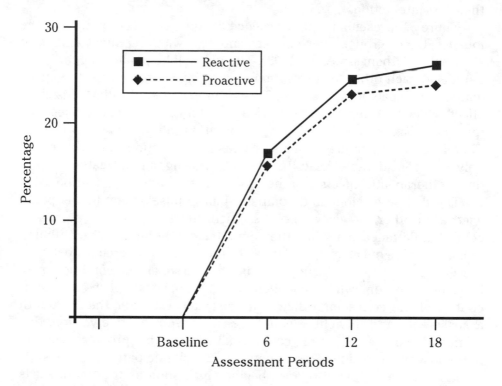

Sources: Prochaska, et al., 1993.
Prochaska, Velicer, Fava, and Rossi, 1996.
Prochaska, Velicer, Fava, and LaForge, 1996.

Summary

Historically, the field focused on two therapeutic alternatives for reaching high-risk populations: voluntary therapy versus mandated treatment. The first form was initiated by the individual clients; the second was ordered by others. Voluntary therapy was viewed as creating more commitment, cooperation, change, and positive outcomes. Mandated therapy was often viewed as increasing participation but at the risk of increasing coercion, conflict, and noncompliance. But research results were clear when comparing voluntary versus mandated drug abuse therapy: mandated treatment did as well as voluntary treatment (Anglin, 1988; Maddux, 1988).

One of the problems with mandated treatment for alcoholism and alcohol abuse is that we have to wait until someone breaks the law before treatment can be ordered by the court. This is still a reactive approach to recruitment. We wait until people come to the court and then we react. Proactive interventions provide our communities with a more promising approach. We do not have to wait for individuals to initiate treatment; remember most will not unless a crisis occurs. We proactively can initiate interventions with entire populations of high-risk people.

If our results can be replicated across addictions and across populations, intervention programs will be able to produce unprecedented impacts on entire populations. We believe that such unprecedented impacts require scientific and professional shifts:

- From an action paradigm to a stage paradigm

- From reactive to proactive recruitment

- From expecting participants to match the needs of our programs to having our programs match their individual needs

- From clinic-based to community-based behavior change programs that still apply the field's most powerful individualized and interactive intervention strategies

With this type of revolution in population-based interventions, our sciences and professions will be able to respond to the huge unmet needs and the great opportunities related to the treatment of the addictions.

Endnote

1 Our research cited in this article was supported by Grants CA 27821, CA 50087, and CA 63745 from the National Cancer Institute.

References

Anglin, D. M.. 1988. The Efficacy of Civil Commitment in Treatment of Narcotics Addiction. *Journal of Drug Use*. 19:527-545.

COMMIT Research Group. 1995. Community Intervention Trial for Smoking Cessation (Commit): I. Cohort Results from a Four-year Community Intervention. *American Journal of Public Health*. 85:183-192.

Donovan, D. M. and G. A. Marlatt. 1982. Personality Subtypes among Driving-while Intoxicated Offenders: Relationship to Drinking Behavior and Driving Risk. *Journal of Consulting and Clinical Psychology*. 50:241-249.

Elkin, I. E., T. Shea, J. T. Watkins, S. D. Imber, S. M. Stotsky, J. F. Collins, D. R. Glass, P. A. Pilkonis, W. R. Leber, J. P. Docherty, S. J. Fiester, and M. B. Parloff. 1989. National Institute of Mental Health's Treatment of Depression Collaborative Research Program: General Effectiveness of Treatment. *Archives of General Psychiatry*. 46:974-982.

Ennett, S. T., N. S. Tobler, C. L. Ringwalt, and R. L. Flewelling. 1994. How Effective Is Drug Abuse Resistance Education? A Meta-analysis of Project DARE Outcome Evaluations. *American Journal of Public Health*. 84:1394-401.

Flores, P. 1982. The Efficacy of the Use of Coercion in Getting DWI Offenders into Treatment. *Journal of Alcohol and Drug Education*. 27:18-27.

Glasgow, R. E., J. R. Terborg, J. F. Hollis, H. U. H. Severson, and S. M. Boles. 1995. Take Heart: Results from the Initial Phase of a Work-site Wellness Program. *American Journal of Health*. 85:209- 116.

Holden, R.T. 1986. Rehabilitative Sanctions for Drunk Driving. In D. Foley, ed. *Stop DWI: Successful Community Responses to Drunk Driving*. Lexington, Massachusetts: Lexington Books.

Hunt, W. A., L. W. Barnett, and L. G. Branch. 1971. Relapse Rates in Addiction Programs. *Journal of Clinical Psychology*. 27:455-459.

Jacobs, J. B. 1989. *Drunk Driving: An American Dilemma*. Chicago: The University of Chicago Press.

Lando, H. A., T. F. Pechacek, P. L. Pirie, D. M. Murray, M. B. Mittelmark, E. Lichtenstein, F. Nothwehyr, and C. Gray. 1995. Changes in Adult Cigarette Smoking in the Minnesota Heart Health Program. *American Journal of Public Health*. 85:201-208.

Lichtenstein, E. and J. Hollis. 1992. Patient Referral to Smoking Cessation Programs: Who Follows Through? *The Journal of Family Practice*. 34:739-744.

Luepker, R. V., D. M. Murray, D. R. Jacobs, M. B. Mittelmark, N. Bracht, R. Carlaw, R. Crow, P. Elmer, J. Finnegan, A. R. Folsom, et al. 1994. Community Education for Cardiovascular Disease Prevention: Risk Factor Changes in the Minnesota Heart Health Program. *American Journal of Public Health*. 84:1383-1393.

Maddux, J. F. 1988. Clinical Experience with Civil Commitment. *Journal of Drug Issues*. 18: 575-594.

Mann, R. E., G. Leigh, E. R. Vingilis, and K. DeGenova. 1983. A Critical Review on the Effectiveness of Drinking Driving Rehabilitation Programmes. *Accident Analysis and Prevention*. 15:441-461.

Medeiros, M. E., and J. O. Prochaska. 1996. Predicting Termination and Continuation Status in Psychotherapy: Using the Transtheoretical Model. Unpublished manuscript.

Nichols, I. L., E. B. Weinstein, V. S. Ellingstad, D. L. Struckman-Johnson, and R. E. Reis. 1981. The Effectiveness of Education and Treatment Programs for Drinking Drivers: A Decade of Evaluation. In L. Goldberg, ed. *Alcohol, Drugs and Traffic Safety* (Vol. 3). Stockholm: Almgvist and Wikskell.

Nickel, W. R. 1990. Programs for the Rehabilitation and Treatment of Drinking-driving Multiple Offenders in the Federal Republic of Germany. In R. J. Wilson and R. E. Mann, eds. *Drinking and Driving: Advances in Research and Prevention*. New York: The Guilford Press.

Peck, R. C., D. D. Sadler, and M. W. Perrine. 1985. The Comparative Effectiveness of Alcohol Rehabilitation and Licensing Control Actions for Drunk Driving Offenders: A Review of the Literature. *Alcohol Drugs and Driving: Abstracts and Reviews.* 1:15-39.

Prochaska, J. O. 1994a. Staging: A Revolution. Master science lecture at the Annual Meeting of the Society for Behavioral Medicine, Boston, Massachusetts.

Prochaska, J. O. 1994b. Strong and Weak Principles for Progressing from Precontemplation to Action Based on Twelve Problem Behaviors. *Health Psychology.* 13:47-51.

Prochaska, J. O. and C. C. DiClemente. 1983. Stages and Processes of Self-change of Smoking: Toward an Integrative Model of Change. *Journal of Consulting and Clinical Psychology.* 51:390-395.

Prochaska, J. O., C. C. DiClemente, and J. C. Norcross. 1992. In Search of How People Change: Applications to the Addictive Behaviors. *American Psychologist.* 47:1102-1114.

Prochaska, J. O., C. C. DiClemente, W. F. Velicer, and J. S. Rossi. 1993. Standardized, Individualized, Interactive, and Personalized Self-help Programs for Smoking Cessation. *Health Psychology.* 12:399-405.

Prochaska, J. O., J. C. Norcross, and C. C. DiClemente. 1994. *Changing for Good.* New York: William Morrow and Company.

Prochaska, J. O., W. F. Velicer, J. S. Rossi, M. G. Goldstein, B. H. Marcus, W. Bakowski, C. Fire, L. L. Harlow, C. A. Redding, D. Rosenbloom, et al. 1994. Stages of Change and Decisional Balance for 12 Problem Behaviors. *Health Psychology.* 13:39-46.

Prochaska, J. O., W. F. Velicer, J. Fava, and R. Laforge. 1996. Toward Disease State Management for Smoking: Stage Matched Expert Systems for a Total Managed Care Population of Smokers. Unpublished manuscript.

Prochaska, J. O., W. F Velicer, J. Fava, and J. Rossi. 1996. A Stage Matched Expert System Intervention with a Total Population of Smokers. Unpublished manuscript.

Prochaska, J.O., W. F Velicer, J. Fava, J. Rossi, and R Laforge. 1996. Stage, Interactive, Dose Response, Counseling and Stimulus Control Computer Effects in a Total Managed Care Population of Smokers. Unpublished manuscript.

Project MATCH. 1996. Matching Alcoholism Treatments to Client Heterogeneity: Project Match Post-treatment Drinking Outcomes. Symposium presented at the Addictions '96 Conference, Hilton Head, South Carolina.

Rossi, J. S. 1992. Stages of Change for 15 Health Risk Behaviors in an HMO Population. Paper presentation at 13th meeting of the Society for Behavioral Medicine, New York, New York.

Schmid, T. L., R. W. Jeffrey, and W. L. Hellerstedt. 1989. Direct Mail Recruitment to House-based Smoking and Weight Control Programs: A Comparison of Strengths. *Preventive Medicine*. 18:503- 517.

Smith, M. L., G. V. Glass, and T. I. Miller. 1980. *The Benefits of Psychotherapy*. Baltimore: John Hopkins University Press.

Sobell, L. C., J. S. Cunningham, M. B. Sobell, S. Agrawal, D. R Gavin, G. I. Leo, and K. N. Singh. 1996. Fostering Self-change among Problem Drinkers: A Proactive Community Intervention. *Addictive Behaviors*. 21:817-834.

Steer, R. A., E. W. Fine, and P. E. Scoles. 1979. Classification of Men Arrested for Driving While Intoxicated, and Treatment Implications: A Cluster-analytic Study. *Journal of Studies on Alcohol*. 40:222-229.

Tsoh, J. Y., J. O. Prochaska, and J. S. Rossi. 1996. Coercion, Stages of Change and Decisional Balance among Drug Addicts in Treatment. Manuscript submitted for review.

Velicer, W. F., J. L. Fava, J. O. Prochaska, D. B Abrams, K. M. Emmons, and J. Pierce 1995. Distribution of Smokers by Stage in Three Representatives Samples. *Preventive Medicine*. 24:401-411.

Veroff, J., E. Douvan, and R. A. Kulka. 1981. *Mental Health in America*. New York: Basic Books.

Wells-Parker, E., J. W. Landrum, and J. S. Topping. 1990. Matching the DWI Offender to an Effective Intervention Strategy: An Emerging Research Agenda. In R. J. Wilson and R. E. Mann, eds. *Drinking and Driving: Advances in Research and Prevention*. New York: The Guilford Press.

Wieczorek, W. and B. Miller. 1992. Preliminary Typology Designed for Treatment Matching of Driving While Intoxicated Offenders. *Journal of Consulting and Clinical Psychology.* 60:757-765.

Wierzbicki, M. and G. Pekarik. 1993. A Meta-analysis of Psychotherapy Dropout. *Professional Psychology: Research and Practice.* 29:190-195.

Wilson, J. 1991. Subtypes of DWIs and High Risk Drivers: Implications for Differential Intervention. *Alcohol, Drugs and Driving.* 7:1-12.

Examining Offender Readiness to Change and the Impact on Treatment Outcome[1]

9

Sharon Kennedy, Ph.D.

Ralph Serin, Ph.D.

Correctional Service of Canada
Ottawa, Ontario
Canada

Introduction

The work of Andrews et al. (1986, 1990) outlines the key principles of effective correctional programming. These principles are based on their detailed analysis of programs that showed above-average success in reducing recidivism. The risk principle states that the intensity of the treatment intervention should correspond with the risk of recidivism. This is because higher-risk cases tend to respond better to intensive service, while low-risk cases respond better to less intensive service.

Once offenders are matched appropriately in this manner, attention should be directed to the sorts of needs that the treatment program should address. The need principle distinguishes between criminogenic and noncriminogenic needs. The former are dynamic risk factors (Gendreau, Cullen, and Bonta, 1994), which, if changed, reduce the likelihood of criminal conduct. In contrast, noncriminogenic needs, which are derived from character variables such as personal distress and self-esteem (Gendreau, Cullen, and Bonta, 1994), are considered inappropriate targets for treatment since their resolution does not have a significant impact on recidivism. Finally, the responsivity principle states that styles and modes of treatment service must be closely matched to the preferred learning style and abilities of the offender (Andrews et al., 1986).

Although the principles of risk and need have been articulated clearly in the literature, the precise role and function of offender responsivity and other variables related to offender motivation are not yet clearly understood. This is despite the fact that they are widely recognized as key factors mediating the success of treatment programs (Brown, 1996). It is our view that treatment readiness and responsivity must be assessed and considered in treatment planning if the maximum effectiveness of treatment programs is to be realized (Kennedy and Serin, 1997).

In many correctional agencies today, treatment is viewed as an integral part of the risk-management continuum, and offender responsivity is a critical issue for correctional programs. This chapter, which is set in the context of a risk/need management framework, will present a theoretical overview of the concept of offender treatment responsivity. Findings from a standardized assessment battery of offender responsivity will be presented and a number of responsivity-related factors will be identified and discussed in terms of their potential impact on treatment outcome. Our objective is to place the construct of treatment responsivity in a context which underscores the importance of allocating offenders to programs in the most effective manner and to identify factors that might mediate the effectiveness of treatment services.

Responsivity and Related Constructs

It is commonly accepted that behavioral, cognitive-behavioral, and multimodal intervention strategies yield the best outcome for correctional samples (Andrews and Bonta, 1994). However, the provision of good programs with high integrity, while necessary, is not a sufficient requirement for effective intervention with offenders. Notably, intervention must target criminogenic needs; therapists and program deliverers must account for offenders' learning styles and characteristics; and efforts must be made to match offenders' and therapists' styles. Several of these issues are fundamental to the principle of treatment responsivity, a term used to describe client-based factors which influence the potential for positive treatment effects.

By conceptualizing responsivity as a broad concept which incorporates treatment readiness (motivation) and is related to treatment response and outcome, it may be possible to advance our efforts at detailed assessments of responsivity. Gains in our understanding of effective correctional programming also will be helpful so that appropriate treatment is provided as a backdrop against which the assessment of responsivity occurs. Concepts such as amenability, motivation, compliance, treatment response, and treatment gain all contribute to the notion of responsivity. Importantly, the extension of the assessment of treatment gain to reflect the degree of change and the identification of thresholds for knowledge and skill have appeal.

The relation of responsivity to outcome and risk are also important issues to investigate. Preliminary research supports the utility of the assessment of motivation in predicting risk of offenders under community supervision (Stewart and Millson, 1995). The potential for interaction between responsivity and risk level and its effect on offender outcome merits further investigation. Below, we review the responsivity principle, its related constructs and their relationship to risk, need, and effective intervention in corrections.

Treatability

Rogers and Webster (1989) suggest that treatability refers to the clinical determination of which patients (offenders), under what treatment modalities and environmental conditions will respond most favorably. Their conclusion was that clinicians who attempt to assess treatability are hampered by a lack of consensual understanding of the construct and its relationship to treatment outcome. This is consistent with data reported by Quinsey and Maguire (1983) which revealed that mental health staff demonstrate poor interclinician reliability when assessing the treatability of offenders with personality disorders. Although most offenders meet the DSM-IV diagnostic criteria for personality disorder (American Psychiatric Association, 1994; Marshall and Serin 1997), clinicians disagree about relevant treatment strategies and treatment efficacy for these offenders. This creates a dilemma for informed treatment planning.

Heilbrun and his colleagues (Heilbrun et al., 1988; Heilbrun et al., 1992) took the initial steps to develop a means of assessing treatability. First, they identified four key aspects: (1) appropriateness (fit between treatment goals and patient deficits), (2) response history (previous experience with this form of treatment), (3) motivation, and (4) contraindications.

Then, they created individual items and organized them into the following areas: a. biological (appropriate disorder, history of response, physical contraindications, and motivation); b. educational/training (lacking in relevant skill, response to past educational/training interventions, likelihood that training will be productive, and motivation for specific training, with these four items rated separately for vocational skills, social skills, living skills, anger management, medication management, and communications skills); c. management (frequency of threatening or aggressive behavior, past response to management interventions, likelihood that management will be effective); and d. psychotherapy (extent of discontent or ineffectiveness, past response to psychotherapy, contraindications, and motivation).

By creating a scale using these items, Heilbrun et al. (1992) demonstrated modest overall reliability, with the strongest findings in the areas of psychotherapy and biological treatment. These data support the view that even the treatability aspect of responsivity is a multifaceted concept and that a great deal more work is required to operationalize the construct in a meaningful and empirically sound manner.

Motivation as a Dynamic Variable

The traditional view of motivation was very narrow and simplistic. Motivation was defined as a personality characteristic or problem. Thus, motivation was used as an adjective, and the desire to change was perceived as a quality one had or did not have. This view failed to include all the factors which influence a person's desire to change his or her behavior. This view has been replaced in recent years with a view that emphasizes the complexity of change. The interactional view asserts that internal and external factors influence the change process. From this perspective, motivation is viewed as an interactional and interpersonal process that can be influenced in a positive way by the professional (Miller and Rollnick, 1991).

In this context, motivation is dynamic and therefore at least some responsibility falls to the therapist to motivate the offender (Miller and Rollnick, 1991). The therapist must create effective motivational choices so that offenders are most likely to respond favorably to correctional programming. This includes enhancing offender motivation and dealing with resistant clients after the pretreatment assessment of treatment readiness. Offenders who are resistant to treatment may require pretreatment priming for the formal treatment program to be effective.

Many offenders view their criminal behavior in an ego-syntonic manner. That is, they are relatively unconcerned about their actions, except in terms of their legal consequences. Accordingly, offenders often feel coerced into treatment, consenting only because the contingencies for refusing to participate are sufficiently negative. Minimization of the effects of their behavior on others, denial of responsibility, and rationalization of their law violations are common among offenders. Treatment engagement must address these obstacles, primarily by focusing on therapeutic alliance and assisting offenders to develop a decisional balance analysis for comparison purposes (Preston and Murphy, 1997; Velicer et al., 1985).

Further, the content, intensity, and style of intervention must be consistent with the offender's current stage in the change process. This complex interaction forms the cornerstone for incorporating motivational interviewing into correctional programming (Miller and Rollnick, 1991). Therefore, treatment progress may depend on the match between the offender and the type of treatment modality, as well as the interaction between therapist and offender. Currently, however, there is little empirical data to indicate the relative contribution of these factors to treatment progress.

Client Characteristics and Program Matching

It is widely accepted that offenders differ substantially, not only in their level of motivation to participate in treatment, but also in terms of their responsivity to various styles or modes of intervention. According to the responsivity principle, these factors impact directly on the effectiveness of correctional treatment and ultimately on recidivism. Consequently, various offender characteristics must be considered when assigning offenders to treatment programs.

Factors that interfere with or facilitate learning can be broken down into internal and external responsivity factors. Internal factors refer to individual client characteristics: motivation, personality characteristics (in other words, psychopathy, anxiety, depression, mental illness, self-esteem, poor social skills) cognitive intellectual deficits (such as low intelligence, concrete-type thinking, inadequate problem-solving skills, poor verbal skills) and other demographic variables (such as, age, gender, race, ethnicity) (Bonta, 1995; Van Voorhis, 1997). External factors refer to therapist and setting characteristics. It is important to understand that external factors, in isolation, do not impact on responsivity, but rather those therapist characteristics or setting characteristics interact with offender characteristics to affect (impede or assist) responsivity.

Specific responsivity factors merit comment in that they are represented in most settings. Consideration of gender issues, ethnicity, age, social background, and life experiences all contribute to the engagement of offenders into treatment and the development of a therapeutic alliance (Dana, 1993). Ignoring these issues will significantly impede offenders' compliance with treatment. Similarly, failure to consider these factors may contribute to an inaccurate assessment of the motivation or readiness of individuals referred for treatment. This is not to imply that offenders and clinicians must share similar characteristics and backgrounds. Rather, treatment will be enhanced with respect to the extent to which such factors are considered. Effective matching of offenders' and therapists' styles, as well as intensity of intervention are central to the principle of treatment responsivity.

Differential Treatment

Efforts to clarify offender subpopulations according to certain clinical and offense-specific variables has furthered our knowledge of effective correctional treatment. For example, differentiating among sex offenders according to type of victim, degree of sexual deviance, and pervasiveness of sexual assault history, among other variables, distinguish empirical " types" (Knight, Prentky, and Cerce, 1994). These types have differential outcomes, both for those who have received treatment and those who have not received treatment (Marques et al., 1994; Barbaree, Seto, and Maric, 1996; Hanson and Bussière, 1996). Similarly, violent offenders can be distinguished in terms of their anger problems, the degree of instrumental violence employed, their use of weapons, their attributions towards others, the degree of planning in their crimes, and their level of impulsivity. This array of variables clearly will yield a heterogeneous sample of violent offenders referred for treatment. In this respect, one treatment strategy cannot be expected to meet all these offenders' needs equally. Additionally, it is reasonable to anticipate such heterogeneity will yield differential treatment effects similar to those seen in the sex offender treatment literature. A good differentiation of offender classification types according to risk and need may further advance the precision by which treatment can be prescriptively applied and should lead to a more comprehensive assessment of responsivity related factors (Serin, 1995).

Treatment effectiveness depends on matching types of treatment and therapists to types of clients. Moreover, the general psychotherapy research has shown that the personal variables of a therapist are very important for effective intervention. However, with the exception of the Canadian Volunteers in Correction (CaVIC) research conducted by Andrews and Kiessling (1980) on characteristics of effective probation officers, and the differential treatment research (Barkwell, 1980), there is little systematic research on the interaction of therapist and offender characteristics on correctional treatment. This is a much needed area of research as we often find a group of therapists working in a common setting and offering the same treatment approach, but producing dramatic differences in terms of client attrition and successful outcome. Therapists' attitudes and competence that do not match the aims and content of a program may lower treatment integrity and reduce its effectiveness.

Stages of Change

Prochaska and his colleagues have conducted important research on the process of psychotherapy change (Prochaska and DiClemente, 1986; Prochaska, DiClemente, and Norcross, 1992), mainly in the area of addictions; particularly in the area of smoking cessation (Davidson, 1992). Four stages of change have been identified: precontemplation, contemplation, action, and maintenance. In the precontemplation stage, the individual is not even considering the possibility of change. Individuals in this stage typically perceive that they are being coerced into treatment to satisfy someone else's need.

The contemplation stage is characterized by ambivalence. In other words, individuals may simultaneously or in rapid alternation consider and reject reasons to change. Individuals in the action stage have made a commitment to change and are engaging in actions to bring about change. Typically, at this stage, they are involved in therapy. Lastly, individuals in the maintenance stage are working to sustain the significant changes they have made and are actively working to prevent relapse. This transtheoretical treatment model (Prochaska, DiClemente, and Norcross, 1992) highlights the importance of treatment readiness and is consistent with the responsivity concept.

To ensure their intervention is sensitive to clients' level of readiness, Prochaska developed and validated a self-report measure, the University of Rhode Island Change Assessment Scale (URICA)—now known as the Stages of Change Questionnaire—on various samples. Although their assessment work is evolving, it provides an initial starting point for our research on the development of a multimethod assessment strategy of treatment readiness and responsivity with offenders. Although there is concern about the predictive validity of the stages of readiness to change (Farkas et al., 1996a, 1996b), we believe its application to correctional intervention with offender populations well may provide the conceptual focus that has been lacking.

Development of a Protocol for the Assessment of Treatment Responsivity in Offenders

A theoretically based, multimethod assessment protocol of treatment responsivity factors was developed to contribute to the broader literature on effective correctional programming. Our intent was to pilot an assessment battery, which could be administered in conjunction with a range of correctional programs. Accordingly, the protocol was developed for generic application rather than for a particular type of treatment program (Kennedy and Serin, 1997; Serin and Kennedy, 1997).

TABLE 9.1. Principal Domains Sampled by the Interpersonal Style Scale and the Treatment Evaluation Scale

Interpersonal Style Ratings Scale

1. Procriminal views
2. Procriminal associations
3. Grandiosity
4. Callousness
5. Neutralization
6. Impulsivity
7. Procrastination
8. Motivation for anger
9. Power and control
10. Problem-solving
11. Victim stance

Treatment Evaluation Scale

1. Knowledge of program content
2. Skills acquisition
3. Disclosure
4. Offender confidence
5. Knowledge application
6. Skills application
7. Understanding of criminality
8. Motivation
9. Insight
10. Attendance
11. Disruptiveness
12. Appropriateness
13. Participation

For our pilot work, the assessment protocol consisted of the following: Stages of Change Questionnaire (SCQ; Prochaska and DiClemente, 1992); Orientation to Treatment Scale (Robinson and Weekes, 1994); Readiness for Change Questionnaire (RCQ; Rollnick et al., 1992); Balanced Inventory of Desirable Responding (BIDR; Paulhus, 1984); Interpersonal Style Scale (Serin and Kennedy, 1998); and the Treatment Evaluation Scale (Serin and Kennedy, 1998). The first four are self-report paper-and-pencil questionnaires, and the last two are interview-based assessments of responsivity factors and treatment gains/participation. The principal domains sampled by the Interpersonal Style Scale and Treatment Evaluation Scale are presented in Table 9.1. Sample items from the Stages of Change Questionnaire, Orientation to Treatment, and Readiness to Change Questionnaire are presented in Table 9.2.

The protocol was completed by ninety-two federal Canadian male prisoners (the total includes twenty-one treated sex offenders, twenty untreated sex offenders, and thirty-one treated nonsex offenders). Data pertaining to the race and ethnicity of the subjects were not collected. The entire protocol was completed both pre- and posttreatment by all offenders, except the untreated sex offenders, who only completed the pretest. The mean age for the sample was 37.7 years. The mean sentence length was fifty-four months, with eleven offenders serving indeterminate sentences. Only 16 percent of the sample had nonviolent index offenses. The majority of offenders were married (61 percent) and were in minimum security (64 percent). Regarding program type, 29 percent completed sex offender treatment, 19 percent completed substance-abuse programs, 18 percent completed cognitive skills, and 5 percent completed anger management.

TABLE 9.2. Sample Items from the Stages of Change Questionnaire, Orientation to Treatment Scale, and Readiness to Change Questionnaire

Stages of Change Questionnaire
(SCQ: Prochaska and DiClemente, 1992)

Precontemplation
As far as I'm concerned, I don't have any problems that need changing.

Contemplation
I think I might be ready for some self-improvement.

Action
I am doing something about the problems that have been bothering me.

Maintenance
It worries me that I might slip back on a problem I have already changed, so I am here to seek help.

Orientation to Treatment Scale
(OTS; Robinson and Weekes, 1994)

I can learn new ways of thinking about my behavior.
I am willing to be open and honest about myself.
If I let down my guard, others will manipulate me.
I don't like it when someone is trying to figure me out.

Readiness to Change Questionnaire
(Rollnick, Heather, Gold, and Hall, 1992)

Precontemplation
I don't think I drink too much.

Contemplation
Sometimes I think I should cut down on my drinking.

Action
I am trying to drink less than I used to.

TABLE 9.3. Mean Scores for the Stages of Change Questionnaire and Readiness for Change Questionnaire for the Four Stages of Change

Stage of Change	SCQ		RCQ	
	Pre $\bar{x}$ (SD)	Post $\bar{x}$ (SD)	Pre $\bar{x}$ (SD)	Post $\bar{x}$ (SD)
Precontemplation	14.68 (4.22)	13.50 (3.80)	12.74 (4.74)	14.83 (4.10)
Contemplation	12.58 (3.25)	13.12 (3.65)	10.89 (4.81)	10.15 (5.04)
Action	13.24 (3.62)	12.68 (3.44)	9.47 (2.74)	10.17 (3.01)
Maintenance	14.93 (3.91)	15.21 (3.40)	NA	NA

SD = standard deviation

Since the Stages of Change Questionnaire (URICA) developers state that there are no cut-off norms established to determine what constitutes high, medium or low on a particular stage, we decided to restrict our analyses of the Stages of Change Questionnaire and the Readiness to Change Questionnaire to continuous rather than discrete procedures. Thus, we decided not to categorize subjects according to stages of change (that is, precontemplation, action, maintenance). Listed in Table 9.3 are the mean scores for the Stages of Change Questionnaire (SCQ) and the Readiness to Change Questionnaire (RCQ) for the four stages of change.

In Table 9.3, we see that there were only slight differences in pre- and posttreatment scores. None of these differences was significant.

The Interpersonal Style Ratings Scale has eleven domains, with two items on each domain that are rated on a four-point scale. Total scores range from 0-66, with higher scores indicating enhanced treatability. Comparisons pre- and posttreatment yielded significantly different total scores in the desired direction. This pattern was similar for each of the eleven domains.

Self-reported current treatment satisfaction was significantly correlated with social desirability as measured by total Balanced Inventory of Desirable Responding scores and Impression Management subscale scores ($r = .48$, $p < .0001$), but this was only significant for nonsex offenders ($r = .40$, $p < .003$). Interpersonal style ratings were significantly correlated with Treatment Evaluation under both pretreatment ($r=.50$, $p<.0002$) and posttreatment ($r=.69$, $p<.0001$) conditions. The pretreatment and posttreatment difference total was also significantly correlated with the Treatment Evaluation Scale (r=.46, p<.005). Interpersonal style ratings and self-reported current treatment satisfaction were not significantly correlated. The only significant difference between sex offenders and non-sex offenders on changes on interpersonal style was victim stance (p<.004), with sex offenders showing decreased victim stance. There were no significant correlations between Readiness to Change Questionnaire scores and Treatment Evaluation or between the Stages of Change Questionnaire scores and Treatment Evaluation. There were no significant correlations between URICA scores and the Treatment Evaluation Scale.

Several key findings resulted from this pilot study. Firstly, many offenders report low readiness for treatment, which did not change as a function of treatment. It is noted that the URICA may be less applicable to offender populations than other clinical populations. The fact that offenders report low readiness for treatment both pre- and posttreatment has important implications for the planning and delivery of correctional programming and intervention. Secondly, the Interpersonal Style Ratings Scale proved to be dynamic, with significant pre/posttreatment changes in the desired direction, and was significantly correlated with treatment gains.

Thirdly, self-report measures are influenced by social desirability and do not significantly correlate with behavioral measures. Related to this finding was the result that offenders' self-report regarding treatment gain was discrepant from clinicians' evaluations. In addition, staff feedback was positive, indicating that the assessment protocol was user friendly, not time consuming, and guided them in completing a posttreatment report by structuring their comments regarding an offender's response to correctional treatment. Optimally, systematic investigations of responsivity will yield potential targets for incorporation into a pretreatment motivational group, such that subsequent correctional treatment would be enhanced.

These data are limited by the small sample and the methodological problem of having the same raters for Interpersonal Style Ratings and Treatment Evaluation. The minimal variance on the Stages of Change Questionnaire and the failure to assess denial and minimization (Barbaree, 1993) for the sex offenders were also limitations. It would be reasonable to expect greater variability in a sample which included offenders under community supervision. Nonetheless, the findings are promising.

This is the first step in our effort to develop a systematic protocol for the assessment of treatment responsivity in the context of a risk/need management framework in which treatment is an integral part of the risk-management continuum. We have completed our second step and developed an interview-based assessment of treatment readiness to complement the Interpersonal Style Ratings and Treatment Evaluation (Serin and Kennedy, 1998). A set of user guidelines and a more explicit scoring scheme have been developed to maximize reliability. Plans also are underway to develop a training package and to implement the revised protocol with a wide range of correctional programs.

Endnote

[1] The authors wish to acknowledge the contribution of Shelley Brown, who entered the data for this paper and completed the statistical analysis.

References

American Psychiatric Association.1994. *Diagnostic and Statistical Manual of Mental Disorders*, 4th ed. Washington, D.C.: American Psychiatric Association.

Andrews, D. A., and J. Bonta. 1994. *The Psychology of Criminal Conduct.* Cincinnati: Anderson Publishing.

Andrews, D. A. and J. J. Kiessling. 1980. Program Structure and Effective Correctional Practice: A Summary of CaVIC Research. In R. Ross and P. Gendreau, eds. *Effective Correctional Treatment.* Toronto: Butterworths.

Andrews, D. A., J. J. Kiessling, D. Robinson, and S. Mickus. 1986. The Risk Principle of Case Classification: An Outcome Evaluation with Young Adult Probationers. *Canadian Journal of Criminology.* 28:377-84.

Andrews, D. A., I. Zinger, J. Hoge, J. Bonta, P. Gendreau, and F. T. Cullen. 1990. Does Correctional Treatment Work? A Clinically Relevant and Psychologically Informed Meta-analysis. *Criminology.* 28:369-404.

Barbaree, H. E. 1993. Denial and Minimization Among Sex Offenders. *Forum on Corrections Research.* 3:30-33.

Barbaree, H. E., M. C. Seto, and A. Maric. 1996. *Sex Offender Characteristics, Response to Treatment, and Correctional Release Decisions at the Warkworth Sexual Behavior Clinic.* Research Report. Forensic Division, Clarke Institute of Psychiatry, Toronto, Ontario.

Barkwell, L. J. 1980. Differential Treatment of Juveniles on Probation: An Evaluative Study. In R. Ross and P. Gendreau, eds. *Effective Correctional Treatment.* Toronto: Butterworths.

Bonta, J. 1995. The Responsivity Principle and Offender Rehabilitation. *Forum on Corrections Research.* 7:34-37.

Brown, M. 1996. Refining the Risk Concept: Decision Context as a Factor Mediating the Relation Between Risk and Program Effectiveness. *Crime & Delinquency.* 42:435-455.

Dana, R. 1993. *Multicultural Assessment Perspectives for Professional Psychology.* Boston: Allyn & Bacon.

Davidson, R. 1992. The Prochaska and DiClemente Model: Reply to the Debate. *British Journal of Addiction.* 87:833-835.

Farkas, A. J., J. P. Pierce, S. Zhu, B. Rosbrook, E. A. Gilpin, C. Berry, and R. M. Kaplan. 1996a. Addiction Versus Stage of Change Models in Predicting Smoking Cessation. *Addiction.* 91:1271-1280.

————. 1996b. Is Stage-of-Change a Useful Measure of the Likelihood of Smoking Cessation? *Addiction.* 18:79-86.

Gendreau, P., F. T. Cullen, and J. Bonta. 1994. Intensive Rehabilitation Supervision: The Next Generation in Community Corrections? *Federal Probation.* 58 (4):72-78.

Hanson, R. K. and M. T. Bussière. 1996. *Predictors of Sexual Offender Recidivism: A Meta- analysis* (User Report: Catalogue No. JS4-1/1996-4E). Ottawa: Solicitor General Canada.

Heilbrun, K. S., W. S. Bennett, J. H. Evans, R. A. Offult, H. J. Reiff, and A. J. White. 1988. Assessing Treatability in Mentally Disordered Offenders: A Conceptual and Methodological Note. *Behavioral Sciences and the Law.* 6:479-486.

————. 1992. Assessing Treatability in Mentally Disordered Offenders: Strategies for Improving Reliability. *Forensic Reports.* 5:85-96.

Kennedy, S. and R. Serin.1997. Treatment Responsivity: Contributing to Effective Correctional Programming. *The ICCA Journal on Community Corrections.* 7:46-52.

Knight, R. A., R. A. Prentky, and D. D. Cerce.1994. The Development, Reliability, and Validity of an Inventory for the Multidimensional Assessment of Sex and Aggression. *Criminal Justice and Behavior.* 21:72-94.

Marques, J. K., D. M. Day, C. Nelson, and M. A. West. 1994. Effects of Cognitive-behavioral Treatment on Sex Offender Recidivism: Preliminary Results of a Longitudinal Study. *Criminal Justice and Behavior.* 21:28-54.

Marshall, W. L., and R. C. Serin. 1997. Personality Disorders. In S. M. Turner and M. Hersen, eds. *Adult Psychopathology and Diagnosis,* Third Edition. New York: Wiley.

Miller, W. R., and S. Rollnick. 1991. *Motivational Interviewing: Preparing People to Change Addictive Behavior.* New York: The Guilford Press.

Paulhus, D. L. 1984. Two-component Models of Socially Desirable Responding. *Journal of Personality and Social Psychology.* 46:598-609.

Preston, D. L. and S. Murphy. 1997. Motivating Treatment Resistant Clients and Therapy. *Forum on Corrections Research.* 9 (2):39-43.

Prochaska, J. O. and C. C. DiClemente. 1986. Toward a Comprehensive Model of Change. In W. R. Miller and S. Rollnick, eds. *Motivational Interviewing: Preparing People to Change Addictive Behavior.* New York: The Guilford Press.

Prochaska, J. O., C. C. DiClemente, and J. C. Norcross. 1992. In Search of How People Change: Applications to Addictive Behaviors. *American Psychologist.* 47:1102-1114.

Quinsey, V. L. and A. Maguire. 1983. Offenders Remanded for a Psychiatric Examination: Perceived Treatability and Disposition. *International Journal of Law and Psychiatry.* 6:193-205.

Robinson, D. and J. R. Weekes. 1992. *The Substance Abuse Problem Recognition Scale.* Ottawa: Correctional Service of Canada.

Rogers, R. and C. D. Webster. 1989. Assessing Treatability in Mentally Disordered Offenders. *Law and Human Behavior.* 13:19-29.

Rollnick, S., N. Heather, R. Gold, and W. Hall. 1992. Development of a Short 'Readiness to Change' Questionnaire for Use in Brief, Opportunistic Interventions among Excessive Drinkers. *British Journal of Addiction.* 87:743-754.

Serin, R. C. 1995. Treatment Responsivity in Criminal Psychopaths. *Forum on Corrections Research.* 7:23-26.

Serin, R. and S. Kennedy. 1997. Treatment Readiness and Responsivity: Contributing to Effective Correctional Programming. *Correctional Services of Canada Research Report, R- 54.*

———. 1998. Assessment Protocol for Treatment Readiness, Responsivity, and Gain. *Correctional Services of Canada Research Report.*

Stewart, L. and W. Millson. 1995. Offender Motivation for Treatment as a Responsivity Factor. *Forum on Corrections Research.* 7:5-7.

Van Voorhis, P. 1997. Correctional Classification and the " Responsivity Principle." *Forum on Corrections Research.* 9 (1):46-50.

Velicer, W. F., C. C. DiClimente, J. O. Prochaska, and N. Brandenburg. 1985. Decisional Balance Measure for Assessing and Predicting Smoking Status. *Journal of Personality and Social Psychology.* 48:1279-1289.

SECTION 4:

EMERGING ISSUES AND TRENDS

TRENDS AND ISSUES IN THE ADULTIFICATION OF JUVENILE JUSTICE

10

David M. Altschuler, Ph.D.
Institute for Policy Studies
The Johns Hopkins University
Baltimore, Maryland

Introduction

Though for several decades states have been debating and passing laws to "get tough" with juvenile offenders in general and violent, serious and chronic juvenile offenders in particular, the last several years have witnessed a veritable tidal wave of such changes. The National Governors' Association reported that more than half of the states—at least a dozen in just 1995—changed their juvenile laws to specify the crimes and minimum ages for which juveniles may be (or must be) prosecuted as adults (National Governors' Association, 1996). Large segments of the public, politicians of all stripes, and the media have been in a virtual stampede in their fury about and attention to the problem of violent juvenile crime. It seems as if hardly a day goes by when there is not another story about a child somewhere maiming or killing others. While questions have been raised as to how swift, certain, and harsh either the juvenile or criminal justice system treats juveniles, there is little question about the swiftness, certainty, harshness, and popularity of the legislative responses from the states.

This paper will do five things: (1) examine the level and nature of the statutory changes nationwide, (2) review in detail several of the most recent studies on the impact of the changes, (3) explore the status of state corrections' incarceration policy and practice, (4) analyze what is currently known about correctional confinement and release, and finally, (5) sketch out ideas on what could constitute a promising and innovative sanctioning framework that seeks both to punish juveniles fairly and enhance public safety in the short-run and long-term.

Key to Types of Changes in Law (Table 10.1)

A TRANSFERRING JUVENILES TO THE ADULT COURT SYSTEM. This covers three types of specific changes: (1) where the legislature has mandated that certain types of crimes automatically be transferred to the adult court; (2) judicial waiver, where judges have the right to transfer youths; (3) prosecutorial discretion, where prosecutors can determine which youths to send to adult courts.

F FINGERPRINTING. Allowing juveniles to be fingerprinted.

O OPENING JUVENILE COURT. Opening court proceedings to the public or opening juvenile records to the public or selected law enforcement.

P PARENTAL RESPONSIBILITY. New laws forcing parents to take responsibility for the crimes of their children, sometimes paying fines or making restitution.

V VICTIMS' RIGHTS. Extending victims' rights to juvenile courts. (Making sure victims get to sit in on juvenile court sessions or are notified of results, or in some cases are paid restitution).

3 THREE STRIKES. Equivalents of the "three strikes and you're out" laws, only in these cases it is three strikes and you are an adult.

TABLE 10.1. Changing Juvenile Laws

State	Changes						State	Changes					
Alaska	A						Missouri	A	F		P	V	
Arizona	A			P	V		Montana*						
Arkansas	A			P			Nevada	A		O			
California	A		O		V		New Hampshire	A		O	P		
Colorado	A			P			New Jersey	A					
Connecticut	A	F	O				New Mexico	A					
Delaware	A						New York	A					
Florida	A		O	P		3	North Dakota	A		O	P	V	
Georgia			O				Ohio	A		O			
Hawaii			O				Oklahoma*						
Idaho	A	F	O	P			Oregon	A	F		P		
Illinois	A		O	P			Pennsylvania		F	O			
Indiana	A		O	P			Rhode Island				P		
Iowa	A	F					South Carolina	A					
Kansas*							Tennessee	A					
Kentucky	A		O	P	V		Texas	A	F				3
Louisiana	A		O	P			Utah	A					
Maine	A				V		Vermont	A			P		
Maryland	A	F					Virginia	A	F	O		V	
Massachusetts	A						West Virginia	A		O			
Minnesota	A						Washington*						
Mississippi	A						Wisconsin	A					

* State making changes other than those listed.
Data Source: National Conference of State Legislatures
Source: *New York Times*, May 12, 1996

The Changing Face of Juvenile Justice

The *New York Times* reported that forty-four states in some way changed their juvenile laws from 1994 to early 1996 (May 12, 1996). Using data from the National Conference of State Legislators, as reflected in Table 10.1, the *Times* showed that beyond those changes that transfer juveniles to criminal court, there were also changes related to fingerprinting, confidentiality of court proceedings and records, parental responsibility, victims' rights, and "three strikes and you are an adult." Clearly, there are sweeping changes underway, and they are not by any means restricted to trying juveniles in criminal court. There is also the issue of the criminal court sentencing of juveniles to adult prisons for adult-length sentences.

In 1992, Congress asked the General Accounting Office (GAO) to study issues related to juveniles sent to criminal court versus juvenile court. One critical question of interest was what effect the various changes in state laws likely would have on the number of juveniles sent to criminal court. The General Accounting Office discovered that this question could not be answered directly because of the fact that of the three mechanisms for transferring juveniles to criminal court, national data existed for only judicial waiver (1995). In contrast, no such national data exist on either prosecutor direct filing, which permits the prosecutor to file charges in either juvenile or criminal court under concurrent jurisdiction authority or legislative exclusion laws, which require the prosecution in criminal court of juveniles charged with certain offenses and/or records. Consequently, the General Accounting Office reviewed state statutes to identify the possible impact of statutory changes since 1978 on the number of juveniles sent to criminal court nationwide.

The General Accounting Office selected 1978 as the baseline year because that was the year in which data systematically were collected by an earlier research team (Hamparian et al., 1982) also looking at youth tried in adult court. It was during the 1970s that trying certain juveniles as adults in state criminal courts became a major issue, driven by a concern about rising juvenile crime, a questioning of the juvenile court's prioritization that placed rehabilitation and treatment ahead of punishment and deterrence, and criticisms (including those embodied in several notable Supreme Court decisions) leveled at the informality of juvenile court proceedings and the resulting inattentiveness to the due process rights of juveniles (Armstrong and Altschuler, 1982; Hamparian, 1981; Thomas and Bilchik, 1985).

TABLE 10.2. Impact of Changes in State Laws on
            Population of Juveniles Potentially Subject
            to Criminal Court Jurisdiction 1978-1994

State	Increase	No Net Change	State	Increase	No Net Change
Alabama	X		Minnesota		X
Alaska		X	Mississippi	X	
Arkansas	X		Missouri		X
California	X		Montana	X	
Colorado		X	Nevada		X
Connecticut	X		New Hampshire		X
Delaware	X		New Jersey	X	
District of Columbia	X		North Carolina	X	
Florida	X		North Dakota	X	
Georgia	X		Ohio		X
Hawaii		X	Oklahoma		X
Idaho	X		Oregon	X	
Illinois		X	Pennsylvania		X
Indiana	X		Rhode Island	X	
Iowa		X	South Carolina	X	
Kansas	X		Tennessee	X	
Kentucky	X		Utah		X
Louisiana	X		Vermont	X	
Maine		X	Virginia	X	
Maryland		X	Washington		X
Michigan		X	Wisconsin	X	

Source: General Accounting Office. 1995. *Juvenile Justice: Juveniles Processed in Criminal Court Case Dispositions*. Washington, D.C.: General Accounting Office.

Hamparian and her colleagues found that even in 1978, thirty-one of the states had statutory provisions excluding certain offenses from juvenile court jurisdiction, eleven of which referenced specific types of serious offenses (Hamparian et al., 1982). As of 1978, every state gave juvenile court judges the authority to make transfer decisions with twenty of the states specifying sixteen years of age as the minimum age for judicial waiver for certain offenses and fourteen years of age for other states permitting the transfer of children as young as fourteen years old. In addition, as of 1978, eight states permitted prosecutors the nonappealable discretion to file criminal charges in either juvenile or criminal court. Clearly then, efforts to get tough with certain kinds of juvenile offenders are not new and neither is questioning the role, structure, procedures and efficacy of the juvenile justice system. What has changed, however, is momentum.

The General Accounting Office study found that of all the statutory changes made on transfer since 1978, a total of forty-four states and the District of Columbia passed new laws that have an impact on which juveniles may be sent to juvenile court. In twenty-four of the states and the District of Columbia, as shown in Table 10.2, the population of juveniles potentially subject to criminal court jurisdiction increased. By contrast, in seventeen of the states, the new laws changed only the method by which certain juvenile cases may be sent to criminal court but did not increase the size of the potential population of juveniles that may be sent to juvenile court. Three states actually passed laws that tended to decrease the population of juveniles potentially subject to criminal court transfer. It is important to note, of course, that changes in law that potentially have an impact on the number of juveniles subject to transfer are not an indication of how many cases actually are transferred. Rather, it is an indication that for nearly half of the states, the legal structure has indeed been set for an increase in the number of transferred youth.

Specifically in terms of legislative exclusion, the National Council of State Legislatures reported that at least thirteen states enacted measures in 1994 alone that required certain juvenile cases be prosecuted in criminal court (Hunzeker, 1995). A report issued by the U.S. Office of Juvenile Justice and Delinquency Prevention indicated that between 1992 and 1995, thirty-five states changed, in some form, their legislative exclusion criteria (Sickmund, Snyder, and Peo-Yamagata, 1997). As a result of all of these recent changes, thirty-seven states now have one or more statutory exclusion laws (*see* Table 10.3).

Table **10.3.** **Summary of Juvenile Transfer Provisions**

State	Judicial Waiver	Prosecutor Direct Filing	Statutory Exclusion Laws	Reverse Waiver	Once Waived/ Always
Alabama	X		X		X
Alaska	X		X		
Arizona	X				
Arkansas	X	X		X	
California	X				
Colorado	X	X		X	
Connecticut			X	X	
Delaware	X		X	X	
District of Columbia	X	X			X
Florida	X	X	X		X
Georgia	X	X	X	X	
Hawaii	X		X		X
Idaho	X		X		X
Illinois	X		X		
Indiana	X		X		
Iowa	X		X		
Kansas	X		X		X
Kentucky	X		X	X	
Louisiana	X	X	X		
Maine	X				X
Maryland	X		X	X	
Massachusetts	X				
Michigan	X	X			
Minnesota	X		X		
Mississippi	X		X	X	X
Missouri	X				

(continued on page 240)

(Table 10.3 continued)

State	Judicial Waiver	Prosecutor Direct Filing	Statutory Exclusion Laws	Reverse Waiver	Once Waived/ Always
Montana	X		X		
Nebraska	X	X		X	
Nevada	X		X	X	X
New Hampshire	X	X		X	X
New Jersey	X				
New Mexico			X		
New York			X	X	
North Carolina	X		X		
North Dakota	X		X		
Ohio	X		X		X
Oklahoma	X		X	X	
Oregon	X		X		X
Pennsylvania	X		X	X	X
Rhode Island	X		X		
South Carolina	X		X	X	X
South Dakota	X				
Tennessee	X		X	X	
Texas	X		X	X	X
Utah	X		X	X	
Vermont	X	X	X	X	X
Virginia	X	X	X	X	X
Washington	X		X		
West Virginia	X		X	X	
Wisconsin	X		X		
Wyoming	X	X		X	

Source: H. N. Snyder and M. Sickmund. 1995. *Juvenile Offenders and Victims: A National Report.* Washington, D.C.: Office of Juvenile Justice and Delinquency Prevention; P. Torbet, R. Gable, H. Hurst IV, I. Montgomery, L. Szymanski, and D. Thomas. July 1996. *State Responses to Serious Juvenile Crime.* Washington, D.C.: Office of Juvenile Justice and Delinquency Prevention, U.S. Department of Justice.

Judicial Waiver

All the states but Connecticut, Nebraska, New Mexico, and New York permit juvenile court judges to transfer jurisdiction over a juvenile case to criminal court. The General Accounting Office obtained data on judicial waiver from the National Juvenile Court Data Archive and found that the percent of formal delinquency cases judicially waived to criminal court jumped from 1.2 percent in 1988 to 1.6 percent in 1992, representing a growth of nearly 5,000 cases a year, as shown in Table 10.4. This 5,000 case increase in the number of judicial waivers is equivalent to a 68 percent jump as compared to a 31 percent rise in the total number of formal delinquency cases.

The General Accounting Office study further showed that judicial waiver rates in 1992 varied by offense type, with judges more likely to waive cases to criminal court involving juveniles charged with person offenses (2.4 percent) than juveniles charged with property offenses (1.3 percent), but the waiver rates for drug offenses, at 3.1 percent, led the pack by far. It is important to note that while the chances of juvenile cases being waived to criminal court were highest for juveniles charged with drug and person offenses, property offenders still made up the largest percentage of waived cases, simply because of the prevalence of property offenses as compared to drug and person offenses.

Looking in detail at data provided by six states (Arizona, California, Florida, Missouri, Pennsylvania, and South Carolina) to the National Juvenile Court Data Archive, the General Accounting Office analyzed the impact of several characteristics on the likelihood of judicial waiver: age (for six states), sex (for six states), race (for six states), and number of prior referrals (for five states). More likely to have their cases waived were males sixteen years or older with three or more prior referrals. In four of the six states, black juveniles were more likely to be transferred than their white counterparts. While this type of analysis is interesting and provocative, it is important to note that it was conducted using data supplied by very few states and thus we cannot be certain of its national applicability.

It is therefore critical to examine the overall offense and demographic profile of waived juvenile cases both for individual years and over time. In doing so from 1988 through 1992, the General Accounting Office found that person offenses increased from 29 percent of the waived cases in 1988 to 34 percent in 1992 (*see* Table 10.5). In addition, the percentage of youth under age sixteen jumped from 7 percent in 1988 to 12 percent in 1992. Blacks represented half of all waived cases in 1992, up from 43 percent in

TABLE 10.4. **Number of Formal Delinquency Cases Nationwide and the Number and Percentage of Cases Judicially Waived to Criminal Court**

Year	Number of formal delinquency cases	Number of formal delinquency cases judicially waived to criminal court	Judicial waiver rate[a]
1988	569,596	7,005	1.2%
1989	608,593	8,350	1.4%
1990	654,742	8,708	1.3%
1991	689,328	10,933	1.6%
1992	743,673	11,748	1.6%

Note: The broad offenses categories used in our analysis included crimes against persons, property, drugs, and public order as defined by the Office of Juvenile Justice and Delinquency Prevention. The person category includes criminal homicide, forcible rape, robbery, aggravated assault, simple assault, and other person offenses—such as kidnapping and harassment. The property category includes burglary, larceny, motor vehicle theft, arson, vandalism, stolen property offenses, trespassing, and other property offenses—such as fraud, counterfeiting, and embezzlement. The drug category includes unlawful sale, purchase, distribution, manufacture, cultivation, transport, possession or use of a controlled or prohibited substance or drug. The public order category includes weapons offenses, nonviolent sex offenses, and liquor law violations.

[a] The waiver rate is the ratio of the number of waived cases to the number of formal delinquency cases. The percentage of all delinquency cases which were handled formally varied across states.

Data Source: Developed by General Accounting Office from NJCDA data.

Source: General Accounting Office. 1995. *Juvenile Justice: Juvenile Processed in Criminal Court and Case Dispositions.* Washington, D.C.: General Accounting Office.

1988. These are more than mere technical points, because from the standpoint of developing a strategy for sanctioning and sentencing offenders, correctional planners and operations staff need to know what the prospects are for the future. While older juveniles more likely may be waived than younger ones, it is still apparently the case nationwide that

TABLE 10.5. Percent of Waived Juvenile Cases by Sex, Age and Race 1988-1992

	Sex		Age	Race			Person Offense
Year	Male	Female	Under 16	White	Black	Other	
1988	96	4	7	54	43	2	29
1989	95	5	11	49	49	2	28
1990	96	4	10	45	52	3	32
1991	96	4	9	47	52	2	32
1992	96	4	12	47	50	3	34

Note: Percentages may not add up to 100 percent due to rounding.

Data Source: Developed by General Accounting Office from NCJJ's data archive.

Source: General Accounting Office. 1995. *Juvenile Justice: Juvenile Processed in Criminal Court and Case Dispositions.* Washington, D.C.: General Accounting Office.

the justice system, both court and corrections, is having to deal with both a growing number of youngsters under age sixteen and a disproportionately black population. This poses a number of substantial challenges and opportunities that will be raised below.

Beyond Judicial Waiver

Beyond judicial waiver, the General Accounting Office study, as shown in Table 10.3, also identified twenty-two states with statutory provisions that allow criminal court judges to transfer cases from their courts to juvenile court (known sometimes as "reverse waiver") under circumstances specified by law. Reverse waiver procedures place the burden of proof on the defense (for the juvenile) to show why he or she should not be subject to criminal court jurisdiction, whereas traditionally the burden of proof has been on the prosecution to prove why the juvenile should not be subject to juvenile court jurisdiction. These are more than mere subtleties of law, as rules of evidence and procedure clearly can have an impact on case flow and volume.

As Table 10.3 demonstrates, moreover, for any particular state, a combination of transfer provisions may apply. By the start of 1996, thirty-nine of the states and the District of Columbia had provisions in their statutes for at least two of the three mechanisms to transfer juveniles to criminal court prosecution. Florida, Georgia, Louisiana, Vermont, and Virginia possessed all three transfer mechanisms.

Focusing on disposition and sentencing, the General Accounting Office review of statutes further identified nineteen states that allow juveniles prosecuted and convicted in criminal court to receive dispositions as a juvenile under specified circumstances. Other states permit extended sentences within the juvenile court itself. For example, Colorado, Connecticut, Hawaii, New Mexico, and New Jersey may retain jurisdiction of the juvenile for disposition purposes for the full term of the disposition order. Texas provides for the juvenile court to retain jurisdiction of the juvenile through age fifty-six, for Massachusetts it is thirty-six and for California, Oregon, and Wisconsin it is twenty-four (see Table 10.6).

Some other states have statutorily removed judicial discretion on the type and length of sanction, and still other states have in effect preempted legislative action by virtue of their juvenile corrections agencies developing classification grids as the means to structure and guide placement decisions and length of stay (see Fagan, 1995). Finally, although not ordinarily considered a transfer, thirteen states presently consider fifteen or sixteen years of age as the upper age of juvenile court jurisdiction in delinquency matters. In thirty-seven states and the District of Columbia, the maximum age for juvenile court jurisdiction is seventeen years (see Table 10.7). In ten states, the maximum age of juvenile court jurisdiction is sixteen years, and it is fifteen years in Connecticut, New York, and North Carolina. In short, while it not known overall how many juveniles in their early and mid-teens are being sent to criminal court and/or adult corrections, there is no doubt that the juvenile justice system is undergoing unprecedented change.

Prosecutorial Direct Filing

While some national data on judicial waiver exist, as discussed above, unfortunately there are no such national data regarding prosecutorial direct filing or legislative exclusion. As shown in Table 10.3, eleven states and the District of Columbia possess prosecutor-initiated direct filing authority (also known as concurrent jurisdiction). To learn more about concurrent jurisdiction practices, the General Accounting Office contacted the office of the state court administrator in ten states with direct filing laws. Statewide data on direct filing existed for only five of the states and

TABLE 10.6. Oldest Age Over Which the Juvenile Court May Retain Jurisdiction for Disposition Purposes in Delinquency Matters

Age	States
17	Arizona, New Hampshire, North Carolina
18	Alaska, Kentucky, Iowa, Nebraska, Oklahoma, Tennessee
19	Mississippi, North Dakota, West Virginia
20	Alabama, Arkansas, Delaware, District of Columbia, Florida, Georgia, Idaho, Illinois, Indiana, Kansas, Louisiana, Maine, Maryland, Michigan, Minnesota, Missouri, Montana, Nevada, New York, Ohio, Pennsylvania, Rhode Island, South Carolina, South Dakota, Utah, Vermont, Virginia, Washington, Wyoming
24	California, Oregon, Wisconsin
36	Massachusetts
56	Texas

Note: 1) Colorado, Connecticut, Hawaii, New Jersey, and New Mexico may retain jurisdiction for the full term of the disposition order.
2) Extended ages of jurisdiction may be restricted to certain offenses or juveniles (such as violent offenses, habitual offenders, and juveniles under correctional commitment).

Data Source: L. Szymanski,1995. *Extended Age of Juvenile Court Delinquency Jurisdiction Statues Analysis (1994 Update)*. Pittsburgh, Pennsylvania: National Center for Juvenile Justice.

Source: Snyder, H. N., and M. Sickmund. 1995. *Juvenile Offenders and Victims: A National Report*. Washington, D.C.: Office of Juvenile Justice and Delinquency Prevention, U.S. Department of Justice; Torbet, P., R. Gable, H. Hurst IV, I. Montgomery, L. Szymanski, and D. Thomas. July 1996. *State Responses to Serious Juvenile Crime*. Washington, D.C.: Office of Juvenile Justice and Delinquency Prevention, U.S. Department of Justice.

the extent of its use varied widely, ranging from less than 1 percent to 13 percent of juvenile court cases. The General Accounting Office data also showed that many of the cases eligible for direct filing did not result in an actual filing, underscoring the wide discretion that is permitted.

It is precisely that wide exercise of prosecutorial discretion that concerns many observers, even some prosecutors (*see* for example, Whitebread and Batey, 1981; Zimring, 1981; Thomas and Bilchik, 1985). The problem is that whereas judicial waiver procedures and decision-making are bounded by a substantial body of law that at least seeks to clarify the right of juveniles (Davis, 1981; Hamparian, 1981), prosecutorial transfer is regarded as equivalent to the routine charging decisions made in criminal cases, and as such, is neither subject to judicial review nor required

TABLE 10.7. Oldest Age for Original Juvenile Court Jurisdiction in Delinquency Matters

15 years old	16 years old	17 years old		
Connecticut	Georgia	Alabama	Kansas	Oklahoma
New York	Illinois	Alaska	Kentucky	Pennsylvania
North Carolina	Louisiana	Arizona	Maine	Rhode Island
	Massachusetts	Arkansas	Maryland	South Dakota
	Michigan	California	Minnesota	Tennessee
	Missouri	Colorado	Mississippi	Utah
	New Hampshire	Delaware	Montana	Vermont
	South Carolina	D. C.	Nebraska	Virginia
	Texas	Florida	Nevada	Washington
	Wisconsin	Hawaii	New Jersey	West Virginia
		Idaho	New Mexico	Wyoming
		Indiana	North Dakota	
		Iowa	Ohio	

Note:
- Many states have higher upper ages of juvenile court jurisdiction in status offense, abuse, neglect, or dependency matters—often through age twenty.
- In many states, the juvenile court has jurisdiction over youthful offenders who committed offenses while juveniles.
- Several states also have minimum ages of juvenile court jurisdiction in delinquency matters—ranging from six to twelve.
- Many states exclude married or otherwise emancipated juveniles from juvenile court jurisdiction.
- * In Vermont, the juvenile and criminal courts have concurrent jurisdiction over all sixteen- and seventeen-year olds.

Source: M. Sickmund, M. N. Snyder, and E. Poe-Yamagata, 1997. *Juvenile Offenders and Victims: 1997 Update on Violence.* Washington, D.C.: Office of Juvenile Justice and Delinquency Prevention.

to meet certain due process standards (Snyder and Sickmund, 1995). There is a certain irony in that some of the very due process protections and procedural safeguards accorded juveniles within the juvenile justice system are, in effect, obviated by the direct filing transfer mechanism. As Thomas and Bilchik (1985) have insightfully noted:

> . . . there is a truly awesome difference in our legal system between the potential for abuse of judicial and of prosecutorial powers. Many if not most of the powers vested in the judiciary are exercised in open court and, at least in relative terms, those offended by the exercise of judicial discretion have access to various avenues of appeal . . . . (Prosecutorial powers) often reflect the preferences of individual and sometimes inexperienced prosecutors rather than officially promulgated administrative guidelines . . . and this is most particularly true with regard to the nation's juvenile court prosecutors. Even when guidelines do exist, mechanisms for effectively monitoring compliance with them seldom exist. . . . Thus, whether for better or for worse, the fact is that the most peculiar feature of our juvenile and criminal justice process is that it involves a fairly elaborate set of checks and balances on the conduct and the decisions of all but one set of actors: prosecutors.

Legislative Waiver

It is the third mechanism of transfer, legislative waiver, that has grown at the fastest rate, and it is this mechanism that appears to have the potential to have the largest impact on the population of juveniles in the adult system. Legislative waiver sometimes is called "automatic" transfer, because state law requires criminal prosecution if juveniles over a certain age are either charged with a particular crime or have reached a threshold on the number of certain types of prior offenses. Interestingly, however, since it is up to the prosecutor to decide on what to charge, it is by no means clear that prosecutorial power and discretion in legislative waiver differs substantially from prosecutorial direct filing. Consequently, the Thomas and Bilchik warning on unchecked prosecutorial power seems equally applicable.

Once again, unfortunately, because national data on the number of cases excluded by law from juvenile court jurisdiction do not currently exist, the General Accounting Office study was unable to determine the frequency of statutory exclusion cases sent to criminal court. The General Accounting Office (1995), however, did analyze all the state legislative waiver laws passed through 1994 and found that:

> In seventeen of the thirty-seven states with statutory exclusion laws, the laws excluded juveniles charged with serious violent offenses and juveniles with prior court records (repeat offenders) from juvenile court. For example, in Pennsylvania, any juvenile charged with murder is excluded from juvenile court as well as any juvenile who has been previously found guilty in a criminal proceeding. In thirteen of the thirty-seven states, the focus of the statutory exclusion laws is to exclude juveniles charged with serious violent offenses from juvenile court . . . In seven of the thirty-seven states and in the District of Columbia, the focus of the statutory exclusion laws is to exclude juveniles with prior criminal court records from juvenile court jurisdiction. These laws apply to all juveniles with specified prior records (i.e., adult court convictions) regardless of their offenses.

It also should be pointed out that the list of excluded offenses is not restricted exclusively to juveniles charged with serious violent offenses. The General Accounting Office found that in fifteen states, at least one other serious offense such as burglary, weapons, and drug offenses is excluded. The National Center for Juvenile Justice, which maintains the National Juvenile Court Data Archive, has observed that in states with legislative exclusion laws, it is quite conceivable that the number of youth affected could exceed those transferred via judicial waiver. While this has not been directly established empirically, Snyder and Sickmund (1995) of the National Center for Juvenile Justice cite Illinois where lawmakers amended the juvenile code in 1982 to exclude juveniles ages fifteen or older charged with murder, armed robbery, or rape. In the seven years prior to 1982, the Cook County juvenile court judicially waived an average of 47 cases annually to criminal court, whereas in the first two years following the enactment of the exclusion legislation, criminal prosecutions of juveniles more than tripled, climbing to 170 per year, 151 of which resulted from the exclusion provision. While other factors such as more violent crime by juveniles may be involved as well as overcharging, the Illinois illustration certainly suggests how legislative waiver might impact case flow.

The General Accounting Office study only covered state developments through the end of 1994, but there has been no let up in 1995-1998. According to a report from the National Conference of State Legislatures on juvenile crime and justice state enactments in 1995 (Lyons, 1995), Alaska, Arkansas, Delaware, Idaho, Indiana, Iowa, Louisiana, Minnesota, Nevada, North Dakota, Ohio, Oregon, Tennessee, Utah, and West Virginia added crimes for which a juvenile may, or must, be prosecuted as an adult.

No less activity has been taking place within the juvenile justice system itself, both in terms of juvenile court proceedings, juvenile corrections, and the entire organization and administration of juvenile justice within state capitals and at the local levels. For example, the National Conference of State Legislatures (Lyons, 1995) reported that at least ten states enacted changes in 1995 related to treating juvenile records or proceedings[1] more like those of adult criminals (such as in Georgia, Hawaii, Idaho, Indiana, Louisiana, Nevada, New Hampshire, North Dakota, Ohio, and Pennsylvania), and at least seven states introduced new laws designed to hold parents accountable (such as in Arizona, Idaho, Illinois, Indiana, New Hampshire, Oregon, and Rhode Island). A number of states also adopted new laws addressing criminal gangs (such as Arkansas, Tennessee, Illinois, Indiana, Nevada, and North Dakota). There also have been several notable statewide juvenile justice reorganizations, such as those in New Jersey, Colorado, Idaho, and Wisconsin. Indeed, even as the opportunity to try juveniles in criminal court and to sentence them like adults is expanding, so too is the face of juvenile disposition and corrections.

Sentencing Goals and Impact

Most of the developments and changes reported thus far relate to transfer provisions, court of original jurisdiction, age limitations, and extended jurisdiction. Little mention has been made of the disposition, sentencing, and the outcome side of the question. After all, whatever changes are being made, the bottom line is whether the intended goals are being met. Interestingly, it turns out that there is no basic agreement on the ultimate intent of the many and varied changes that have been discussed. Those advocating for more reliance on criminal court and adult corrections are quite expressly looking for harsher and more punitive sanctions than those typically provided by the juvenile justice system. Some of those espousing this view are driven by retributive punishment motives, and for them, deterring others from committing similar crimes or even deterring the offender from committing more crime when released, is not really the issue. Rather, the desired outcome is quite simply to deliver punishment that fits the crime, not the criminal; the call is usually for "justice" and what is desired is "just deserts," the more the better and please no less.

Others who subscribe to more reliance on criminal court and adult corrections firmly believe that harsh and very punitive responses can act as a deterrent to other would-be criminals, but regardless, at least the public (or the victim) will be protected for the length of the punishment, especially if the punishment is incarceration. Finally, there are those who support the various approaches to getting tough with juveniles on the basis of making it clear that accumulating a criminal record, with subsequent punitive consequences attached to that accumulating record, is what is at stake. The reasoning is that only so many strikes can accumulate, and knowing that, the offender will either desist (be deterred) or pay the consequences with certain and lengthy punishment.

The ultimate test of each of these propositions can be found in research that examines sanctioning patterns in the juvenile and criminal justice systems, respectively, and tests whether the sanctions have the intended retributive, incapacitative, and deterrent impacts being sought. A complete examination of these propositions requires information on both the certainty and harshness of the sanction, as well as the impact on recidivism.

In terms of the disposition and sentencing of such juveniles, a number of different questions are important to ask. What happens to juveniles when they are tried in criminal court? Do they get convicted? If convicted, are they sentenced to a period of incarceration and for how long? Where are they incarcerated, under what conditions, and are any services provided? Are they placed on some form of supervision when released into the community and are any services provided at that point? Finally, do they end up more law abiding and is the public safer? Some of these questions have been examined before, particularly those related to factors influencing who gets transferred and how they are sanctioned. Of course, there have been so many recent changes so fast, that the applicability of findings from previous studies to today's situation must be assessed very carefully.

Recent Research on Convictions, Incarceration, and Recidivism

The General Accounting Office analyzed the Bureau of Justice Statistics' Offender Based Transition Statistics data from California, Minnesota,

Missouri, Nebraska, New York, Pennsylvania, and Vermont for 1989 and 1990 combined. The conviction rates varied across states, ranging from 32 percent in New York to 100 percent in Minnesota for serious violent offense cases. In comparing conviction rates in the seven states, the General Accounting Office found generally that transferred juveniles were, for some offenses, as likely as persons age eighteen to twenty-four to be convicted in criminal court, though in New York, transferred cases had a greater likelihood of acquittal. There was no consistency when comparing the incarceration rates of juveniles with persons age eighteen to twenty-four.

Additional data were available for New York and Missouri, permitting the General Accounting Office to compare the conviction rates of transferred juveniles in New York and Missouri, respectively, with those of other youths age sixteen and seventeen in criminal court in New York and other youths age seventeen in criminal court in Missouri. The General Accounting Office found that conviction rates in New York were lower for transferred serious violent offense cases than for both other New York youths age sixteen and seventeen prosecuted in criminal court for the same type of offenses and for young adults age eighteen through twenty-four who were prosecuted for serious violent offenses. By contrast, conviction rates in Missouri were higher for transferred serious violent offense cases than for other Missouri youths age seventeen who were prosecuted in criminal court for serious violent offenses. Information on "findings" (in other words, convictions) for similar cases in New York and Missouri that remain in the juvenile court was not examined, but this would be very important to know as well, especially since the intent of transfer is to get more certainty and punishment from the criminal court than that thought possible from juvenile justice.

The General Accounting Office study did not focus on the ultimate impact on public safety, though this is certainly key when the goal involves deterrence. It is actually quite curious and perhaps telling that Congress did not request information from the General Accounting Office on recidivism and public safety impacts. Fortunately, however, two very recent studies explored the question of whether transfer to criminal court makes a difference and how. One study in Florida was conducted by Bishop et al. (1996) and it involved comparing the outcomes of nearly 3,000 transferred juvenile offenders in 1987 with those of a matched sample of delinquents who were retained in the juvenile justice system. The researchers found that transferred youth were more likely to be incarcerated and for longer periods of time than those retained in the juvenile justice system.

Those favoring transfer as the means to impose retributive punishment and short-run incapacitative benefits might find these results encouraging. On the other hand, only approximately 30 percent of the transferred youths were sentenced to prison, most for periods of one-to-five years. And not only were transferred youths more likely to reoffend when released, but they were more likely to reoffend faster than their nontransferred matches. Any incapacitative benefit achieved in the short-run was apparently negated by the accelerated recidivism upon release. In short, those favoring transfer as a means to enhance public safety in the long-term (in other words, achieve a "specific deterrent" effect) may be disappointed. The authors speculate on a number of possible explanations for their findings:

1. Transfer to the adult system heightens law enforcement vigilance and increases the risk of rearrest more than reoffending.

2. Offenders transferred to criminal court are more closely supervised on probation and parole than are youths retained in the juvenile justice system, making detection of repeat offenses more likely.

3. Officials have a lower threshold of tolerance for violations committed by offenders transferred to adult court.

4. Transfer to criminal court may increase the likelihood of recidivism through either the adverse impact of sanctions that reject, exclude, and stigmatize or the angry pride and defiance induced by the perception of unjust and unfair treatment.

Another study by Fagan (1995) compared the sanctioning patterns and recidivism rates of approximately 400 adolescents age 15 and 16 charged with felony robbery and burglary in juvenile court in New Jersey's Essex and Passaic Counties with similar juveniles from Brooklyn and Queens, where felony robbery and burglary are routinely tried in criminal court. Study data indicate that sanctioning patterns and recidivism differ somewhat by type of offense. For example, as compared to robbery cases in juvenile court, those in criminal court were more likely to be found guilty and to be incarcerated when found guilty. On the other hand, several other important findings emerged. First, sentence length did not differ. Second, fewer robbery offenders were rearrested who either were incarcerated or sentenced to probation in the juvenile court than in the criminal court. Third, the time to rearrest for robbery offenders who were sentenced to incarceration in juvenile court was longer than those similarly sentenced in criminal court. Last, the annualized rearrest rate (computed by annualizing total arrests over the at-risk time during the follow-up period) was the same, whichever court issued the incarceration sentence. In short, the specific deterrent effect of sanctions on recidivism was greater for robbery cases in the juvenile court. At the same time, criminal court was more likely than juvenile court to convict and to incarcerate juvenile robbers.

Burglary cases revealed a slightly different pattern. The likelihood of being found guilty was unaffected by court jurisdiction but for those found guilty in criminal court, incarceration was more likely. At the same time, incarceration sentence lengths were no different between juvenile and criminal court. Regardless of the sentencing sanction, there were no significant differences by type of court in either percent rearrested or time to first rearrest. It was only for burglary offenders who were incarcerated that annualized rearrest rates were significantly lower for those sentenced in criminal court. Rearrest rates did not differ significantly by other types of sanction.

In both of these studies, it is mostly the case that recidivism is less among those juveniles retained in the juvenile justice system. It was only burglary offenders in the New York/New Jersey study where transferred juveniles incarcerated by the criminal court evidenced lower recidivism for one of the three recidivism measures. To the extent that deterrence is a goal in transferring youths, the recidivism data strongly suggest that the goal is not being met, at least in these two studies. To the extent that the goals relate to achieving a greater certainty for "severe" punishment (in other words, retributive punishment) and incapacitation whereby the offender is not committing crimes while incarcerated, the data are mixed. It thus must be said quite soberly that there can be no assurance that a criminal court proceeding as opposed to a juvenile proceeding is likely to produce a conviction and subsequent incarceration. It also appears that incapacitative benefits achieved during incarceration may be at the expense of longer-run recidivism and public safety.

While research on these questions is still in its infancy and a limited number of studies have produced somewhat mixed results, perhaps the best that can said at this moment is that it would be foolish to proceed as if there were clarity on what impact transferring juveniles into criminal court may have. Given the level and variety of changes that have been made by the states, there is surely a dire need for rigorous research and evaluation to determine under what conditions and circumstances it is likely that juveniles will receive lenient or harsher sentences in criminal court and with what impact on short-run and long-term public safety.

Incarceration Policy and Practice

One of the problems confronting adult corrections is that they mostly have their hands full in dealing with the far more numerous adult offenders confined in their correctional facilities. Taking on uncertain numbers of juveniles, in fact, is introducing among adult corrections officials much uncertainty and a scramble for programmatic and custodial responses. The concern in adult corrections on how to handle juveniles has produced one irony that may give pause to some of the more ardent supporters of retributive punishment for juveniles within adult corrections. After a meeting with forty-nine of the commissioners of adult corrections at the American Correctional Association annual conference, the Director of Youth Services in North Dakota, reported (NAJCA News, 1996) that the commissioners seemed less afraid to sound like "bleeding heart liberals" than did juvenile corrections officials!

Moreover, incarcerating violent or other serious juvenile offenders appears to be creating at least as much of a problem for adult corrections as it has for juvenile corrections. In fact, there are indications that adult corrections officials feel that they are being asked to develop a programmatic and custodial capacity for handling juveniles they neither want nor have the expertise to address (Torbet et al., 1996; Parent et al., 1997). In addition, as discussed above, there is some evidence to suggest that transfer into the adult system can backfire and produce less public safety.

Juveniles in Adult Corrections

The General Accounting Office reported that there were no national estimates on the number of inmates at or below the maximum age of juvenile court jurisdiction in each state and that the only information available was that from the 1991 Survey of State Prison Inmates (Bureau of Justice Statistics, 1993), which indicated that less than 1 percent of the 712,000 state prison inmates were seventeen years or younger. The General Accounting Office research team went to four states (Florida, Michigan, North Carolina, and Ohio) and visited a total of seven prisons that housed the majority of inmates under age eighteen. The General Accounting Office found that the juveniles in the seven adult prisons ranged from less than 1 percent to 15 percent of the inmates and that they were generally subject to the same policies and procedures as other inmates regarding housing, education, vocation programs, recreation, and so forth.

In a separate survey sent to state contact persons for the National Institute of Corrections Prisons Division and Information Center (LIS, Inc., 1995), twenty-two agencies projected increases over the next five years in the number of persons under the age of eighteen entering adult corrections. Respondents anticipated growth ranging from 1 percent to 730 percent.

Projected Increases By States

1-5%   Colorado, Maine, Missouri, Oregon, South Dakota, Vermont

6-10%   Alabama, Florida, West Virginia

11-20%   District of Columbia, New Jersey, North Carolina, North Dakota, Wyoming

21-50%   Minnesota, Puerto Rico

Over 50% Arizona, Delaware, Idaho (100%); Washington (370%); New Mexico (500%); Alaska (730%)

Respondents from Georgia, Kansas, and Kentucky reported anticipating an increase, but did not project a specific growth rate.

The survey also collected information on the number of juveniles under age eighteen in adult correctional facilities on June 30, 1994. Including Connecticut (n=334), New York (n=487), and North Carolina (n=451), where sixteen- and seventeen-year-olds are considered adults, there were 3,816 sixteen-seventeen-year-olds in adult corrections' custody on that date.[2] Florida (n=740), New York (n=487), North Carolina (n=451), Connecticut (n=334), Illinois (n=168), Georgia (n=163), Arkansas (n=140), Puerto Rico (n=138), and Oklahoma (n=110) reported the largest number of sixteen and seventeen-year-olds in adult facilities. Just over 100 thirteen-to-fifteen-year-olds were in adult corrections' custody, the most in Florida (n=39), North Carolina (n=18), Arkansas (n=11), and Georgia (n=8).[3]

A number of state-by-state reviews and profiles (LIS, Inc., 1995; Lyons, 1995; Torbet et al., 1996; Parent et al., 1997) have examined policies on housing juveniles and how juveniles sentenced to incarceration by criminal courts are being handled. There is clearly a great deal of regrouping and ferment both within adult and juvenile corrections. Many state adult corrections' departments are looking closely at their policies and practices on housing and managing juveniles and various states are formulating new procedures. For example, authorities in Delaware, North Dakota, and Washington in certain circumstances can choose between a juvenile or adult facility. The decision is based on a number of factors, including age and sentence length.

Torbet et al. (1996) identify four types of correctional responses potentially involving the adult system:

1. Straight adult incarceration, allowed in nearly all states, where transferred juveniles of a certain age can be housed in adult facilities either with younger adult offenders or in the general adult population. (Only Arizona, Hawaii, Kentucky, Montana, Tennessee, and West Virginia either prohibit an adult commitment altogether or require juveniles be housed separately from adults. California and North Dakota prohibit housing any juvenile under sixteen years old in an adult prison.)

2. Graduated incarceration, where transferred juveniles can be incarcerated in juvenile correctional facilities or in a separate facility/unit operated by adult corrections until they reach a certain age (usually eighteen), at which time they can be transferred to an adult facility or released. (Examples of states using juvenile institutions are Delaware, Missouri, North Dakota, Oregon, Tennessee, Texas, Washington, and West Virginia. States with special juvenile facilities or units within their adult correction systems include Georgia, Maryland, and Ohio. Utah maintains a facility operated by juvenile corrections on the grounds of an adult institution.)

3. Segregated incarceration, where transferred juveniles can be housed in separate facilities for young adult offenders, usually eighteen to twenty-one to twenty-five years of age. (Examples include facilities in Florida and South Carolina.)

4. Youthful offenders, where special legal protections (such as expunging records) are accorded successful completion of sentence served in either the adult or juvenile corrections systems. (For example, states with such designations include California, Colorado, Kentucky, New Mexico, New York, and Wisconsin.)

In some states, handling juveniles within adult corrections poses a serious programming and housing challenge since the juveniles are too few in number to merit specialized attention or care. Forty states and the District of Columbia prohibit committing juveniles below certain ages to adult corrections, and some states further prohibit the placement of juveniles below certain ages in adult facilities. States with prohibitions on housing offenders under a certain age with adults may have to establish entirely new secure facilities or units for juvenile inmates. State adult corrections' departments who may be responsible for housing thirteen- or fourteen-year-old children clearly must confront the reality of housing and managing these juveniles (*see* Glick and Sturgeon, 1998).

The Toughening of Juvenile Corrections

Quite another approach is that involving some fairly fundamental changes in the goals, policies, and practices being pursued within the juvenile justice system itself (Guarino-Ghezzi and Loughran, 1996). Many states, some of them trying to preempt other more drastic changes or even abolition, are giving primacy to punishment, accountability, and the nature of the crime(s) committed over treatment, rehabilitation, and the well-being of the offender. Other states are adopting language within their juvenile codes that depart from the traditional juvenile justice emphasis on prevention, diversion, and treatment to a balance between punishment and treatment (*see*, for example, Snyder and Sickmund, 1995). In either case, however, the trend away from a juvenile justice system giving primacy to rehabilitation and secondary importance to retributive punishment is unmistakable, and at least for the foreseeable future, probably unstoppable.

It has been argued for quite some time (initially by liberal reformers that supported juvenile justice) that juvenile justice has not been able to succeed ". . . significantly in rehabilitating delinquent youth, in reducing or even stemming the tide of delinquency, or in bringing justice and compassion to the juvenile offender (U.S. President's Commission, 1967). A variety of solutions have been advanced, including more resources, a wider array of dispositional alternatives and intermediate sanctions, greater emphasis on prevention, more attention to opportunities and supports involving family, peers, education, employment, and neighborhood, and, of course, getting tougher with the violent and serious juvenile offender, even within the framework of the juvenile justice system.

Reintegrative-oriented Incarceration of the Few Violent Juveniles: Balancing Punishment and Treatment

One aspect of reform focuses on the use of incarceration for juvenile offenders who have committed the most violent and predatory crimes. Regardless of which court has jurisdiction and even which corrections system operates the institution, the experience of the juvenile justice system in this area is instructive and offers some important insights on offender targeting, program design, and supervision approaches.

Research has shown that youths are incarcerated in juvenile correctional facilities for a number of very different reasons and under a variety of circumstances (Bureau of Justice Statistics, 1989; Champion, 1992; Krisberg et al., 1993). Some have been involved in a violent crime, but have no prior record of violence; others are confined because of having committed a serious property crime. Still others are incarcerated because they have an "extensive" arrest history, considered more serious because of the large number of arrests rather than the severity of any individual charge. Precisely because of this heterogeneity, it is hardly surprising that prior research has found that some incarcerated juveniles are much less likely to reoffend than others (see, for example, Altschuler and Armstrong, 1990; Baird, 1986; Bleich, 1987; Clear, 1988; Petersilia, Greenwood, and Lavin, 1977; Strasburg, 1984; Zimring, 1978; Zimring and Hawkins, 1973). Simply stated, the likelihood of reoffending upon release varies enormously for different subgroups of incarcerated individuals.

Prediction research repeatedly has shown that the relationship between seriousness of the presenting offense and the likelihood of committing future offenses is extremely weak, if not inverse (see, for example, Baird, 1986; Baird, Storrs, and Connelly, 1984; Clear, 1988; Petersilia et al., 1977; Zimring and Hawkins, 1973). The research also suggests that it is largely property offenders, not violent offenders, who are most prone toward reoffending (Bleich, 1987; Strasburg, 1984; Zimring, 1978). Altschuler and Armstrong's (1990) review of prediction research revealed that risk factors associated with juvenile reoffending behavior, broadly defined, include a combination of justice system contact factors (for example, age of youth at first justice system contact, number of prior offenses and referrals) and need-related factors (for example, family dysfunction, school disciplinary problems, negative peer-group influences, and drug involvement).

One effect of the upswing in the use of juvenile incarceration during the last decade is the mixing in juvenile correctional facilities of the comparatively few violent juvenile offenders with other nonviolent and less serious offenders. Another effect is that juveniles who have committed a violent crime and on the basis of risk assessment are judged to be at low risk to reoffend are mixed with other juveniles who also have committed a violent crime but are determined to be at high risk to reoffend. Thus, offenders who have been committed for a violent offense are literally packed into crowded facilities with the more numerous nonviolent juveniles, and second, all the juveniles committed on the basis of a violent crime typically are handled the same way during both incarceration and aftercare, regardless of their risk of reoffending. It is no wonder that many juvenile correctional facilities are little more than revolving doors for many, if not most, of their resident offenders.

Adult facilities housing juveniles will not likely be immune from this same problem. A recent national study of juvenile detention and correctional facilities (Parent et al., 1994) concluded that substantial and widespread deficiencies existed in terms of living space, security, control of suicidal behavior, and health care. The authors of the study note "if the objective is to substantially improve conditions that confined juveniles experience, then efforts to improve or close a few 'bad' facilities, while laudable, will have little overall impact."

One hardly can argue that the conditions of juvenile confinement are not harsh enough. In addition, the adult system is in even worse shape, where crowding, litigation on conditions of confinement, and substantial increases in costs predate the emergence of these very same problems in juvenile facilities. Already overburdened adult corrections' facilities may be even less equipped to tend to the housing and custody needs of their very youngest inmates.

The difficulty juvenile institutions have had can be linked to three challenges they have had to confront. First, it is exceedingly difficult to successfully punish, deter, and treat incarcerated juvenile offenders in large, locked, secure training schools that are operating at overcapacity; yet, this is the norm in juvenile corrections nationwide. While the training school experience is likely to be punishing and harsh, if for no other reason than the abysmal conditions documented in the recently completed national study (Parent et al., 1994), by all accounts, it appears not to have made much of a dent in the violent juvenile crime problem and neither has the increase in juvenile admissions to adult prison.

However, to the extent that addressing both risk factors and specific deterrence objectives becomes an explicit, formal, and accepted part of the incarceration approach to punishment, attention is shifted to elements of treatment and advocacy. Large, locked, secure training schools frequently function like other closed, self-contained, and insulated social systems, in that outsiders and outside influences are viewed with suspicion, if not disdain. Particularly when offenders are involved, there are those in the community who are all too pleased to rely on others to handle their problems at a distance. Unfortunately, prosocial supports in the community are not cultivated, and the youths return either less capable of functioning autonomously or more attached to their deviant peers and patterns (Altschuler, 1984; Coates, Milller and Ohlin, 1978; Empey and Lubeck, 1971; Haley, 1980; Shannon, 1982; Whittaker, 1979; Wolfensberger, 1972). Whether and how adult corrections will confront this same phenomenon in their system remains to be seen.

Second, large, locked, secure training schools frequently fall prey to an institutional culture in which the measures of success relate only to compliance with institution rules and norms, as well as in-program progress in relation to whatever services are available (*see*, for example, Jackson, 1998). The problem is that progress within such settings generally is short-lived, unless it is followed-up, reinforced, and monitored in the community (Whittaker, 1979; Altschuler and Armstrong, 1984). Having no responsibility, authority, or involvement for anything other than institutional adjustment and progress, the institution and its staff have little incentive or interest in what ultimately happens to youths in the community, and why should they? Just maintaining control and order inside the institution is more than a full-time job.

Third, the complexity and fragmentation of the justice system works against the reintegration of offenders back into the community; this requires a comprehensive and collaborative approach. As the existing system is presently structured in most states, administering and managing juvenile justice poses particularly tough challenges, a problem not unknown to the criminal justice system. The division of authority and responsibility is dispersed among state and local levels of government, conflicting bureaucratic and organizational interests, as well as divergent professional orientations.

Depending upon the state, the key decision-makers involved with juvenile justice include judges, prosecutors, state youth corrections agencies, institution staff, parole authorities and community review boards, county government, and court service staff, plus other public and private service providers. The sheer size and organizational complexity of the juvenile justice "system" make it exceedingly difficult to achieve basic communication, much less collaboration. Furthermore, the forces that support leaving institutional corrections to function as they always have are well organized, entrenched, and formidable (Miller, 1991). There is no reason to believe that the adult system faces less of a challenge on this front.

There are also pressures and directives affecting juvenile corrections that emanate from still other sources, including the public, judiciary, public defenders, and private defense attorneys, governors, legislatures and state agencies, career civil servants, unions, private-sector contractors and service providers, victims' groups, child advocates, and the media. They represent an almost overwhelming collection of vying interests and countervailing forces, many of which by their very nature are adversarial. The net effect is a kind of inherent organizational schizophrenia, that if not very consciously, carefully, and properly treated and soothed, can result in chaos, fingerpointing, and scapegoating. The question to ask is whether adult corrections systems are better situated so that these same challenges are not merely replicated within their existing systems. One way to approach this question is to examine some potential solutions and judge their applicability to the corrections system that will have jurisdiction.

Critical Issues in the Incarceration of Juveniles: What Has Been Learned?

A number of concrete steps can be taken to deal with the three challenges posed above. These steps should be viewed as important guideposts in the development, design, and implementation of reintegration-oriented sanctioning of juvenile offenders. Which system or combination of systems may be in the best position to accomplish these steps is a separate concern.

Downsizing populations confined in locked, secure training schools is one important option worth considering. It is highly unlikely that any meaningful problem-solving related to specific deterrence and rehabilitation can occur in large, crowded, unsafe, and understaffed locked facilities, whether they are lodged within the juvenile or adult corrections system. Chronic nonviolent juveniles who require residential placement can be considered for alternatives to institutionalization, such as group homes, halfway houses, therapeutic foster care, outward bound, therapeutic communities, boot camps, and so forth. Since most juvenile offenders and most institutionalized juveniles are nonviolent, restricting institutional confinement to only violent juveniles would represent for most institutions a viable downsizing strategy. If juveniles in the adult system include both violent and nonviolent offenders, which is certainly true, it is very important to consider the downside to indiscriminately mixing these classes of offenders.

Placing nonviolent juveniles in a range of so-called intermediate sanction programs, such as group homes, therapeutic foster care, day treatment centers, alternative schools, intensive probation, outreach and tracking, house arrest, or electronic monitoring leaves costly and limited institutional space for those individuals truly requiring the most secure correctional incarceration. In addition and more to the point, it means that those youth who pose the greatest danger can be held accountable and punished for what they have done, but in ways that simultaneously promote the goals of specific deterrence and rehabilitation. Confining the smaller number of violent juveniles in locked, secure facilities that are intensively staffed and demanding in program content and activity opens a whole new set of possibilities. On the one hand, day-to-day programming in locked, secure facilities can be very demanding and strict. On the other hand, services can be individualized and keyed to identified risk factors.

It is also critically important to objectively assess and classify juveniles incarcerated for committing even a violent offense in terms of their risk of reoffending upon release. Assessing and classifying juveniles on their risk of reoffending potential is crucial, whether the juvenile or criminal corrections department has jurisdiction. High-risk juvenile offenders who are incarcerated for violent offenses require much more than punishment and incarceration if they are to succeed when released into the community, a fact that few will deny and that the research bears out. It is imperative that such juvenile offenders have sustained and concerted attention devoted to the very risk factors that have been shown to predict further offending. It is unrealistic to expect that the chances of success in the community can be improved without actively addressing family dysfunction, educational and vocational deficiencies, employment opportunities, peer-group influences, and drug-related problems (abuse as well as drug dealing).

Serious attention to the identified risk factors means that aftercare concerns and stakeholders must be directly incorporated into institutional operations. Aftercare case managers, service providers, and sources of community support should have a presence at the institution and be part of a closely knit team. When distance is a problem because a secure facility is not available nearby, it is important to have access to a transitional residential setting within reach of the home community. Even in that instance, however, explicit and formal arrangements need to be made so that aftercare case managers, community service providers, and sources of community support maintain ongoing contact that begins early-on during the confinement period, not just toward the very end during some prerelease period. It is extremely unwise and irresponsible to release into the community high-risk offenders without community supervision, support, and intensified service delivery particularly focused on risk factors.

The cost-effectiveness of both secure confinement and aftercare, as well as the extent and nature of community, family, and peer involvement during these two stages, must be closely monitored and evaluated: what is the extent and nature of contact with youth, how is the transition initiated and supported, and what does a youth's ultimate success or failure after release say about how well the corrections system (for example, institution and aftercare), the service providers, and the sources of community support have performed? Just as punishment alone during confinement is inadequate, so too is surveillance-oriented aftercare. Merely monitoring offender conduct and functioning without services hardly can be expected to have an impact upon known risk factors (Petersilia and Turner, 1993; Petersilia, Turner, and Deschenes, 1992, Byrne and Brewster, 1993).

In addition, more surveillance unaccompanied by a structured system of graduated consequences and alternatives to revocation is likely to lead to more incarcerations, not less. The reason is that higher levels of surveillance increase the ability to detect infractions and violations, which can result in reincarceration, which in turn contributes to the crowding problem. Moreover, there is no evidence to suggest that technical violations are a proxy for criminal activity (Petersilia and Turner, 1991; Turner and Petersilia, 1992). Consequently, while getting tough on technical violators does not appear to buy more crime control, it certainly contributes to institutional crowding.

Finally, the use of electronic monitoring equipment and drug testing has gained popularity but as with other aspects of surveillance, there is little reason to believe that these approaches alone will be of much help. The reason is that the use of high-tech surveillance techniques is not a substitute for services and support and what is more, they only trigger a reaction after misconduct already has occurred. Therefore, they do serve as an early warning signal; they do not address precipitating circumstances; and they do not directly detect accomplishment. Detecting accomplishment, however, is extremely important with youths who often are starving for some form of recognition and achievement. Positively reinforcing and acknowledging achievement establishes the means to provide such recognition, offers an incentive, and also can act as a deterrent in the sense that there is something to lose in the form of withdrawn recognition or the loss of an earned privilege.

A Tough and Smart Juvenile Corrections Policy that Sacrifices Neither Punishment nor Rehabilitation: Some Closing Observations

While discussion over the merits, philosophy, and impacts of handling particular classes of juvenile offenders and offenses most assuredly is going to continue with fervor over the years ahead, a fundamental question central to this paper remains: how might it be possible and what would it take for the juvenile and criminal justice systems, to at once provide punishment and accountability proportionate to the criminal act, promote public safety, reduce an offender's future reoffending, prevent or deter others from reoffending in the first place, accomplish these goals in a cost-effective manner, and appropriately take into account the age-related, developmental circumstances and prospects of children and adolescents? Can accountability and punishment co-exist with rehabilitation and treatment?

It is extremely important to recognize that while juvenile justice is in theory primarily committed to rehabilitation, it is still very much the case that the juvenile court considers the severity of the act and the record of the juvenile in determining an appropriate response, which includes institutionalization. Indeed, it has been precisely because of a concern over the deprivation of liberty and even lack of rehabilitative treatment in some juvenile facilities and institutions that a series of court decisions starting in the 1960s began to address rights of due process and equal protection of the law. It is also the case that while the criminal justice system is primarily committed to retribution, deterrence, and punishment, it still very much seeks rehabilitation as one result of its intervention, and even penal institutions are not without a concern for restoring most of their subjects to constructive social roles (Zimring, 1981). The point is that the punishment versus rehabilitation missions attached to criminal and juvenile justice, respectively, can help to explain some of the distinctions between the two systems, but in practice both systems venture deeply into punishment and treatment arenas.

The unprecedented change that is occurring within both the juvenile and criminal justice systems throughout the country is testimony to how much deep dissatisfaction there is with the current system. While some in juvenile justice would rather not deal at all with violent and very dangerous juvenile offenders, others in juvenile justice would prefer to have more facilities, resources, and extended time to address these individuals. Some in criminal justice would rather not deal with the very young offender because of a lack of expertise, shortage of space, and concern over the far more numerous young adult offenders in their custody. As shown, states are experimenting, and many are incorporating a wide variety of changes all at once. Sorting out various impacts through rigorous research is complex and made all the more thorny by very inconsistent and conflicting goals held by different interests, advocates, and organizations. What is more likely to change an offender, punishment or treatment? What about retributive punishment, which may place no value on offender change, or what about marathon incapacitation, which places great value on stopping crime commission during confinement but remains silent about long-term impacts on recidivism and cost?

What is at stake here is sorting out which goals should prevail or what the balance should be among potentially conflicting goals. The problem of handling violent and other serious juvenile offenders is perplexing because in a real sense, neither system has offered an optimal solution. The juvenile justice system has been criticized as not sufficiently punitive for at least some types of offenders and too time limited in its jurisdiction. The criminal justice system has been criticized as not sufficiently rehabilitative and potentially detrimental to public safety in the long run. These criticisms can be addressed through thoughtful and conscientious reform, but it must be said that retribution unaccompanied by a concern for the impact on both short-term and long-run recidivism as well as cost-effectiveness, is imprudent from the standpoint of sound public correctional policy.

Given the fundamental distinction between juvenile justice—with its primary focus on the offender and providing treatment and advocacy to promote change—and criminal justice—with its primary focus on the crime and the imposition of retributive punishment and deterrence, it should be obvious that both systems must retool somewhat to meet the challenge posed by violent and other serious juvenile offenders. Neither system is inherently incapable of meeting the challenge of balancing punishment with rehabilitation, but to do so, changes such as those mentioned are clearly required. The challenge is to establish a framework for change.

Within the context of the juvenile justice system, it is clear that handling cases of extreme predatory violence will require a concession on how long jurisdiction can last. This can be established in terms of a maximum age of extended jurisdiction or a minimum number of years, perhaps whichever is longer. Dispositions with minimums that are more in line with the gravity of the violent crime should be considered. One virtue of handling such cases within some special unit within the juvenile system is that the potential problem of leniency accorded juveniles within the criminal justice system may be countered. It is also crucial to incorporate within a disposition involving incarceration or placement the share of time allotted to postinstitutional supervision and enhanced service delivery. Adequate resources and staffing for supervision and services in the community are needed to ensure that gains made and lessons learned while confined can persist.

Last, confinement of juveniles without taking into consideration their age and developmental status—including their behavioral, cognitive, emotional, and physical state—is very risky business and not advisable. Problems can arise both in terms of vulnerabilities among the juveniles and the impact on the overall maintenance of order for the older, adult population. It is for this reason that placing juveniles in a general adult population can lead to serious problems and disorder. Graduated and dedicated incarceration arrangements, as well as daily routines that are geared specifically to adolescents are recommended.

It is truly ironic that the move to handle more juvenile offenders within the adult system is contributing to a broader debate on juvenile correctional reform in general. Questions such as which juvenile offenders should be incarcerated and why, how it should be accomplished and where, and with what goals and outcomes are all being asked and discussed by more and more people in more and more places. While the overall direction being taken may not be viewed by some as positive, the more attention and discussion placed on the issue hopefully will pave the way for a rational juvenile crime control and corrections policy that promotes both accountability through punishment and offender change through habilitation, rehabilitation, and support.

Endnotes

[1] Also see Torbet et al., 1996.

[2] This number excludes reporting from Iowa, New Jersey, and South Carolina because of insufficient age breakouts. Maryland did not report. While Connecticut, New York, and North Carolina consider sixteen- and seventeen-year-olds as adults, ten other states treat seventeen-year-olds as adults, as shown in Table 10.7.

[3] This number excludes reporting from Iowa and New Jersey because of insufficient age breakouts. Maryland did not report.

References

Altschuler, D. M. 1984. Community Reintegration in Juvenile Offender Programming. In R. Mathias, P. DeMuro, and R. Allinson, eds. *Violent Juvenile Offenders: An Anthology*. San Francisco: National Council on Crime and Delinquency.

Altschuler, D. M. and Troy Armstrong. 1995. Managing Aftercare Services for Delinquents. In Barry Glick and Arnold P. Goldstein, eds. *Managing Delinquency Programs that Work*. Lanham, Maryland: American Correctional Association.

Armstrong, T. L., and D. M. Altschuler. 1982. Conflicting Trends in Juvenile Justice Sanctioning: Divergent Strategies in the Handling of the Serious Juvenile Offender. *Juvenile and Family Court Journal*. 33 (4):15-30.

————. 1984. Intervening with Serious Juvenile Offenders: Summary of a Study on Community-based Programs. In R. Mathias, P. DeMuro, and R. Allinson, eds. *Violent Juvenile Offenders: An Anthology*. San Francisco: National Council on Crime and Delinquency.

————. 1990. Intensive Community-based Aftercare Programs: Assessment Report. Report submitted to Office of Juvenile Justice and Delinquency Prevention, Washington, D.C.

Baird, S. C., G. M. Storrs, and H. Connelly. 1984. *Classification of Juveniles in Corrections: A Model Systems Approach*. Washington, D.C.: Arthur D. Little, Inc.

Baird, S. C. 1986. The Usefulness of Risk Scales to the Treatment of Offenders. Paper presented at the Conference on Statistical Prediction in Corrections, Rutgers University. Washington, D.C.: Arthur D. Little, Inc.

Bishop, D. M., C. E. Frazier, L. Lanza-Kaduce, and L. Winner. 1996. The Transfer of Juveniles to Criminal Court: Does it Make a Difference? *Crime & Delinquency.* 42:171-191.

Bleich, J. 1987. Toward an Effective Policy for Handling Dangerous Juvenile Offenders. In F. S. Hartman, ed. *From Children to Citizens: The Role of the Juvenile Court,* Vol. II. New York: Springer-Verlag.

Bureau of Justice Statistics. 1989. *Children in Custody, 1975-85*. Washington, D.C.: Bureau of Justice Statistics, U.S. Department of Justice.

———. 1993, March. *Survey of State Prison Inmates, 1991*. Washington, D.C.: Bureau of Justice Statistics, U.S. Department of Justice.

Byrne, J. and M. Brewster. 1993. Choosing the Future of American Corrections: Punishment or Reform? *Federal Probation*. 57(4):3-9.

Champion, D. J. 1992. *The Juvenile Justice System: Delinquency, Processing, and the Law*. New York: Macmillan Publishing Company.

Clear, T. R. 1988. Statistical Prediction in Corrections. *Research in Corrections*, Vol. 1. Washington, D.C.: National Institute of Corrections.

Coates, R. B., A. D. Miller, and L. E. Ohlin. 1978. *Diversity in a Youth Correctional System: Handling Delinquents in Massachusetts*. Cambridge: Ballinger Publishing Company.

Davis, S. M. 1981. Legal and Procedural Issues Related to the Waiver Process. In J. C. Hall, D. M. Hamparian, J. M. Pettibone, and J. L. White, eds. *Major Issues in Juvenile Justice Information and Training: Readings in Public Policy*. Columbus, Ohio: Academy for Contemporary Problems.

Empey, L.T. and S. G. Lubeck. 1971. *The Silverlake Experiment: Testing Delinquency Theory and Community Intervention*. Chicago: Aldine Publishing Company.

Fagan, J. 1995. Separating the Men from the Boys: The Comparative Advantage of Juvenile Versus Criminal Court Sanctions on Recidivism Among Adolescent Felony Offenders. In J. C. Howell, B. Krisberg, J. D. Hawkins, and J. J. Wilson, eds. *A Sourcebook: Serious, Violent and Chronic Juvenile Offenders*. Newbury Park, California: Sage Publications.

General Accounting Office. 1995, August. *Juvenile Justice: Juveniles Processed in Criminal Court and Case Dispositions*. Washington, D.C.: General Accounting Office.

Glick, Barry, and William Sturgeon, with Charles R. Venator-Santiago. 1998. *No Time to Play: Youthful Offenders in Adult Correctional Systems*. Lanham, Maryland: American Correctional Association.

Guarino-Ghezzi, S. and E. J. Loughran. 1996. *Balancing Juvenile Justice*. New Brunswick, New Jersey: Transaction Publishers.

Haley, J. 1980. *Leaving Home: The Therapy of Disturbed Young People*. New York: McGraw-Hill Book Company.

Hamparian, D. M. 1981. Introduction to Section II: Youth in Adult Courts. In J. C. Hall, D. M. Hamparian, J. M. Pettibone, and J. L. White, eds. *Major Issues in Juvenile*

Justice Information and Training: Readings in Public Policy. Columbus, Ohio: Academy for Contemporary Problems.

Hamparian, D. M., L. K. Estep, S. M. Muntean, R. R. Priestino, R. G. Swisher, P. L. Wallace, and J. L. White. 1982. *Major Issues in Juvenile Justice Information and Training-Youth in Adult Courts: Between Two Worlds.* Washington, D.C.: Office of Juvenile Justice and Delinquency Prevention, U.S. Department of Justice.

Hunzeker, D. 1995. Juvenile Crime, Grown Up Time. *State Legislatures.* 21(5):15-19.

Jackson, Lonnie. 1998. *Gangbusters: Strategies for Prevention and Intervention.* Lanham, Maryland: American Correctional Association.

Krisberg, B., D. Onek, M. Jones, and I. Schwartz. 1993. Juveniles in State Custody: Prospects for Community-based Care of Troubled Adolescents. *NCCD Focus.* San Francisco: National Council on Crime and Delinquency.

LIS, Inc. 1995, February. *Offenders Under Age 18 in State Adult Correctional Systems: A National Picture.* Special Issues in Corrections. Longmont, Colorado: National Institute of Corrections Information Center, U.S. Department of Justice.

Lyons, D. 1995, November. *Juvenile Crime and Justice State Enactments 1995.* State Legislative Report. 20(17).

Miller, J. 1991. *Last One Over the Wall: The Massachusetts Experiment in Closing Reform Schools.* Columbus, Ohio: Ohio State University Press.

NAJCA News. 1996, Spring. Annual Forum Focuses on Changes Leading to the Adultification of the Juvenile Justice System. *NAJCA News.* IX(1):1.

National Governors Association. 1996. States Crack Down on Juveniles. *Governors' Bulletin.* 1. March 11.

Parent D. G., V. Leiter, S. Kennedy, L. Livens, D. Wentworth, and S. Wilcox. 1994. *Conditions of Confinement: Juvenile Detention and Correctional Facilities.* Washington, D.C.: Office of Juvenile Justice and Delinquency Prevention.

Parent, D., T. Dunworth, D. McDonald, and W. Rhodes. 1997. *Transferring Serious Juvenile Offenders to Adult Courts.* NIJ Research in Action. Washington, D.C.: National Institute of Justice.

Petersilia, J., P. W. Greenwood, and M. Lavin. 1977. *Criminal Careers of Habitual Felons.* Santa Monica, California: Rand Corporation.

Petersilia, J. and S. Turner. 1991. An Evaluation of Intensive Probation in California. *The Journal of Criminal Law and Criminology.* 82:610-658.

————. 1993. *Evaluating Intensive Supervision Probation/Parole: Results of a Nationwide Experiment.* NIJ Research in Brief. Washington, D.C.: National Institute of Justice.

Petersilia, J., S. Turner, and E. P. Deschenes. 1992. The Costs and Effects of Intensive Supervision for Drug Offenders. *Federal Probation.* 56(4):12-17.

Shannon, L. W. 1982. *Assessing the Relationship of Adult Criminal Careers to Juvenile Careers: A Summary.* Washington, D.C.: Office of Juvenile Justice and Delinquency Prevention, U.S. Department of Justice.

Sickmund, M., H. N. Snyder, and E. Peo-Yamagata. 1997. *Juvenile Offenders and Victims: 1977 Update on Violence.* Washington, D.C.: Office of Juvenile Justice and Delinquency Prevention, U.S. Department of Justice.

Snyder, H. N. and M. Sickmund. 1995. *Juvenile Offenders and Victims: A National Report.* Washington, D.C.: Office of Juvenile Justice and Delinquency Prevention, U.S. Department of Justice.

Strasburg, P. A. 1984. Recent National Trends in Serious Juvenile Crime. In R. Mathias, P. DeMuro, and R. Allinson, eds. *Violent Juvenile Offenders: An Anthology.* San Francisco: National Council on Crime and Delinquency.

Szymanski, L. A. 1995. *Extended Age of Juvenile Court Delinquency Jurisdiction Statues Analysis.* Pittsburgh, Pennsylvania: National Center for Juvenile Justice.

Thomas, C. W. and S. Bilchik. 1985. Prosecuting Juveniles in Criminal Courts: A Legal and Empirical Analysis. *The Journal of Criminal Law and Criminology.* 76:439-479.

Torbet, P., R. Gable, H. Hurst IV, I. Montgomery, L. Szymanski, and D. Thomas. 1996. *State Responses to Serious Juvenile Crime.* Washington, D.C.: Office of Juvenile Justice and Delinquency Prevention, U.S. Department of Justice.

Turner, S., and J. Petersilia. 1992. Focusing on High-risk Parolees: An Experiment to Reduce Commitments to the Texas Department of Corrections. *The Journal of Research in Crime and Delinquency.* 29:34-61.

U.S. President's Commission on Law Enforcement and the Administration of Justice. 1967. *The Challenge of Crime in a Free Society.* Washington, D.C.: Government Printing Office.

Whitebread, C. H. and R. Batey. 1981. The Role of Waiver in the Juvenile Court: Questions of Philosophy and Function. In J. C. Hall, D. M. Hamparian, J. M. Pettibone, and J. L. White, eds. *Major Issues in Juvenile Justice Information and Training: Readings in Public Policy.* Columbus, Ohio: Academy for Contemporary Problems.

Whittaker, J. K. 1979. *Caring for Troubled Children: Residential Treatment in a Community-based Context.* San Francisco: Jossey-Bass Publishers.

Wolfensberger, W. 1972. *Normalization.* New York: National Institute on Mental Retardation.

Zimring, F. E. and G. Hawkins. 1973. *Deterrence: The Legal Threat in Crime Control.* Chicago: University of Chicago Press.

————. 1978. Background paper. *Confronting Youth Crime: Report of the Twentieth Century Fund on Sentencing Policy Toward Young Offenders.* New York: Holmes and Meier Publishers.

————. 1981. Notes Toward a Jurisprudence of Waiver. In J. C. Hall, D. M. Hamparian, J. M. Pettibone, and J. L. White, eds. *Major Issues in Juvenile Justice Information and Training: Readings in Public Policy.* Columbus, Ohio: Academy for Contemporary Problems.

Restorative Justice: What Works

11

Mark S. Umbreit, Ph.D.
Center for Restorative Justice and Mediation
School of Social Work
University of Minnesota, St. Paul, Minnesota

Introduction

At a time when the public debate around issues of crime and punishment is driven largely by political leadership embracing the conservative or liberal solutions of the past, restorative justice offers a fundamentally different framework for understanding and responding to crime and victimization within American society. Restorative justice emphasizes the importance of elevating the role of crime victims and community members, holding offenders directly accountable to the people they have violated, restoring the emotional and material losses of victims, and providing a range of opportunities for dialog, negotiation, and problem solving, whenever possible, which can lead to a greater sense of community safety, conflict resolution, and closure for all involved.

In contrast to the offender-driven nature of our current systems of justice, restorative justice focuses upon three client groups: crime victims, offenders, and community members. It represents a growing international movement with a relatively clear set of values, principles, and guidelines for practice, while at this point in its development lacking a comprehensive plan for broad implementation as a new paradigm to fully replace our current systems of juvenile and criminal justice. As a relatively new practice theory (though based upon many old-fashioned principles) that is gaining support among a growing number of correctional policymakers and practitioners, victim advocates, court officials, and law enforcement officials, it is important to examine the current development and impact of this movement. At its best, restorative justice truly represents a very different way of responding to crime through more active involvement of crime victims and the community. It goes far beyond the traditional liberal and conservative positions of the past by identifying underlying truths and joint interests of all of those concerned about crime policy in a democratic society. At its worst, restorative justice could become another generation of correctional euphemisms to make current highly retributive practices look more effective or fair. Such a "window dressing" effect clearly is not the intent of restorative justice advocates, yet could become the eventual reality of this movement if the underlying vision of the movement becomes lost.

The purpose of this chapter is to examine the development and impact of the restorative justice movement. Because the relatively new and emerging practice theory of restorative justice is still in its developmental phase and not widely understood by many policymakers and practitioners, a significant amount of background and descriptive material about this concept will be presented before highlighting what has been learned through research. First, a number of underlying problems facing the current systems of juvenile and criminal justice will be identified. Second, a description of the values and principles that drive the restorative justice movement will be presented, including characteristics of how the movement has grown in the United States and abroad. Third, data that have emerged from a number of empirical studies will be presented in the context of policies and interventions that are uniquely restorative in nature. Finally, a number of unresolved issues and implications for practice will be offered, along with identifying the need for further research into this important justice reform movement.

What Are the Major Unresolved Issues with the Current System?

Many, if not most, criminal and juvenile justice systems in the United States are faced with numerous unresolved problems that have been particularly evident during recent decades. With an ever-increasing emphasis on retribution, contradictory impulses still exist between punishment and rehabilitation among many correctional policymakers and practitioners. A lack of clarity exists about the basic purpose of sentencing. Is it meant to rehabilitate and change offender behavior? Are criminal sentences meant to deter others from committing crimes? Or, should the purpose of sentencing be simply to incapacitate or remove the criminal from circulation in society for a set period of time? These and other goals contribute to ongoing confusion about what courts are trying to achieve.

Victims of crime feel increasingly frustrated and alienated by our current systems of justice. Even though the justice system exists precisely because individual citizens have been violated by criminal behavior, crime victims have virtually no legal standing in the process of doing justice in American courts. The crime is against "the state" and state interests drive the process of doing justice. Individual crime victims are left on the sidelines of justice, with little, if any, input.

Crime victims frequently feel twice victimized: first, by the offender, second, by the criminal justice system for which their tax dollars are expended. For many crime victims, their encounter with the justice system leads to increasing frustration and anger as they largely are ignored, and often are not even provided with information about the process, court date changes, and the final disposition of the case. Rarely do criminal justice professionals take the time to listen to the fears and concerns of crime victims and then seek their input and invite their participation in holding the offender accountable.

The failure of increasing punishments to change criminal behavior is another problem facing our nation's juvenile and criminal justice systems. If severe punishment and incarceration were effective, America should be one of the safest societies in the world. Despite the common perception among many citizens that the United States is too lenient on criminals, the fact is that more Americans are locked up in prisons, per capita, than in any developed nation in the world. In a similar vein, sentences in the United States are far in excess of other democratic western nations. The United States is the only developed nation to advocate and use capital punishment routinely. Finally, the skyrocketing cost of corrections, and incarceration specifically, is driving a growing number of legislatures and policymakers to reconsider the wisdom of the current retributive system of justice which relies so heavily on incarceration, while largely ignoring the needs of crime victims.

What Is Restorative Justice?

Restorative justice provides an entirely different way of thinking about crime and victimization (Van Ness and Strong, 1997). Rather than the state being viewed as the primary victim in criminal acts and placing victims and offenders in passive roles, as is the case in the prevailing retributive justice paradigm, restorative justice recognizes crime as first and foremost being directed against individual people. It assumes that those most affected by crime should have the opportunity to become actively involved in resolving the conflict. Restoration of losses, allowing offenders to take direct responsibility for their actions, and assisting victims in their journey of moving beyond their frequent sense of vulnerability by means of achieving some closure, stand in sharp contrast to focusing on past criminal behavior through ever-increasing levels of punishment (Umbreit, 1996, 1995b, 1994a, 1991a; Wright, 1991; Zehr, 1990). Restorative justice attempts to draw upon the strengths of both offenders and victims, rather than focusing upon their deficits. While denouncing criminal behavior, restorative justice emphasizes the need to treat offenders with respect and to reintegrate them into the larger community in ways that can lead to lawful behavior. It represents a truly different paradigm based on the following values (Bazemore and Umbreit, 1995).

1. Restorative justice is far more concerned about restoration of the victim and victimized community than simply ever more costly punishment of the offender.

2. Restorative justice elevates the importance of the victim in the criminal justice process, through increased involvement, input, and services.

3. Restorative justice requires that offenders be held directly accountable to the person and/or community they victimized.

4. Restorative justice encourages the entire community to be involved in holding the offender accountable and promoting a healing response to the needs of victims and offenders.

5. Restorative justice places greater emphasis on the offenders accepting responsibility for their behavior and making amends, whenever possible, than on the severity of punishment.

6. Restorative justice recognizes a community responsibility for social conditions which contribute to offender behavior.

In a very real sense, the theory of restorative justice provides a blueprint for moving into the next century by drawing upon much of the wisdom of the past. Dating all the way back to twelfth-century England, following the Norman invasion of Britain, a major paradigm shift occurred in which there was a turning away from the well-established understanding of crime as a victim-offender conflict within the context of community. William the Conqueror's son, Henry I, issued a decree securing royal jurisdiction over certain offenses (robbery, arson, murder, theft, and other violent crimes) against the King's peace. Prior to this decree, crime always had been viewed as conflict between individuals with an emphasis on repairing the damage by making amends to the victim.

Restorative justice also draws upon the rich heritage of many recent justice reform movements, including: community corrections, victim advocacy, and community policing. The principles of restorative justice are particularly consistent with those of many indigenous traditions, including Native American, Hawaiian, Canadian First Nation people, and Maori people in Australia and New Zealand. These principles are also consistent with values emphasized by nearly all of the world religions.

The distinction between the old paradigm of retributive justice and the new paradigm of restorative justice has been developed by Zehr (1990). As Table 11.1 illustrates, whereas retributive justice focuses on punishment, the restorative paradigm emphasizes accountability, healing, and closure.

What Does Restorative Justice Look Like in Practice?

As communities move more toward a fully developed restorative justice system of responding to crime and victimization, juvenile and criminal justice practice would include the following characteristics, some of which are already in place.

- Victims and families of victims receive support and assistance.

- If they wish, victims have a chance to help shape how the offender will repair the harm done.

TABLE 11.1. Paradigms of Justice

Retributive	Restorative
1. Crime defined as violation of one person by another	1. Crime defined as violation of the state
2. Focus on establishing blame, on guilt, on past (did he or she do it?)	2. Focus on problem solving, on liabilities and obligations, on future (what should be done?)
3. Adversarial relationship and process normative	3. Dialog and normative negotiation
4. Imposition of pain to punish and deter/prevent	4. Restitution as a means of restoring both parties' goal of reconciliation/restoration
5. Justice defined by intent and process: right rules	5. Justice defined as right relationships; judged by outcome
6. Interpersonal, conflictual nature of crime obscured, repressed; conflict seen as individual versus the state	6. Crime recognized as interpersonal conflict; value of conflict is recognized
7. One social injury is replaced by another	7. Focus on repair of social injury
8. Community on sideline, represented abstractly by state	8. Community as facilitator in restorative process
9. Encouragement of competitive, individualistic values	9. Encouragement of mutuality
10. Action directed from state to offender —victim ignored —offender passive	10. Victim and offender's roles recognized in problem/solution —victim rights/needs recognized —offender encouraged to take responsibility
11. Offender accountability defined as taking punishment	11. Offender accountability defined as understanding impact of action and helping decide how to make things right
12. Offense defined in purely legal terms, devoid of moral, social, economic, and political dimensions	12. Offense understood in whole context—moral, social, economic, and political dimensions
13. "Debt" owed to state and society in the abstract	13. Debt/liability to victim recognized
14. Response focused on offender's past behavior	14. Response focused on harmful consequences of offender's behavior
15. Stigma of crime unremovable	15. Stigma of crime removable through restorative action
16. No encouragement for repentance and forgiveness	16. Possibilities for repentance and forgiveness
17. Dependence upon proxy professionals	17. Direct involvement by participants

- Restitution is more important than other financial obligations of the offender.

- Victim-offender mediation is available for victims who want to have a mediation meeting with the offender to discuss how the crime affected them and how the offender can repair the harm. Victim-offender mediations are conducted by trained mediators who are sensitive to the needs of victims and their families.

- Community volunteers are working with offenders.

- The community provides work for offenders to be able to pay back restitution to victims.

- Offenders participate in community service projects which are valued by the community.

- Educational programs for offenders include becoming aware of how victims feel and being able to empathize with victims. Education also helps offenders see their responsibilities as members of a community.

- Offenders face the personal harm caused by their crime through victim-offender mediation, hearing panels or groups of victims or community members talk about their experiences with crime and how crime has affected their lives.

- Orders for repairing the harm caused by crime are more important than orders imposed just for punishment.

- The courts and corrections provide annual reports on how reparation is made.

- Community members advise the courts and corrections by being on advisory boards.

- Business and community groups work with offenders to bring them back into the community as the offenders make good on their obligations.

- Faith communities sponsor support groups for offenders trying to change their lives.

- Offenders end up with greater skills than when they entered the corrections system.

How Widespread Is Interest in Restorative Justice?

The initial concept of restorative justice began in the late 1970s and was first clearly articulated by Zehr (1980). At that time, the discussion of this new paradigm was based largely in North America and with a small network of academicians and practitioners in Europe. At this time, restorative justice was not being considered seriously by the mainstream of criminal and juvenile justice policymakers and practitioners.

By 1990, an international conference supported by NATO funds was convened in Italy to examine the growing interest in restorative justice throughout the world. Academicians and practitioners from a wide range of countries (Austria, Belgium, Canada, England, Finland, France, Germany, Greece, Italy, Netherlands, Norway, Scotland, and Turkey) presented papers related to the development and impact of restorative justice policies and practice. International interest in restorative justice has continued to grow.

In 1995, the New Zealand Ministry of Justice issued a working paper on restorative justice for serious consideration as a federal policy. During 1996 and 1997, a group of scholars in North America and Europe interested in restorative justice will be meeting in the United States and Belgium to examine this emerging practice theory. A second international book on restorative justice (following the initial book about the NATO conference in Italy) is forthcoming. Finally, a working subcommittee of the United Nations currently is examining the concept of restorative justice and will be preparing a draft resolution for presentation at a United Nation's conference in the year 2000.

Interest in the United States has grown extensively during the past five years. Representing one of the oldest and most visible expressions of restorative justice, the practice of victim-offender mediation, which began in the late 1970s, now is occurring in more than 280 communities throughout the United States and a considerably larger number in Europe as noted in Table 11.2.

The American Bar Association has played a major leadership role in the area of civil court mediation for more than two decades. After many years of little interest in criminal mediation, if not skepticism, the American Bar Association in the summer of 1994 fully endorsed the practice of victim-offender mediation and recommended its development in courts throughout the country.

Hundreds of restorative justice information packets have been sent out by the Center for Restorative Justice and Mediation at the University

TABLE 11.2. International Development of Victim-offender Mediation Programs

Country	Number of Programs
Australia	5
Austria	Available in all jurisdictions
Belgium	8
Canada	26
England	43
Finland	130
France	40
Germany	293
New Zealand	Available in all jurisdictions
Norway	54
South Africa	1
Scotland	2
United States	300

of Minnesota to correctional officials, policymakers, and practitioners throughout the country and abroad. In January of 1996, the U.S. Department of Justice convened their first national conference on restorative justice, bringing together policymakers and practitioners from throughout the country. Perhaps one of the clearest expressions of the growing support for restorative justice is seen in the National Organization for Victim Assistance's monograph endorsing "restorative community justice." During the early years of this movement, most victim advocacy groups were quite skeptical. Many still are; however, there are a growing number of victim support organizations actively participating in the restorative justice movement.

Have Restorative Justice Practices Been Implemented?

In contrast to many previous reform movements, the restorative justice movement points the way to systemwide change in how justice is done in American society. While initiating restorative justice interventions such as victim-offender mediation, family group conferences, restorative community service, victim panels, and other forms of victim-offender dialog or neighborhood dispute resolution is important, restorative justice places a heavy emphasis on systemic change. As a result of the Balanced and Restorative Justice project supported by the Office of Juvenile Justice and Delinquency Prevention of the U.S. Department of Justice, numerous county and state jurisdictions throughout the country are examining the merits of restorative justice.

Fifteen states have drafted and/or introduced legislation promoting a more balanced and restorative juvenile justice system. The Balanced and Restorative Justice Project has been working extensively with six juvenile justice systems (Deschutes and Lane counties in Oregon, Travis county in Texas, Dakota county in Minnesota, Allegheny county in Pennsylvania, and Palm Beach county in Florida) which are actively involved in implementing restorative justice polices and practices. Mission statements are being reexamined and rewritten, job descriptions changed, policies revised to include more victim and community involvement, resources are being redeployed, new restorative interventions are being initiated, and a far greater awareness of victim needs for involvement and services are being developed.

In 1994, the Vermont Department of Corrections embarked on one of the most ambitious systemwide restorative justice initiatives. Following a public opinion poll, which indicated broad dissatisfaction with the criminal justice system and openness to more restorative and community-based responses to nonviolent crime, the department "took a wrecking ball" and demolished a 100-year-old correctional system built upon the options of either prison or probation.

They were able to identify up to 50 percent of the current probation caseload which they believed could be held accountable by Reparative Probation Community Boards made up of citizen volunteers. Instead of traditional probation supervision, a wide range of property offenders would be referred directly to a Reparative Community Board, before which they would have to appear. In dialog with the offender, the Board determines a community-based restorative sanction, oftentimes including victim-offender mediation, community service, or meeting with a victim panel. The department now is encouraging crime victims to be represented on each Reparative Probation Community Board. No other known current restorative justice initiative represents such a major structural change, which clearly elevates the role of community volunteers and crime victims in the process of holding offenders accountable to the community they violated.

Individual restorative program initiatives, rather than systemwide initiatives, are much more widely dispersed throughout the country, in addition to the more than 150 victim-offender mediation programs throughout the United States. There are numerous other programs (such as creative community service, neighborhood dispute resolution, financial restitution with victim input, victim/offender dialog groups or panels) incorporating many or all of the principles of restorative justice. While hard figures are difficult to obtain, a conservative estimate would suggest at least 200 to 300 of these programs are developing in urban and rural communities throughout the country.

Is There Public Support for Restorative Justice?

Even in view of the growing interest and support of restorative justice theory and practice, the question remains "Is the larger public really interested?" Certainly the data that have emerged from examination of a number of individual programs, as noted below, are rather persuasive. Yet, is there evidence of public support for the principles of restorative justice? The strong "law and order" and "get tough" rhetoric that dominates most political campaigns would suggest not. After all, how often have we heard ambitious politicians or criminal justice officials state that "the public demands that we get tougher with criminals"? This perception, or some would argue, misperception, fuels the engine that drives our nation toward ever-increasing and costly criminal punishments, as seen in lengthy sentences and the highest per capita incarceration in the world (Mauer, 1991).

There is, however, a growing body of evidence to suggest that the general public is far less vindictive than often portrayed and far more supportive of the basic principles of restorative justice than many might think, particularly when applied to property offenders. Studies in Alabama, Delaware, Maryland, Michigan, Minnesota, North Carolina, Oregon, and Vermont consistently have found a public deeply concerned with holding offenders accountable while being quite supportive of community-based sanctions, which allow for more restorative outcomes.

A study in Minnesota is particularly illustrative. A statewide public opinion survey, conducted by the University of Minnesota (Pranis and Umbreit, 1992) using a large probability sample, challenged conventional wisdom about public feelings related to crime and punishment. A sample of 825 Minnesota adults, demographically and geographically balanced to reflect the state's total population, was asked three questions with implications for restorative justice as part of a larger omnibus survey. A sampling of this size has a sampling error of plus or minus 3.5 percentage points. The first question was: "Suppose that while you are away, your home is burglarized and $1,200 worth of property is stolen. The burglar has one previous conviction for a similar offense. In addition to four years on probation, would you prefer the sentence include repayment of $1,200 to you or four months in jail?" Nearly three out of four Minnesotans indicated that having the offender pay restitution was more important than a jail sentence for a burglary of their home.

To examine public support for policies that address some of the underlying social problems that often cause crime, a concern that is closely related to restorative justice, the following question was asked: "For the greatest impact on reducing crime, should additional money be spent on more prisons, or spent on education, job training, and community programs?" Spending on education, job training, and community programs rather than on prisons to reduce crime was favored by four out of five Minnesotans.

The third and final question related to restorative justice addressed the issue of interest in victim-offender mediation. This question was presented in the following manner: "Minnesota has several programs which allow crime victims to meet with the person who committed the crime, in the presence of a trained mediator, to let this person know how the crime affected them, and to work out a plan for repayment of losses. Suppose you were the victim of a nonviolent property crime committed by a juvenile or young adult. How likely would you be to participate in a program like this?"

More than four of five Minnesotans expressed an interest in participating in a face-to-face mediation session with the offender. This finding is particularly significant in that criminal justice officials and program staff who are unfamiliar with mediation often make such comments as "there is no way in the world that victims in my community would ever want to confront the offender" or "only a small portion of victims would ever be interested." The finding is particularly important since the vast majority of crime is committed by either juveniles or young adults. Some would suggest that the victim-offender mediation process is likely to be supported only for crimes involving juvenile offenders. This is certainly not the case in Minnesota. Eighty-two percent of respondents indicated they would be likely to participate in a program that would allow them to meet the juvenile or young adult who victimized them.

A picture of a far less vindictive public than often portrayed emerges from this statewide survey. Respondents indicated greater concern for restitution and prevention strategies that address underlying issues of social injustice than for costly retribution. Holding offenders personally accountable to their victim is more important than incarceration in a jail. Public safety is understood to be more directly related to investing in job training, education, and other community programs than incarceration.

While it might be tempting to suggest that this public opinion survey simply reflects the rather unique liberal social policy tradition of Minnesota, its findings are consistent with a growing body of public opinion research across the United States (Bae, 1992; Gottfredson and Taylor, 1983; Clark, 1985; Public Agenda Foundation, 1987; Public Opinion Research, 1986). These previous studies have found broad public support for payment of restitution by the offender to their victim instead of incarceration for property crimes, and support for crime-prevention strategies instead of prison strategies to control crime. The studies did not explicitly ask respondents if they supported "restorative justice." The questions asked, however, addressed important underlying principles that are fundamental to the theory of restorative justice, which places far more value on crime prevention and restoration of physical and emotional losses than on retribution and blame for past behavior.

Is Restorative Justice a Public or Private Responsibility?

Restorative justice requires an active partnership between the public and private sectors. While many of the early restorative justice interventions, such as victim-offender mediation and reconciliation, were initiated by private community-based agencies, increasingly, local and statewide correctional and law enforcement departments, including victim-service units, are developing new programs. They are becoming active stakeholders in the restorative justice movement.

Can Restorative Justice Apply Within Correctional Institutions and Residential Programs?

Some of the most creative restorative justice interventions have occurred in correctional institutions. Structured and facilitated dialog sessions between a small group of inmates and crime victims (not their own victims) periodically have been conducted in prisons in the United States and England. Two of the more well-known programs were developed in the maximum-security prisons in Vacaville, California and

Graterford, Pennsylvania. Several prisons in different states (including Alaska, California, Minnesota, New York, Ohio, Pennsylvania, Texas, and Wisconsin) have allowed parents of murdered children or other victims of severe violence to meet with the offender/inmate in the presence of a highly trained and skilled mediator and following lengthy and intensive preparation of both parties over a period of many months.

While such prison-based restorative justice programs are few in number, the potential for wider implementation in the future is large. Only a few residential programs are known to have initiated a restorative justice program involving some form of direct victim offender communication and problem solving. The Minnesota Restitution Center, a nationally recognized residential program in the early 1970s, was a pioneer in experimenting with direct victim and offender communication, long before the theory of restorative justice was formally conceptualized. As with prison-based restorative justice programs, residential community correctional facilities hold a great deal of potential for further implementation of restorative justice practices in the future. It is important to note that community-based residential programs nearly always have offered services that are restorative in nature for offenders and their reintegration into the community. Restorative justice, however, moves beyond just the offender focus and requires more active involvement of crime victims and citizen volunteers in the process of holding offenders accountable through maximizing opportunities for the offenders to restore the emotional and material losses that resulted from their behavior.

Is Restorative Justice Meant for Only Minor Property Offenses?

The vast majority of current restorative justice programs, representing primarily victim-offender mediation programs, work with first- or second-time property offenders, particularly juvenile offenders. On the other hand, many programs have worked with minor assaults and with adult offenders for many years. A small number of programs are beginning to offer restorative justice interventions such as mediation, family-group conferencing, or victim-offender dialog groups in prisons for persons involved in severely violent crime, often at the request of victims.

There are few instruments that have been developed specifically for restorative justice interventions to identify appropriate participants. Existing correctional assessment instruments typically are used for offenders, whether or not in the context of restorative justice.

Several programs have developed brief-assessment checklists for staff or mediators to use with crime victims or offenders. The best example has been developed by a victim-offender mediation program in Leeds, England. While not a thoroughly developed and validated instrument, these brief-assessment forms developed by the program in Leeds provide some helpful guidance. Far more work is needed in the area of client assessment, particularly when dealing with more serious and violent offenses that may be appropriate for a restorative justice intervention.

Precisely because of the intense emotional trauma experienced by victims of violence, as well as the impact (or lack of impact) on the offender, the potential benefits of restorative interventions in violent offenses is significant for those interested victims. A level of healing and closure may be possible that is unlikely to occur through any other intervention. Far greater risk, however, is also present when providing a restorative justice intervention such as victim-offender mediation to parties involved in severely violent crime, such as attempted homicide or murder. Almost by definition, interventions in such offenses are prison-based, while interventions with property offenders and minor assaults are nearly always community-based.

What Policies and Practices Are Uniquely Restorative?

Policies

Criminal and juvenile justice system policies that hold the greatest promise for restorative justice practice include those that allow for the following:

- greater participation of crime victims in the criminal justice process; enhanced and systematic training of correctional staff related to victim needs

- greater involvement of citizen volunteers and community agencies in the process of holding offenders accountable and building safer communities

- provision of a range of opportunities for appropriate crime victims and offenders to engage in dialog, problem solving, and restoration of victim losses; competency-development opportunities for offenders that emphasize their strengths and obligation to make things right with their victims and communities; provision of victim awareness and empathy development training for all offenders

- major emphasis and investment in crime prevention and community safety

- reduced and selective use of incarceration for only the most violent and predatory offenders

While many other policies may also emphasize restorative outcomes, the policies noted above highlight the distinctive qualities of a truly restorative justice based system as opposed to merely enhancing our current systems of justice with a few marginal policies that may be restorative.

Practices

Programs that provide a safe and structured setting for victim-sensitive communication between appropriate offenders and their victims that can lead to restorative outcomes (often using trained citizen volunteers) are particularly restorative interventions. Victim-offender mediation is the best-known guided communication between victims and offenders; however, there are other similar interventions that also have been found to be very effective (Umbreit, 1995b, 1995c). While not always described as mediation or using the specific techniques of mediation, these forms of communication can be very positive for both victims and offenders. The full range of victim-offender communication should be recognized as related; otherwise, they will continue to be disconnected from each other and from the broader principles of restorative justice.

The different types of victim-offender communication can be placed on a continuum ranging from low-intensity meetings involving victim representatives and limited communication in a community setting, to high-intensity direct involvement meetings between victims or survivors and offenders convicted of first-degree murder in a high-security correctional institution. Other types of communication between victims and offenders also can be placed along this continuum between those two extremes. Note that these high-intensity meetings that involve violent crimes require extensive preparation and highly trained mediators.

Victim and Offender Panels and Groups. Through panels of representative victims, who share their stories with large groups of offenders or through small groups of inmates and "surrogate" victims who have been harmed by similar crimes who meet several times and work at coming to a better understanding of the full human impact of crime in our communities, both groups feel the transformative power of victims communicating with offenders. Feelings are expressed. Information is shared. Stereotypes are destroyed. Both victims and offenders often become understood as the real people that they are, rather than the labels that the justice system has given them. Many victims of crime have found this type of communication with offenders helpful, as have the offenders.

Family Group Conferencing. The victim, the offender, and key members of their support community meet face to face. A trained conference coordinator (usually a law-enforcement officer) guides them through a generally emotional discussion of how the crime occurred, how it has affected their lives, and how the crime's harm can be repaired. All participants are allowed to ask questions and to express their feelings. In the conference, the offenders are faced with the full impact of their behavior on the victim, people close to the victim, and the offender's own family and friends. The process condemns the behavior but does it in the context of separating the behavior from the person. The entire group works out an agreement about how the offender best may repair the harm done and receive support in being reintegrated into the life of the community.

Victim Offender Mediation. Victim-offender mediation is used most frequently in property crimes and minor assaults. In victim-offender mediation, the victim and offender meet face to face with a trained mediator and perhaps a support person for each of them. During the mediation session, the victim and offender discuss the incident and its emotional impact on them, ask questions, and negotiate an appropriate form of restitution. Prior to the mediation session, the mediator meets separately with each party to listen to their story, explain the program, invite their participation, and prepare them for the face-to-face meeting. Potential benefits of victim-offender mediation include: receiving needed information about the crime; expressing the full emotional impact of the offense to the person responsible for it; reducing the sense of vulnerability for the victim after meeting the offender; and having direct input into the process of holding the offender accountable. For both victim and offender, the formal and bureaucratic process of justice often is transformed into a far more understandable and humane process focused on restoring the emotional and material losses left in the wake of criminal behavior.

Victim-Offender Dialog in Crimes of Severe Violence. In recent years, a small but growing number of victims—often surviving family members of people who were murdered—have asked to meet and speak with the offender. The victims' goals generally are to ask questions, tell the offender about the lasting harm he or she caused, and express their feelings. Survivors come with the hope that they can make some peace with the trauma they still suffer. The dialog usually takes place years after the crime and in the offender's prison with guards present in the background. A mediator specially trained about crimes of severe violence usually spends many months preparing the victim and offender, and then facilitates their dialog using a style which encourages them to speak directly to each other. The focus of this intervention is on offering a safe and structured setting that can provide the greatest opportunity for both parties to achieve a greater sense understanding, healing, and closure through a process of dialog and mutual aid, while not minimizing in any way the horrible crime that occurred and the devastating impact it has had on many people.

Restorative Victim Offender Communication. All communication between crime victims and offenders needs to be particularly sensitive to the unique needs of victims (Bazemore, 1994; Umbreit and Greenwood, 1997). While also addressing the needs of the offenders, communication with victims requires a thorough understanding of the experience of victims and collaboration with victim advocacy and service groups. Communication between victims and offenders is not, by definition, "restorative." For example, some early victim programs included stalking paroled sex offenders on the streets and confronting them in public through name calling and expressing rage. This type of victim-offender contact or "communication," while a release for the victim, is certainly not restorative. And similarly, some victim panels may be so one directional and shaming in the tone of telling victims' stories that they hardly could be considered a restorative justice intervention.

Even the victim-offender mediation process could become less than truly restorative if the entire effort consists of a brief meeting focused only on developing a restitution plan through a highly directive mediator, with little time for dialog and expression of feelings.

There are a number of characteristics that are likely to facilitate a more restorative experience of communication between victims and offenders (Umbreit, 1996). These include:

1. Having an impartial facilitator present who keeps the process focused on addressing the concerns of both the victims and offenders, who participate voluntarily

2. Allowing the process of communication to go both ways between the parties

3. Preparing both groups for direct communication with each other by the facilitator having separate contact with the victim group and with the offender group prior to any joint session(s)

4. Preparing of the victim, which includes:

— explaining the purpose of victim-offender communication

— clarifying expectations

— understanding the limits and boundaries of victim-offender communication

— coaching on effective communication of sensitive and hurtful feelings

— talking about criminal-justice system language, culture, protocols, and so forth

5. Preparing of offenders includes:

— explaining the purpose of victim-offender communication

— understanding the impact of crime on victims

— examining their own level of ownership for their criminal behavior, including the issue of remorse

— clarifying expectations

— participating in victim-empathy exercises

— understanding the limits and boundaries of victim-offender communication

— coaching on victim-sensitive communication through avoidance of offensive language

6. When the joint session is held, allowing the victim the opportunity to initiate the storytelling phase of the intervention, in which the victim shares the full human impact of the crime

7. Developing of the victim-offender communication intervention with a local victim services agency, which would have a major role in recruiting victim participation in the meeting

8. Avoiding of the words "reconciliation" or "forgiveness" in the title or descriptive material related to the intervention because both words tend to devalue or deny the initial anger and rage

felt by many crime victims. Any reconciliation and forgiveness that may occur must be entirely the choice of the people involved. An apology, if offered by an offender, must be genuine and not forced. Victims must not be made to accept an apology or be made to feel guilty because they do not choose to forgive at the time of the meeting.

Have Studies Been Conducted To Assess the Impact of Restorative Justice?

While the restorative justice movement emphasizes broad systemic change that redefines the purpose of criminal justice, the key players, and the desired outcomes, virtually no research is yet available to assess the impact of this movement on criminal and juvenile justice systems. Given the fact that a small but growing number of justice systems either are examining or implementing major changes in how they operate, such research is likely to occur in the coming years. In fact, the Reparative Probation Community Boards initiative of the Vermont Department of Corrections is being evaluated to determine its statewide impact. Nonetheless, no studies on the systemwide impact of restorative justice have yet been completed.

Several important studies, however, have been conducted on specific restorative justice interventions such as victim-offender mediation (Coates and Gehm, 1989; Dignan, 1990; Marshal and Merry, 1990; Neimeyer and Shichor, 1996; Umbreit and Coates, 1992; Umbreit and Greenwood, 1998; Umbreit and Roberts, 1996; Umbreit, 1989a, 1991a, 1993a, 1994a, 1995b) and family group conferencing (Maxwell and Morris, 1993; McCold and Wachtel, 1998; Umbreit and Fercello, 1997; Wundersitz and Hetzel, 1996), both here and abroad. A number of other studies have examined interventions that are likely to be restorative, such as financial restitution (Butts and Snyder, 1991; Galaway and Hudson, 1990; Schneider, 1986), and community work service (Bazemore and Maloney, 1994). While clearly restorative in nature, these interventions, however, are not by definition consistent with the core principles of restorative justice. For example, most financial restitution and community service programs have little direct involvement of crime victims or citizen volunteers (other than work supervisors). Similarly, most of these programs were not intentionally developed or evaluated within the conceptual framework of restorative justice.

Particularly because financial restitution and community service have intrinsically restorative elements, it would be tempting to include studies of these interventions in this chapter. To do so would come dangerously close to simply renaming interventions of the past while ignoring foundational values of restorative justice. This would lead to far more active and direct involvement of crime victims, citizen volunteers, and community groups in the process of holding offenders accountable through restitution and community service. Moreover, both of these interventions also can be, and probably in many jurisdictions are, administered in a highly retributive offender-driven juvenile or criminal justice system. Therefore, the studies reported on in this chapter will focus on interventions that are clearly restorative in nature and include the following criteria:

1. The offender is held directly accountable to the victim.

2. Restoration of victim losses by the offender is emphasized.

3. Both the victim and offender play active roles in the process.

4. Citizen volunteers and/or community groups play facilitative and/or supportive roles.

5. Opportunities for mediation and dialog between the victim and offender are present.

The interventions of victim-offender mediation, family-group conferencing, circle sentencing and talking circles (in Native American and Canadian First Nation communities), victim-offender dialog groups in prisons and related programs all meet the criteria of uniquely restorative justice grounded initiatives. Empirical data, however, are only currently available on victim-offender mediation and family-group conferencing. While anecdotal data from these other interventions appear to be quite favorable, and research is likely to emerge in these areas in the coming years, for the purposes of this chapter only studies related to victim-offender mediation and family-group conferencing will be reported.

What Have We Learned about Victim Offender Mediation for Property Crimes and Minor Assaults?

As the oldest and most well-developed restorative justice intervention (Wright and Galaway, 1989), the practice of victim-offender mediation with juvenile and adult offenders has been the subject of seventeen studies in the United States (Coates and Gehm, 1989; Gehm, 1990; Neimeyer and Shichor, 1996; Nugent and Paddock, 1995; Umbreit and Coates, 1992; Umbreit and Greenwood, 1998; Umbreit, 1994a, 1991a, 1989a), Canada (Collins, 1984; Fischer and Jeune, 1987; Perry, Lajeunesse and Woods, 1987; Roberts, 1995; Umbreit, 1995a), and England (Dignan, 1990; Marshal and Merry, 1990; Umbreit and Roberts, 1996).

A small but growing amount of research in the field of victim-offender mediation has provided increasing insight into how the process works and the impact it is having on its participants and the larger justice system. All of these studies have found the vast majority of victims and offenders to benefit from the process of meeting each other, talking about the offense and its impact on all involved, and developing a plan for restoring losses. While not the "cure all" for crime and delinquency, victim-offender mediation programs also have been found to yield a number of benefits for the justice system, as well. The most essential findings that have emerged are as follows.

Program Characteristics

Of the nearly 300 (Umbreit and Greenwood, 1998) victim-offender mediation programs in the United States, the vast majority continue to be administered by private community-based nonprofit agencies. A growing number of probation departments and other public agencies, however, are beginning to develop these programs, frequently with the involvement of community volunteers to serve as mediators. Most programs employ a four-phase process consisting of: (1) case referral and intake; (2) preparation for mediation, during which the mediator meets with each party separately prior to the mediation session to listen to their story, explain the program, invite their participation, and prepare them for the face-to-face meeting; (3) mediation, during which a trained third-party mediator (most often a community volunteer) facilitates a dialog, which allows the victim and offender to talk about the impact of the crime on their lives, provide information about the event to each other, and work out a mutually agreeable written restitution agreement; and (4) follow-up, during which restitution agreements are monitored and follow-up mediation sessions are scheduled, if problems arise.

Table 11.3 identifies some characteristics of four programs working with juvenile offenders in different parts of the country. All four programs were part of a multisite evaluation of victim-offender mediation (Umbreit,

TABLE 11.3. Program Characteristics (1991)

Characteristic	Albuquerque	Austin	Minneapolis	Oakland
Start date	1987	1990	1985	1987
Primary referral source	Probation	Probation	Probation	Probation
Sponsor/Management	Private	Public	Private	Private
Total 1991 budget	$31,530	$106,241	$123,366	$127,176
Number of staff	1.5 FTE	3.5 FTE	3.6 FTE	3.5 FTE
Use of comediators	Always	Always	Sometimes	Always
Number of volunteer mediators	32	NA	30	80
Length of mediation training	40 hours	40 hours	25 hours	30 hours
Total 1991 case referrals	391	853	453	368
Total mediations in 1991	108	246	179	129
Proportion of mediations to case referrals in 1991	28%	29%	40%	35%

1994a, 1994b, 1993b). Three of the programs were managed by community-based agencies and one was administered by a probation department. While these four programs had about 30 to 40 percent of their case referrals result in a face-to-face mediation session, many other programs report rates of 50 to 60 percent, or even higher (Coates and Gehm, 1989; Galaway, 1988, 1989; Gehm, 1990; Marshal and Merry, 1990; Umbreit, 1988, 1989a, 1991a; Wright and Galaway, 1989).

Case Referral

Referrals of both juvenile and adult cases to victim-offender mediation programs have been made by judges, probation officers, prosecutors, police, and at times, defense attorneys or victim advocates, at both a pre- and postadjudication level. The majority of programs in the United States serve as a diversion from the juvenile justice system for primarily first- or second-time offenders and receive most of their referrals from the local probation department. The range of referrals to programs can be as few as 100 a year of even less to as many as 1,000 or more (Neimeyer and Shichor, 1996). Table 11.4 indicates referral characteristics of four juvenile system-based programs.

TABLE 11.4. Referral Characteristics (Two-year Period, 1990-1991)

Variable	Albuquerque	Austin	Minneapolis	Oakland	Total
1. Cases referred	591	1,107	903	541	3,142
2. Preadjudication	76%	98%	72%	91%	85%
3. Postadjudication	24%	2%	28%	9%	15%
4. Individual victims	654	1,058	633	454	2,799
5. Individual offenders	604	1,087	658	310	2,659
6. Types of offenses					
a. against property	73%	81%	89%	87%	83%
b. against people	27%	19%	11%	17%	17%
7. Most frequent property offense	burglary	burglary	vandalism	burglary	burglary
8. Most frequent violent offense	assault	assault	assault	assault	assault

Immediate Outcomes of Mediation

There exist a number of immediate outcomes of the victim-offender mediation process. In the four programs identified in Table 11.5, a total of 1,131 face-to-face mediation sessions occurred, and in 95 percent of these cases, a mutually agreeable restitution plan was negotiated. These restitution plans included primarily financial restitution, although community service or personal service for the victim also were included in many agreements.

Victim Participation

The majority of victims of property crime have been quite willing to participate in a mediation session with their offender, when given the opportunity (Coates and Gehm, 1989; Gehm, 1990; Galaway, 1988; Marshall and Merry, 1990; Umbreit, 1985, 1989a, 1991a, 1992a). In a study (Niemeyer and Shichor, 1995) of the Victim Offender Reconciliation Program in Orange County, California, representing the largest victim-offender mediation program in North America with more than 1,000 referrals a year, 75 percent of victims of minor property and personal offenses were interested in participating in the mediation process. In a large multisite study

TABLE 11.5. Immediate Outcomes (Two-year Period, 1990-1991)

Variable	Albuquerque	Austin	Minneapolis	Oakland	Total
1. Number of mediations	158	300	468	205	1,131
2. Successfully negotiated restitution agreements	99%	98%	93%	91%	95%
3. Agreements with:					
a. Financial restitution	82	171	239	111	603
b. Personal service	57	21	31	36	145
c. Community service	29	130	107	39	305
4. Total financial restitution	$23,542	$41,536	$32,301	$23,227	$120,606
5. Average financial restitution	$287	$243	$135	$209	$200
6. Total personal service	1,028 hr	439 hr	508 hr	585 hr	2,560 hr
7. Average personal service	18 hr	21 hr	16 hr	16 hr	18 hr
8. Total community service	1,073 hr	4,064 hr	1,937 hr	588 hr	7,662 hr
9. Average community service	37 hr	31 hr	18 hr	15 hr	25 hr

(Umbreit, 1994), 70 percent of victims who were never even referred to mediation indicated their interest in meeting with the juvenile offender if the opportunity were presented to them. In a statewide public opinion poll in Minnesota, 82 percent of citizens (many of whom were crime victims) indicated that they would be likely to consider participating in a mediation session with a juvenile or young adult offender if they were the victim of a nonviolent property crime (Pranis and Umbreit, 1992). While the possibility of receiving restitution appears to motivate victims to enter the mediation process, following their participation they report that meeting the offender and being able to talk about what happened was more satisfying than receiving restitution (Coates and Gehm, 1989; Umbreit, 1988, 1991a, 1994a, 1995c, 1996).

Offender Participation

Offenders involved in mediation programs, while anxious about a confrontation with their victim, report that meeting the victim and being able to talk about what happened was the most satisfying aspect of the program (Coates and Gehm, 1989; Umbreit, 1991a, 1994a). Juvenile offenders do not seem to perceive victim-offender mediation to be a significantly less demanding response to their criminal behavior than other options available to the court. The use of mediation is consistent with the concern to hold young offenders accountable for their criminal behavior (Umbreit, 1994b).

Voluntary Participation in Mediation

Mediation is perceived to be voluntary by the vast majority of victims and juvenile offenders who have participated in it. In the largest multisite study (Umbreit, 1994a) of victim-offender mediation in the United States, 91 percent of victims indicated they participated voluntarily, and 81 percent of juvenile offenders indicated voluntary participation. A particularly interesting finding that emerged from this large multistate study was related to examining a comparison group of victims and offenders who did not actually participate in mediation. Had they been given the opportunity, 72 percent of juvenile offenders (a matched sample with offenders in mediation) would have chosen to participate in mediation and 70 percent of victims would have chosen mediation.

Client Satisfaction

Victim-offender mediation results in high levels of client satisfaction with the mediation process and outcome for both victims and offenders (Coates and Gehm, 1989; Dignan, 1990; Marshall and Merry, 1990; Umbreit, 1988, 1989a, 1991b, 1993b, 1994a, 1995a, 1995b, 1996; Umbreit and Coates, 1992, 1993). The victim-offender mediation process has a strong effect in humanizing the justice system's response to crime, for both victims and juvenile offenders.

The following comments by victims of juvenile crime are illustrative of how they experienced mediation. "I was allowed to participate and I felt I was able to make decisions rather than the system making them for me." "The mediation made me feel like I had something to do with what went on . . . that justice had been served." "I liked the personal quality of mediation . . . it made me feel less like a victim, but still a victim."

Comments by juvenile offenders about their experience in mediation are represented by the following statements. "I liked the fairness of it." "To understand how the victim feels makes me different. . . . I was able to understand a lot about what I did." "I realized that the victim really got hurt and that made me feel really bad." "I had a chance of doing something to correct what I did without having to pay bad consequences."

As Table 11.6 indicates, after participating in a mediation session, victims and juvenile offenders in four states were far more likely to indicate that they were satisfied with the manner in which the justice system disposed of their case through mediation than a matched sample of similar victims and offender who were not able to participate in mediation.

Most Important Mediator Tasks

In a large multisite study of victim-offender mediation (Umbreit, 1994a), the following items were identified by victims of juvenile crime as the most important tasks of the mediator:

1. Mediator provided leadership.

2. Mediator made us feel comfortable.

3. Mediator helped us develop a restitution plan.

4. Mediator allowed us (victim and offender) to talk.

TABLE 11.6. Client Satisfaction with Case Processing by System Mediation Sample Compared with Sample of Those Not Referred to Mediation

Combined sites	Victims % (N)	Offenders % (N)	Probability
Mediation sample (experimental group)	79% (204)	87% (181)	$p < .0001$*
Nonreferral sample (comparison group)	57% (104)	78% (110)	$p = .055$

* Finding of significant difference

For juvenile offenders, the following items were identified as the most important tasks of the mediator:

1. Mediator made us feel comfortable.

2. Mediator allowed us (victim and offender) to talk.

3. Mediator helped us develop a restitution plan.

4. Mediator was a good listener.

Restitution Agreements—Successful Completion

Restitution agreements that are perceived as fair to both parties are negotiated in nine out of ten cases that enter mediation. A number of programs report successful completion of restitution agreements in the range of 79 to 98 percent (Coates and Gehm, 1989; Galaway, 1988, 1989; Gehm, 1990; Neimeyer and Shichor, 1996; Umbreit, 1986a, 1986b, 1988, 1991a, 1994a).

In a study of programs in Albuquerque, New Mexico and Minneapolis, Minnesota, victim-offender mediation had a significant impact on the likelihood of offenders successfully completing their restitution obligation to victims, when compared to similar offenders in a court-administered restitution program without mediation (Umbreit, 1993b, 1994a, 1994b; Umbreit and Coates, 1992, 1993). As Table 11.7 notes, 81 percent of offenders in mediation successfully completed their restitution obligation compared to 58 percent who were referred to a court-administered restitution program with no mediation component.

TABLE 11.7. Restitution Completion by Offenders (Percent of Restitution Completed)

Sample	Minneapolis % (N)	Albuquerque % (N)	Both sites % (N)
Mediation sample (experimental group)	77% (125)	93% (42)	81% (167)
Nonreferral matched sample (comparison group)	55% (179)	69% (42)	58% (221)
Probability	p < .0001*	p = .005*	p < .0001*

* Finding of significant difference.

TABLE 11.8. Emotional Impact of Mediation on Victims

Combined Sites	Premediation % (N)	Postmediation % (N)	Probability (N)
Upset about crime	67% (155)	49% (162)	p < .0001*
Afraid of being revictimized by offender	23% (154)	10% (166)	p = .003*

* Finding of significant difference

Reduction of Victim Fear and Anxiety

Victim-offender mediation programs in Albuquerque, Minneapolis, and Oakland, California made a significant contribution to reducing fear and anxiety among victims of juvenile crime (Umbreit, 1991a, 1994a, 1994b). Prior to meeting the offender, 23 percent of victims were afraid of being revictimized by the same offender. After actually meeting the offender and talking about the offense and its impact on all involved, only 10 percent of victims were still fearful of being revictimized. Similarly, prior to mediation, 67 percent of victims were upset about the crime, while after mediation, only 49 percent were upset. These findings, depicted in Table 11.8, are consistent with similar studies in England (Umbreit and Roberts, 1996) and Canada (Umbreit, 1995a).

Recidivism

Considerably fewer and less serious additional crimes are committed by juvenile offenders in several victim-offender mediation programs in the United States, when compared to similar offenders who did not participate in mediation (Nugent and Paddock, 1995; Umbreit, 1993b, 1994a, 1994b; Umbreit and Coates, 1993). This finding is consistent with two recent English studies (Marshal and Merry, 1990; Dignan, 1990) which examined programs working with adult offenders as well. With the exception of the Nugent and Paddock (1995) study, however, all of the other studies approached but did not achieve a finding that was statistically significant.

Cross-national Comparison on Key Outcomes

In the first cross-national assessment (Umbreit, Coates, and Roberts, 1997) of victim-offender mediation programs in four states of the United States, four Canadian provinces, and two cities in England that is being finalized, fairly consistent outcome data have emerged. Specific outcome measures examined include: victim and offender satisfaction with the criminal justice system response to their case by referring it to mediation; victim and offender satisfaction with the outcome of mediation; victim and offender perception of fairness in the criminal justice system

TABLE 11.9. Comparison of English, Canadian, and United States Studies of Victims and Offenders Participating in Mediation

Respondents' Perception	Combined English sites (2)	Combined Canadian sites (4)	Combined United States sites (4)
Victim satisfaction with criminal justice system response to their case; referral to mediation	62%	78%	79%
Offender satisfaction with criminal justice system response to their case; referral to mediation	79%	74%	87%
Victim satisfaction with mediation outcome	84%	89%	90%
Offender satisfaction with mediation outcome	100%	91%	91%
Victim fear of revictimization by same offender, following mediation	16% (50% less than victims who were not in mediation)	11% (64% less than victims who were not in mediation)	10% (56% less than prior to mediation for same victims)
Victim perceptions of fairness in criminal justice system response to their case; referral to mediation	59%	80%	83%
Offender perceptions of fairness of criminal justice system response to their case; referral to mediation	89%	80%	89%

response to their case through mediation; and victim fear of revictimization by the same offender following mediation. Findings are summarized in Table 11.9.

What Have We Learned about Victim-offender Mediation for Crimes of Severe Violence?

During the early years of development in the field of victim-offender mediation, in the mid to late 1970s, most practitioners believed that mediation was appropriate for primarily, if not exclusively, property crimes and minor assaults. Over the past few years, however, it has become increasingly clear that a growing number of victims of severe violence, and at times offenders, are requesting a mediated dialog so that they can talk about the impact of the crime and seek a greater sense of healing and closure.

These cases involving such offenses as sexual assault, attempted homicide, and murder (involving surviving family or friends) require a far more intense and lengthy process. It is not uncommon in such cases for the mediator to meet with each party three-to-five times over a ten-to-twelve-month period, in addition to coordinating this intervention with other caregivers, such as therapists or support people. A highly skilled mediator trained in advanced victim-sensitive offender dialog is required. The only such advanced training currently is offered at the Center for Restorative Justice and Mediation at the University of Minnesota.

While the numbers of severely violent cases in mediation/dialog are still relatively small and typically are handled on a limited case-by-case basis, the demand for such an intervention is clearly going to increase in the years ahead. The Victim Services Unit of the Texas Department of Criminal Justice is the only state that currently offers this service to any victim of severe violence in the state. This program is currently being evaluated by the author. Several other state departments of corrections, through their victim services units, are considering similar mediation/dialog services to victims and offenders involved in severely violent crime. Nearly always, these sessions are held in a maximum-security prison.

There are many anecdotal stories from victims and offenders who often speak of their participation in a mediated dialog as a powerful and transformative experience, which helped them in their healing process. Parents of murdered children have expressed their sense of relief after meeting the offender/inmate and sharing their pain as well as being able to reconstruct what actually happened and why. One such mother whose son was murdered stated "I just needed to let him see the pain he has caused in my life and to find out why he pulled the trigger." A school teacher who was assaulted and nearly killed commented after meeting the young man in prison, "it helped me end this ordeal . . . for me, it has made a difference in my life, though this type of meeting is not for everyone." An offender/inmate who met with the mother of the man he killed stated "it felt good to be able to bring her some relief and to express my remorse to her." A doctor in California whose sister was killed by a drunk driver and who was initially very skeptical about meeting the offender, following the mediation session, stated "I couldn't begin to heal until I let go of my hatred. . . . after the mediation I felt a great sense of relief. . . . I was now ready to find enjoyment in life again."

Only two small studies involving four case studies each have been conducted in the United States. The first study (Umbreit, 1989b) found that offering a mediated dialog session in several very violent cases, including a sniper-shooting case, was very beneficial to the victims, offenders, and community members or family members who were involved in the process. Three of these four cases (all adult offenders) were handled by a police department in upstate New York (Genesee County) that operates a comprehensive restorative justice program. The other study involving four cases of severely violent crime committed by juvenile offenders found very high levels of satisfaction with the process and outcomes, from both victims and offenders. The offenders were inmates in a juvenile correctional facility in Alaska.

The only study (Roberts, 1995) that has examined a larger number of cases examined the Victim-offender Mediation Project in Langley, British Columbia. This community-based Canadian program, after having pioneered the early development of victim-offender mediation and reconciliation with property offenses and minor assaults many years ago, initiated in 1991 a new project to apply the mediation process with crimes of severe violence involving incarcerated inmates. Prior to initiating this project, a small study (Gustafson and Smidstra, 1989) had been conducted by the program to assess whether victims and offenders involved in severely violent crime would be interested in meeting with each other in a safe and structured manner, after intensive preparation, if such a service were available. A very high level of interest in such meetings was found.

In the study conducted by Roberts (1995), virtually all of the twenty-two offenders and twenty-four victims who participated indicated support for the program. This support included their belief that they found considerable specific and overall value in the program, felt it was ethically and professionally run, and would not hesitate to recommend it to others. The overall effects of the mediation session expressed by victims included:

- They finally had been heard.

- The offender no longer exercised control over them.

- They could see the offender as a person rather than a monster.

- They felt more trusting in their relationships with others.

- They felt less fear.

- They were not preoccupied with the offender any more.

- They felt peace.

- They would not feel suicidal again.

- They had no more anger.

For offenders, the overall effects of a mediated dialog with the victim included:

- They discovered emotions, feelings of empathy.

- They gained increased awareness of the impact of their acts.

- They developed an increased self-awareness.

- Their eyes were open to the outside world, rather than their prior closed institutional thinking.

- They felt good about having tried the process.

- They achieved peace of mind in knowing they have helped a former victim.

What Have We Learned about Family Group Conferencing?

Similar to victim-offender mediation, the process of family group conferencing involves a face-to-face meeting between the victim and offender. The conferencing model, however, draws upon traditional Maori values in Australia and New Zealand (where it originated) by inviting a much larger group of family members and key support people for both the victim and the offender. For example, the Australian legislation authorizing family group conferencing states that the following persons must be invited to the conference: the guardians of the youth and victim; any relatives of, or any other person who has had a close supportive association with the youth and victim and who may, in the coordinator's opinion, be able to participate usefully in the conference; and a representative of the police. Whereas victim-offender mediation programs typically receive referrals from probation officers, make use of a trained community mediator to facilitate a meeting between the victim and offender and perhaps one or two other people, and encourage the mediator to meet with the parties separately before ever bringing them together, family group conferencing usually has police officers serving as the "coordinator," which is a mediator type of role. This person handles all cases at a very early pretrial point of intervention. Conferencing typically deals with the entire sanctioning process, not just the restitution portion as in victim-offender mediation.

The family group conferencing model clearly is a restorative justice based intervention with many very similar outcomes to victim-offender mediation, but with the added benefit of having all those affected by the crime present with the potential for greater community support for both the victim and offender. It is based on the concept of "reintegrative shaming" developed by the Australian criminologist John Braithwaite (1989). This concept focuses on the importance of denouncing or shaming the criminal behavior while affirming, supporting, and helping to reintegrate the offender back into the community.

Only four studies have been conducted to assess the impact of family-group conferencing with young offenders. The largest study was conducted by Maxwell and Morris (1993) to assess the impact of a new law in New Zealand that requires broad use of family-group conferencing for young offenders. A second and very preliminary study was conducted by Wundersitz and Hetzel (1996). This study examined the initial impact of family-group conferencing for young offenders in South Australia. A small exploratory study of client satisfaction with a police-based conferencing program in Minnesota was completed by a team of researchers from the University of Minnesota (Umbreit and Fercello, 1997). A larger study of a police-based family-group conference program in Bethlehem, Pennsylvania was completed recently (McCold and Wachtel, 1998).

Because of the large amount of interest in the conferencing model in North America and Europe, two additional larger studies have been initiated, but the findings are not yet available. A study initiated by John

Braithwaite of conferencing in Canberra, Australia is nearing completion, as is a multisite exploratory study of client satisfaction with family-group conferencing in Minnesota conducted by the author and Claudia Fercello at the Center for Restorative Justice and Mediation at the University of Minnesota, School of Social Work.

The data from these initial four completed studies are encouraging. Far more frequent and active involvement of families in the justice process has occurred. Young offenders and victims, as well as their families and support people, indicate that the conferencing process had been helpful. As noted below, however, to gain more participation by victims, and serve their needs, more victim-sensitive procedures were needed in the New Zealand model. These procedures have been developed following the study.

Immediate Outcomes

As a result of the Children, Young Person and Their Families Act that was enacted in New Zealand in 1989 and which requires broad national use of family-group conferencing, far fewer young offenders appeared in court and received convictions compared to before the Act was introduced. There were between 10,000 and 13,000 court cases each year compared to 2,587 in 1990. Commitments of young people to correctional institutions was cut by more than 50 percent following the Act; in 1988, 262 young offenders were imprisoned compared to only 112 in 1990. This represents the largest systemic impact of a single restorative justice intervention anywhere in the world.

While not leading yet to change in the entire criminal justice system, the broad use of family-group conferencing in New Zealand bodes well for further systemwide restorative initiatives. An 86 percent offender compliance rate with the decision of the family-group conference was found in the Australian study (Wundersitz and Hetzel, 1996) and an even higher offender compliance rate of 94 percent was found in the more recent Bethlehem, Pennsylvania study (McCold and Wachtel, 1998).

Victim Participation

As a restorative justice intervention, the active involvement of crime victims in the family group conference model is crucial. In the large study conducted by Maxwell and Morris (1993) in New Zealand, in which they examined 692 cases, they found far less frequent victim involvement than anticipated. Only 41 percent of crime victims attended family group conferences. Much of this was due to procedures that did not clearly communicate to victims or effectively invite their participation. Sometimes, the program coordinator simply forgot to invite them. This disturbing finding led to a major review of procedures and a greater emphasis on the restorative justice principle of truly involving and serving victims in a respectful manner.

In the Australian study (Wundersitz and Hetzel, 1996), preliminary evidence indicates that 75 to 80 percent of those conferences in which a victim-based crime occurred had at least one victim present.

When offered, 67 percent of victims in the Bethlehem, Pennsylvania study agreed to participate, representing 43 percent of victims of violence (primarily disorderly conduct and harassment) and 88 percent of victims of property (primarily retail theft) offenses (McCold and Wachtel, 1998). When offered a conference, both victim and offender agreed to participate 53 percent of the time. Sixty-one percent of the victims in this study were institutions (retail stores or schools).

Offender Participation

In New Zealand, family-group conferences often resulted in moderately severe penalties for young offenders. More young people were held accountable for their behavior than previously. Some form of penalty was decided in 94 percent of the conferences. This study found that sometimes the young persons were pressured to admit their guilt since a denial would mean a court hearing and long delays. The majority of cases referred to family group conferencing in the New Zealand study were primarily property offenders, although other violent crimes could be referred, except manslaughter and murder. Only a third of the young offenders indicated that they felt actually involved in the family group conference and many did not say very much in the conference. This is clearly a concern that needs to be addressed.

In the Australian study (Wundersitz and Hetzel, 1996), the offenders most frequently referred to conferencing were involved in burglary, theft, or damage to property. In the Bethlehem study, 79 percent of offenders agreed to participate in a conference, although when matched with the victim, this resulted in an actual participation rate of 53 percent (McCold and Wachtel, 1998).

Family Participation

Families played an active role in conferences and frequently participated. Nearly two-thirds of participating families felt very much involved

(Maxwell and Morris, 1993). Families also were involved actively in conferences in the Australian study (Wundersitz and Hetzel, 1996).

Client Satisfaction

Considerably lower levels of satisfaction with the family group conferencing model, for both victims and offenders, were found in the New Zealand (Maxwell and Morris 1993) when compared to the victim-offender mediation studies. Nearly half of the victims said they were satisfied, and a third went away feeling better. A very disturbing finding, however, was that about a third of the victims left the family group conference feeling worse. This dissatisfaction usually related to: feeling the offender was not really sorry; not receiving any repayment for damage; feeling that the family was making excuses for what happened; and, some expressed fear that the offender would seek revenge on them. While the conferencing model represents a highly restorative type of intervention, the fact that nearly a third of victims felt worse, once again, indicates the need for far more victim-sensitive procedures in the process.

The Australian study (Wundersitz and Hetzel, 1996), however, found a much higher level of satisfaction with the family group conferencing model. Participation in the conference was found to be helpful to 93 percent of the victims.

Offenders in the New Zealand study seemed satisfied with the conference, but it was clear that they played a rather passive role, often speaking very little in the actual conference. The largest portion of offenders felt that the family essentially decided the outcome. More than 80 percent of these young offenders said that they were not involved in deciding the outcome. As with victims, this finding also is disturbing given the fact that restorative justice emphasizes the need for offenders to be in active roles, drawing on their strengths, to take responsibility and make amends to their victims. The satisfaction of families with the outcome of the conference in the New Zealand study was particularly high at 85 percent. The study concluded that there is now far more involvement of families in the justice process.

An exceptionally high rate of client satisfaction with the conferencing process was found in the Bethlehem, Pennsylvania study where satisfaction rates were 96 percent of the victims and 97 percent of the offenders (McCold and Wachtel, 1998).

The small exploratory study of a police-based conferencing program in Minnesota found that 90 percent of participating victims were satisfied as were 80 percent of offenders. Among victims, 94 percent thought they were treated fairly, and 90 percent of offenders indicated they were treated fairly (Umbreit and Fercello, 1997).

Conclusions

The restorative justice movement is having an increasing impact on criminal justice system policymakers and practitioners. While it yet remains a movement and not a fully developed new system or paradigm, the data emerging from studies that have examined uniquely restorative interventions are encouraging.

Through the more than 600 victim-offender mediation programs in North America and Europe, as well as the growing number of family-group conference programs, opportunities for victims, offenders, families, and other community members to be actively involved in a restorative process of justice is maximized. Offenders learn of the real human consequences of their behavior and can be held directly accountable to the person(s) they violated through making amends. Victims are invited to play a more active role in holding the offender accountable, letting them know how the crime affected them, and working toward some form of resolution. Family members and community volunteers can provide support and assistance.

The lengthy twenty-year experience of victim-offender mediation, and the newer experience of family group conferencing, breathe life into the emerging practice and theory of restorative justice. While clearly leading the way toward greater implementation of restorative justice principles, by themselves, they are not the exclusive expression of restorative justice. Nor do these two interventions fully address the larger systemic change implications of restorative justice as a fundamentally different paradigm.

Far more experimentation is needed as the restorative justice movement matures. Several studies have been initiated to assess the broader systemwide impact of adopting this new paradigm. Additional interventions that maximize the unique qualities of restorative justice need to be developed and assessed. Circle sentencing, a very promising intervention developing in several Canadian First Nation communities, is being studied. In addition to examining the immediate outcomes for the individuals involved and the justice system, longitudinal studies are needed to assess the longer-term durability of the positive outcomes we are beginning to see.

The restorative justice movement also faces a number of important risks. Perhaps the greatest risk is that of "window dressing," in which criminal and juvenile justice systems redefine what they have always done with more professionally acceptable and humane language while not really changing the policies and procedures of their system. A few pilot projects may be set up on the margins of the system, while the mainstream of business is entirely offender driven and highly retributive with little victim involvement and services, and even less community involvement.

The other major risk facing the movement is that of being so focused on restorative justice interventions that can more effectively serve victims, victimized communities, and offenders that the larger issue of the tremendous overuse of costly incarceration in American society is ignored. Unless the issue of overuse of incarceration is ultimately dealt with, there will not be the financial resources available to move toward a truly restorative justice model. In a similar vein, concern for the over-representation of people of color in our juvenile and criminal justice systems easily could be lost in the haste of an exclusive focus on restorative interventions alone.

As a relatively young reform effort, the restorative justice movement holds a great deal of promise as we move toward the next century. By drawing on many traditional values of the past, from many different cultures, we have the opportunity to build a far more accountable, understandable, and healing system of justice that can lead to a greater sense of community through active victim and citizen involvement in restorative initiatives.

References

Bae, I. 1992. A Survey on Public Acceptance of Restitution as an Alternative to Incarceration for Property Offenders in Hennepin County, Minnesota. In H. Messmer and H. U. Otto, eds. *Restorative Justice on Trial*. Dordrecht, NETH: Kluer Academic Publishers.

Bazemore, G. 1994. Developing a Victim Orientation for Community Corrections: A Restorative Justice Paradigm and a Balanced Mission. *Perspectives* (Special Issue): 19-24.

Bazemore, G. and D. Maloney. 1994. Rehabilitating Community Service: Toward Restorative Service in a Balanced Justice System. *Federal Probation*. 58 (1):24-35.

Bazemore, G. and M. S. Umbreit. 1995. Rethinking the Sanctioning Function in Juvenile Court: Retributive or Restorative Responses to Youth Crime. *Crime & Delinquency*. 41:296-316.

Braithwaite, J. 1989. *Crime, Shame and Reintegration*. New York: Cambridge University Press.

Butts, J. A. and H. N. Snyder. 1991. *Restitution and Juvenile Recidivism*. Pittsburgh, Pennsylvania: National Center for Juvenile Justice.

Clark, P. 1985. *Perception of Criminal Justice Surveys: Executive Summary*. The Michigan Prison and Jail Overcrowding Project.

Coates, R. B. and J. Gehm. 1989. An Empirical Assessment. In M. Wright and B. Galaway, eds. *Mediation and Criminal Justice*. London: Sage Publications.

Collins, J. P. 1984. *Evaluation Report: Grande Prairie Reconciliation Project for Young Offenders*. Ottawa: Ministry of the Solicitor General of Canada, Consultation Centre (Prairies).

Dignan, J. 1990. *Repairing the Damage*. Sheffield, UK: Centre for Criminological and Legal Research, University of Sheffield.

Fischer, D. G. and R. Jeune. 1987. Juvenile Diversion: A Process Analysis. *Canadian Psychology*. 28:60-70.

Galaway, B. 1988. Crime Victim and Offender Mediation as a Social Work Strategy. *Social Service Review*. 62:668-683.

————. 1989. Informal Justice: Mediation Between Offenders and Victims. In P. A. Albrecht and O. Backes, eds. *Crime Prevention and Intervention: Legal and Ethical Problems*. Berlin: Walter de Gruyter.

Galaway, B. and J. Hudson. 1990. *Criminal Justice, Restitution, and Reconciliation*. Monsey, New York: Criminal Justice Press.

Gehm, J. 1990. Mediated Victim-offender Restitution Agreements: An Exploratory Analysis of Factors Related to Victim Participation. In B. Galaway and J. Hudson, eds. *Criminal Justice, Restitution and Reconciliation*. Monsey, New York: Criminal Justice Press.

Gottfredson, S. and R. Taylor. 1983. *The Correctional Crisis: Prison Overcrowding and Public Policy*. Washington, D.C.: U.S. Department of Justice, National Institute of Justice.

Gustafson, D. L. and H. Smidstra. 1989. *Victim Offender Reconciliation in Serious Crime: A Report on the Feasibility Study Undertaken for the Ministry of the Solicitor General (Canada)*. Langley, B.C.: Fraser Region Community Justice Initiatives Association.

Marshall, T. F. and S. Merry. 1990. *Crime and Accountability*. London: Home Office.

Mauer, M. 1991. *Americans Behind Bars: A Comparison of International Rates of Incarceration.* Washington, D.C.: The Sentencing Project.

Maxwell, G. and A. Morris. 1993. *Family, Victims and Culture: Youth Justice in New Zealand.* Wellington, New Zealand: Institute of Criminology, Victoria University of Wellington.

McCold, P. and B. Wachtel. 1998. *Restorative Policing Experiment: The Bethlehem, Pennsylvania Police-family Group Conferencing Project.* Pipersville, Pennsylvania: Community Service Foundation.

Niemeyer, M. and D. Shichor. 1996. A Preliminary Study of a Large Victim Offender Reconciliation Program. *Federal Probation.* 60 (3):30-34.

Nugent, W. R. and J. B. Paddock. 1995. The Effect of Victim-offender Mediation on Severity of Reoffense. *Mediation Quarterly.* 12:353-367.

Perry, L., T. Lajeunesse and A. Woods. 1987. *Mediation Services: An Evaluation.* Manitoba: Research, Planning and Evaluation Office of the Attorney General.

Pranis K. and M. Umbreit. 1992. *Public Opinion Research Challenges Perception of Widespread Public Demand for Harsher Punishment.* Minneapolis: Citizens Council.

Public Agenda Foundation. 1987. *Crime and Punishment: The Public's View.* New York: The Edna McConnell Clark Foundation.

Public Opinion Research. 1986. *Report Prepared for the North Carolina Center on Crime and Punishment.* Washington, D.C.: Public Opinion Research.

Roberts, T. 1995. *Evaluation of the Victim Offender Mediation Program in Langley, B.C.* Victoria, British Columbia: Focus Consultants.

Schneider, A. L. 1986. Restitution and Recidivism Rates of Juvenile Offenders: Results from Four Experimental Studies. *Criminology.* 24:533-552.

Umbreit, Mark S. 1985. *Crime and Reconciliation: Creative Options for Victims and Offenders.* Nashville, Tennessee: Abingdon Press.

———. 1986a. Victim Offender Mediation: a National Survey. *Federal Probation.* 50 (4):53-56.

———. 1986b. Victim Offender Mediation and Judicial Leadership. *Judicature.* 9:202-204.

———. 1988. Mediation of Victim Offender Conflict. *Journal of Dispute Resolution.* 1988:85- 106.

————. 1989a. Victims Seeking Fairness, Not Revenge: Toward Restorative Justice. *Federal Probation*. 53 (3):52-57.

————. 1989b. Violent Offenders and Their Victims. In M. Wright and B. Galaway, eds. *Mediation and Criminal Justice*. London: Sage.

————. 1991a. Minnesota Mediation Center Gets Positive Results. *Corrections Today*. (August):194-197.

————. 1991b. Mediation of Youth Conflict: A Multi-system Perspective. *Child and Adolescent Social Work*. 8:141-153.

————. 1993a. Crime Victims and Offenders in Mediation: An Emerging Area of Social Work Practice. *Social Work*. 38:69-73.

————. 1993b. Juvenile Offenders Meet Their Victims: The Impact of Mediation in Albuquerque, New Mexico. *Family and Conciliation Courts Review*. 31:90-100.

————. 1994a. *Victim Meets Offender: The Impact of Restorative Justice and Mediation*. Monsey, New York: Criminal Justice Press.

————. 1994b. Crime Victims Confront Their Offenders: The Impact of a Minneapolis Mediation Program. *Journal of Research on Social Work Practice*. 4:436-447.

————. 1995a. *Mediation of Criminal Conflict: An Assessment of Programs in Four Canadian Provinces*. St. Paul, Minnesota: Center for Restorative Justice and Mediation, University of Minnesota.

————. 1995b. The Development and Impact of Victim-offender Mediation in the United States. *Mediation Quarterly*. 12:263-276.

————. 1995c. *Mediating Interpersonal Conflicts: A Pathway to Peace*. West Concord, Minnesota: CPI Publishing.

————. 1996. Restorative Justice through Mediation: The Impact of Offenders Facing Their Victims in Oakland. *Law and Social Work*.

Umbreit, M. S. and R. B. Coates. 1992. The Impact of Mediating Victim Offender Conflict: An Analysis of Programs in Three States. *Juvenile and Family Court Journal*. 43:21-28.

————. 1993. Cross-site Analysis of Victim Offender Mediation in Four States. *Crime & Delinquency*. 39:565-585.

Umbreit, M. S., R. Coates, and A. Roberts. 1997. Cross-national Impact of Restorative Justice through Mediation and Dialog. *The ICCA Journal on Community Corrections*. 8:46-50.

Umbreit, M. S. and C. Fercello. 1997. *Woodbury, Minnesota Police Department's Restorative Justice Conferencing Program: An Initial Assessment of Client Satisfaction*. St. Paul, Minnesota: Center for Restorative Justice and Mediation, University of Minnesota.

Umbreit, M. S. and J. Greenwood. 1997. *Guidelines for Victim-sensitive Victim Offender Mediation*. St. Paul, Minnesota: Center for Restorative Justice and Mediation, University of Minnesota.

———. 1998. *National Survey of Victim Offender Mediation Programs in the U.S.* St. Paul, Minnesota: Center for Restorative Justice and Mediation, University of Minnesota.

Umbreit, M. S. and A. W. Roberts. 1996. *Mediation of Criminal Conflict in England: An Assessment of Services in Coventry and Leeds*. St. Paul, Minnesota: Center for Restorative Justice and Mediation, University of Minnesota.

Van Ness, D. and K. Strong. 1997. *Restoring Justice*. Cincinnati, Ohio: Anderson Publishing Company.

Wright, M. 1991. *Justice for Victims and Offenders*. Philadelphia: Open University Press.

Wright, M. and B. Galaway. 1989. *Mediation and Criminal Justice*. London: Sage.

Wundersitz, J. and S. Hetzel, S. 1996. Family Conferencing for Young Offenders: The South Australian Experience. In J. Hudson, A. Morris, G. Maxwell, and B. Galaway, eds. *Family Group Conferences*. Monsey, New York: Criminal Justice Press.

Zehr, H. 1980. *Mediating the Victim-offender Conflict*. Akron, Pennsylvania: Mennonite Central Committee.

———. 1990. *Changing Lenses: A New Focus for Crime and Justice*. Scottsdale, Pennsylvania: Herald Press.

Index

T

ABOUT THE AUTHORS

David M. Altschuler is principal research scientist at the Johns Hopkins Institute for Policy Studies in Baltimore, Maryland and Adjunct Associate Professor in Sociology. He is also coprincipal investigator on the Intensive Juvenile Aftercare Demonstration Initiative, funded by the Office of Juvenile Justice and Delinquency Prevention, U.S. Department of Justice.

Donald A. Andrews received his Ph.D. in psychology from Queen's University at Kingston Ontario. He is a professor of psychology at Carleton University, Ottawa Ontario. His research interests include a variety of assessment, intervention, evaluation, and theoretical issues in juvenile and criminal justice, corrections, and other human service agencies. He is also interested in the social psychology of criminological knowledge. He is codeveloper of risk/need assessment instruments in wide-scale use with young offenders and adult offenders. Recent consultation and training efforts have involved the National Institute of Corrections (U.S.), National Parole Board of Canada, Ontario Ministry of Community and Social Services, Ontario Ministry of Correctional Services, and the states of Vermont, Ohio, and Colorado. The first edition of his book, *The Psychology of Criminal Conduct*, was nominated for the Hindelang Award of the American Society of Criminology. His research and theoretical contributions to correctional policy and practice were recognized by the American Probation and Parole Association through the University of Cincinnati award in 1997. In addition, he received the Margaret Mead award for contributions to social justice and humanitarian advancement from the International Community Corrections Association.

Alan Harland is a faculty member in the Department of Criminal Justice at Temple University, Philadelphia, where he has served as chairman of the department and of the graduate program. His undergraduate and graduate teaching interests include criminal justice, criminal law, legal philosophy, victimology, sentencing, community corrections, organizational management and change, and criminal justice policy. Professor Harland received his Ph.D. in Criminal Justice from the State University of New York at Albany, where he was Director of the Hindelang Criminal Justice Research Center before joining the faculty at Temple. He also holds law degrees from the University of Pennsylvania and from Oxford University, England. He is executive editor of the *Prison Journal*, a quarterly refereed publication by Sage Publications, with whom he also recently published the book, *Choosing Correctional Options that Work: Assessing the Demand and Evaluating the Supply*.

Patricia M. Harris (Ph.D., Rutgers University) is an Associate Professor of Criminal Justice at the University of Texas at San Antonio. She has published numerous articles on offender treatment evaluation and policy, offender supervision and classification practices, and crime prevention.

Sharon Kennedy's most recent publications have appeared in the International Community Corrections Association's *Journal on Community Corrections*, *Corrections Today*, and research reports on correctional research and corporate development. She recently coauthored an assessment protocol for treatment readiness, responsivity, and gain. She has conducted training workshops for the American Probation and Parole Association, the International Community Corrections Association, and the National Institute of Corrections. Her current research interests include risk/need assessment, treatment responsivity and readiness, and violent offenders.

Mark Harrison Moore is the Guggenheim Professor of Criminal Justice Policy and Management at the Kennedy School of Government. He was the founding chairman of the Kennedy School's Committee on Executive Programs, and served in that role for over a decade. He is also the Director of the Hauser Center for Nonprofit Organizations and the Faculty Chairman of the School's Program in Criminal Justice Policy and Management. His research interests are in public management and leadership; in criminal justice policy and management; in community mobilization and nonprofit organizations, and in the intersection of the three domains. In the area of public management, his most recent book is *Creating Public Value: Strategic Management in Government.* He has written (with others) *Public Duties: The Moral Obligations of Public Officials*; *Ethics in Government: The Moral Challenges of Public Leadership*; *Inspectors-General: Junkyard Dogs or Man's Best Friend*; *Accounting for Change: Reconciling the Demands for Accountability and Innovation in the Public Sector.* In the area of criminal justice policy, he has written *Buy and Bust: The Effective Regulation of an Illicit Market in Heroin* and *Dangerous Offenders: Elusive Targets of Justice.* In the intersection of public management and criminal justice, he has written (with others) *From Children to Citizens: Vol. 1: The Mandate for Juvenile Justice* and *Beyond 911: A New Era for Policing.* Much of his work in public management and criminal justice has focused on the ways in which leaders of public organizations can engage communities in supporting and legitimating the work of the public organizations, and in the role that value commitments play in enabling leadership in public sector enterprises. It is these strands that link his past work to the future challenge of learning about nonprofit enterprises.

Larry Motiuk received his Ph.D. in psychology from Carleton University and currently is the Director General, Research Branch, of the Correctional Service of Canada. He began his correctional career in the psychology department at the maximum-security Ottawa-Carleton Detention Center in 1979 and was an employee of the Ontario Ministry of Correctional Services until 1988. During this period, he provided direct clinical services to remanded and sentenced offenders, conducted research, and coauthored publications on restitution, halfway house selection, diversion, and inmate classification. Dr. Motiuk is also an adjunct professor in the Psychology Department of Carleton University, Ontario. His recent publications have included a textbook chapter, "Intel-ligence and Personality in Criminal Offenders," a coedited book, *Forensic Psychology: Policy and Practice in Corrections*, and journal articles such as "What Works in Corrections: A Blueprint for Action." He also is the editor of *Forum on Corrections Research.* Current research interests include offender assessment, population profiling, and reintegration potential.

Ellen Neises is the associate director of Working Today, a national membership organization that promotes the interests of people working in flexible employment arrangements as temporary, part-time, contract or independent workers. Prior to joining Working Today, Ellen was the special assistant to the president of the Edna McConnell Clark Foundation, the associate director of the Clark Foundation's Justice Program, and director of public policy and director of employment services at the Center for Alternative Sentencing and Employment Services in New York. She has a Bachelor of Science from Carnegie Mellon University and a Masters of Public Policy from Harvard.

James O. Prochaska is director of the Cancer Prevention Research Consortium and Professor of Clinical and Health Psychology at the University of Rhode Island. He is the author of more than 150 publications, including three books, *Changing for Good*, *Systems of Psychotherapy*, and *The Transtheoretical Approach*. He is internationally recognized for his work as developer of the stage model of behavior change. He is the principal investigator on more than $50 million dollars in research grants for the prevention of cancer and other chronic diseases. In addition, he has served as a consultant to the American Cancer Society, Centers for Disease Control, Health Maintenance Organizations, National Health Service of Great Britain, California Tobacco Control Program, major corporations, and numerous universities and research centers. Dr. Prochaska has won several awards including the top five most cited authors in psychology from the American Psychology Society and an honorary chair of medicine from the University of Birmingham, England. He is an invited speaker at many regional, national, and international meetings and conferences.

Ellen Schall has been the Martin Cherkasky Professor of Health Policy and Management at the Robert F. Wagner Graduate School of Public Service at New York University since 1992. Ms. Schall served from 1983-1990 as Commissioner of the New York City Department of Juvenile Justice and before that as Deputy Commissioner for Program Services and Legal Policy for the New York City Department of Correction. She also spent six and one-half years working as a criminal defense attorney for the Legal Aid Society in New York City.

Ralph Serin is a Senior Research Manager with the Research Branch of the Correctional Service of Canada. He has held various positions within the Service since 1975 and currently manages programs research within the Research Branch. He received his Ph.D. from Queen's University and maintains adjunct appointments in the Department of Psychiatry at Queen's University and the University of Toronto, as well as the Department of Psychology at Carleton University. He has more than thirty publications in the areas of psychopathy, risk assessment, sexual offenders, the assessment and treatment of violent offenders, and treatment responsivity. Current research interests include treatment readiness and responsivity, measurement of program effectiveness, typologies in sexual offenders and violent offenders, and systematic assessment protocols and clinical decision-making.

Michael E. Smith is a member of the faculty of at the University of Wisconsin Law School, where he is also Research Director of the Frank J. Remington Center for Education, Research and Service in Criminal Justice. From 1978 through 1994, he was Executive Director of the Vera Institute of Justice in New York. At the Vera Institute, he oversaw the design, implementation, and evaluation of new practice in policing, court administration, sentencing and corrections, and various other fields (for example, employing recently released inmates and other hard-to-employ populations and housing the homeless). He is a member of the Guidelines Subcommittee of Wisconsin's Criminal Penalties Committee, the National Commission on the Future of DNA Evidence (chairing its Legal Issues Working Group), the Editorial Board of Crime and Justice, and the Advisory Board of the Federal Sentencing Reporter. He served on the National Research Council's Committee on Assessment of Family Violence Interventions (1994-1997), and on a variety of federal, local, and state advisory bodies such as the New York State Sentencing Guidelines Committee (1983-86), U.S. Sentencing Commission Advisory Committee on Alternatives to Imprisonment (1989-91).

Wayne N. Welsh is an Associate Professor of Criminal Justice at Temple University. He received his Ph.D. in Social Ecology from the University of California, Irvine, in 1990 and his M.A. in Applied Social Psychology from the University of Saskatchewan (Canada) in 1986. Dr. Welsh has conducted research in two broad areas: (1) applications of organizational theory to criminal justice and examinations of organizational change, and (2) theories of violent behavior and intervention/prevention programs. Recent articles have appeared in *Criminology*, *Journal of Research in Crime and Delinquency*, and *Crime and Delinquency*. He is author of *Counties in Court: Jail Overcrowding and Court-Ordered Reform* (Temple University Press, 1995). In the book and in several journal articles, he examined the impacts of court-ordered correctional reform, especially responses and adaptations by criminal justice agencies. A second book, *Criminal Justice Policy and Planning* (with Phil Harris), was published by Anderson. A third book is in progress: *Criminal*

Violence: Patterns, Causes, and Prevention, with Marc Riedel (Roxbury Press). This book presents an interdisciplinary approach to the study of violence that cuts across research and theories at the individual, group, organizational, community, and social structural levels. Dr. Welsh's recent research has focused on delinquency prevention and school violence. He was principal investigator on a three-year study, funded by the Pennsylvania Commission on Crime and Delinquency, that evaluated nine community-based prevention programs aimed at reducing the overrepresentation of minorities in the juvenile justice system. A school violence study, funded by the National Institute of Justice, examined multilevel predictors (individual, neighborhood, and school characteristics) of school violence in Philadelphia, and examined recommendations for violence prevention. Currently, he is principal investigator on a project titled "Building an Effective Research Collaboration between the Pennsylvania Department of Corrections and the Center for Public Policy At Temple University." The purpose of this project, funded by the National Institute of Justice, is to develop a collaborative research partnership between the Pennsylvania Department of Corrections and Temple University's Center for Public Policy, with a demonstration research project.

Mark Umbreit is director of the Center for Restorative Justice and Mediation and the National Restorative Justice Training Institute and is an associate professor at the University of Minnesota School of Social Work, St. Paul Campus. He is also codirector of the National Balanced and Restorative Justice Project, funded by the Office of Juvenile Justice and Delinquency Prevention of the U.S. Department of Justice. He is an internationally recognized trainer, mediator, author, and researcher in the field of restorative justice and mediation, with more than twenty-five years of experience as a practitioner. He has been a featured speaker on restorative justice and mediation throughout the United States and in Canada, England, Belgium, Italy, Denmark, and China. As a consultant for the U.S. Department of Justice for the past eighteen years, Dr. Umbreit has provided technical assistance and mediation training to community-based programs, correctional agencies, victim service providers, and courts in more than thirty-five states throughout the Untied States. He has completed the first cross-national studies of victim offender mediation in four United States' cities, four provinces in Canada, and two cities in England. Dr. Umbreit is a practicing mediator with expertise in facilitating victim sensitive mediation/dialogs with offenders in crimes of severe violence.

He is the author of two books: *Victim Meets Offender: The Impact of Restorative Justice* (1994) and *Mediating Interpersonal Conflicts: A Pathway to Peace* (1995), as well as numerous articles and monographs on restorative justice and mediation practice.